Reasons

**Edited by
Thomas E. Gaston**

and they shall spring up as among the grass,
as willows by the water course

For

Daniel Wright

"a time is coming when all who are in the tombs will hear his voice"
(John 5:28)

Published by:

WILLOW PUBLICATIONS
13 St. Georges terrace
East Boldon
Tyne and Wear
NE36 0LU, U.K.

ISBN 978-0-9563841-4-0

Available from:

www.lulu.com/willowpublications

This book was written as a project sponsored by the Christadelphian EJournal of Biblical Interpretation, a quarterly e-journal freely available to Christadelphians and others with a like Abrahamic monotheistic faith and available at www.christadelphian-ejbi.org

Contents

Preface

The objective of this book is to present **reasons** for believing in God, Jesus and the Bible. The book does not merely respond to modern attacks by critics of the Bible and Christian faith but presents positive reasons for belief in the original Christian faith.

All the contributors to this volume, both authors and reviewers, are committed believers in God, Jesus and the Bible, and are Christadelphians.[1] They share this common understanding, but might have divergent views on other issues. They have committed themselves to this project on a personal basis and their views may not be representative of their institution or employer.

The Bible declares that God does not show partiality, and as believers we do not judge by the standards of this world. We live in an age when it is not uncommon for believers to be portrayed as eccentric or dim-witted, unable to judge the facts of the matter. For this reason, the authors who contributed to this volume were chosen, in part, for their qualifications and credentials. In addition, each essay has been peer-reviewed to ensure its accuracy. Nevertheless, the arguments should be judged on their merits alone.

One of the reasons presented in this book is the witness of the people of Israel. This should not be read as an endorsement of the actions of the Israeli government, past or present. To be the people of God implies a responsibility to act justly, to love mercy and to walk humbly with God.

This volume is not exhaustive; for each topic covered entire books could have been written. Each chapter includes some suggestions for further reading. These sources are recommended for the relevant material they contain, and, of course, their recommendation does not imply an endorsement of everything written by that author.

I would like to thank all those who have contributed to this book. As well as the named authors and reviewers, I would like to thank all those who gave their advice during the planning stages and those who read early

---

[1] For more information on the Christadelphians see Harry Tennant's *The Christadelphians: What They Believe and Teach,* or the following website can be consulted: www.thechristadelphians.org.uk.

drafts. I would particularly like to thank Kate Stewart for proof-reading the final draft and Mary Gaston for designing the cover.

The individual authors are responsible only for their own contributions and do not necessarily share all the views of the other contributors. Final responsibility for the content of this book rests with the editor alone.

I hope and pray that this book will be of benefit for its readers as they seek after God.

Authors

David Alexander PhD
Research Scientist, Commonwealth Scientific and Industrial Research Organisation

Paul Boyd PhD
Biochemist for major international pharmaceutical company

Jonathan Burke MIMS
PhD student, National Taiwan University of Science and Technology, Taipei

Reg Carr MA DLitt FRSA
Bodley's Librarian Emeritus and formerly Director of Oxford University Library Services

Simon Dean MA (Cantab)

L. Alan Eyre PhD
Senior Research Fellow, University of the West Indies

Thomas E. Gaston MPhil(b)
DPhil Theology student, University of Oxford

Peter Jeavons PGCE MSc PhD
Professor of Computer Science, University of Oxford

John Launchbury MA (Oxon) MSc PhD FACM
Chief Scientist, Galois, Inc. Formerly Professor of Computer Science, Oregon Graduate Institute

David P. Levin MS LPC
Psychotherapist in private practice, Pennsylvania, USA

Andrew Perry BA (Theol) MA PhD

Reviewers

David Brown MA PhD CPhys CSci FInstP
Chief Executive, Institution of Chemical Engineers

Mike Bull

David Burke
B.Th. Student, Tabor College, Adelaide.

Rob J Hyndman PhD A.Stat.
Professor of Statistics, Monash University

Merrilyn Mansfield
PhD Studies in Religion student, University of Sydney

Philip Mallinder PhD
Professional Molecular Biologist

Mark Morris PhD

Joe Pitt-Francis DPhil
Research Assistant, University of Oxford

Stephen D. Snobelen MA MPhil PhD
Professor of History of Science and Technology, University of King's
College, Halifax, Nova Scotia

Robert Wilkinson PhD
Research Fellow, Wesley College Bristol

Introduction: Faith in the Modern World

The Decline of Christianity in Britain

Christianity is in a state of decline in Britain. According to the National Centre for Social Research, the majority of British people (just over 50%) consider themselves to be of no religion. Figures collected by the Catholic Church and the Church of England indicate that just over 3% of the British population attends church services.[1] Some commentators believe that Christianity is in terminal decline. For example, certain analysts have predicted that Methodism will be extinct by the middle of the twenty-first century.[2]

Contrary to popular conception, the decline of Christianity in Britain was not caused by the Enlightenment; it was not caused by the theory of evolution; and it certainly was not caused by increased education. In 1916 James Leuba carried out a survey of 1,000 randomly selected scientists regarding their belief in a personal God. Leuba thought that with increased education, religious belief would inevitably decline. However, when the survey was repeated in 1996 by Edward Larson and Larry Witham, they found that the level of belief amongst scientists was roughly the same, around 40%.[3] The British Social Attitudes survey revealed that amongst those describing themselves as "religious", 40% are educated to degree level, whereas this figure is only 25% for those describing themselves as "non-religious".[4] There seems to be no correlation between atheism (and agnosticism) and higher levels of education.

It was previously thought that Christianity had been declining steadily in Britain since the Industrial Revolution. In *The Death of Christian Britain* (Routledge, 2000), Callum Brown re-examines the figures for church attendance and re-evaluates some of the assumptions on which the idea of steady decline was based. He discovered that church attendance in Britain remained fairly stable throughout the twentieth century until a sudden and rapid decline in the late fifties and early sixties. Brown's initial thesis to explain this decline was about the liberation of women. Brown regarded

---

[1] www.bbc.co.uk/news/11297461 [cited Sept 2010].

[2] "Leader signals end of Methodism", *Independent* (12 February 2010).

[3] E. J. Larson & L. Witham, "Scientists are still keeping the faith", *Nature* 386 (1997): 435 - 436.

[4] L. Lee & S. Bullivant, "Where do atheists come from?", *New Scientist* 205:2750 (2010): 26-7.

wives and mothers as the wardens of religiosity in the traditional British family, and when the role of women changed, with increasing numbers of women working and/or choosing to remain single, so the levels of national religiosity began to crumble. This thesis was probably too simple, and revisiting the issue in *Religion and Society in Twentieth Century Britain* (Longman, 2006), Brown posits a number of other factors, including the rise of popular culture and increasing cultural diversity. A great cultural shift took place in the sixties, affecting not only music and art, but also moral and social values. Legislation on "traditional" values, particularly on sexual ethics (e.g. divorce, adultery, homosexuality, etc.), were all relaxed during the sixties. The driving force of these changes was popular culture, rock stars and actors, whilst Christianity, which represented "traditional" values, was seen as outdated and authoritarian. Rather than being the source of freedom and empowerment, Christianity was presented as the old man holding back change.

It is cultural trends that have had the most influence on the public's attitudes towards Christianity. This is nowhere more obvious than in the media. In recent years, a steady stream of broadcasters has complained about how they feel religion is repressed within the British media.[5] In fact, the executives of the BBC have stated that it is the policy of the BBC that "secularism is the only philosophy to which others must eventually come".[6] This bias within the media is due in part to sensationalism. Books such as *The God Delusion* and *The Da Vinci Code* were always going to sell well, not because they are particularly enlightening or well-written, but because they are sensational; a book entitled *Jesus was right all along* would only sell a fraction in proportion but would probably be more accurate. There is also a growing trend towards viewing religion as a private matter of conscience and not a subject of public discourse.

The Rise of Secularism

Recent years have witnessed the publication of a number of books by the so-called "New Atheists", like Richard Dawkins, Christopher Hitchens and Sam Harris. These books are not representative of any significant

---

[5] For example: "Composer James MacMillan warns of liberal elite's 'ignorance-fuelled hostility to religion'", *Telegraph* (01 October 2008); "Christians are becoming social pariahs in Britain, claims Jeremy Vine", *Sunday Telegraph* (17 January 2009); "BBC News needs a religion editor, says Radio 4's Roger Bolton", *Guardian* (26 May 2010).
[6] *Daily Mail* (24 October 2006); cf. "We are biased, admit the stars of BBC News", *Evening Standard* (21 October 2010).

development in the argument: philosophy has largely moved on from the modernism espoused in these books. These atheists are rank amateurs compared with the eloquence and intellectual prowess of Friedrich Nietzsche, the nineteenth-century philosopher. Nietzsche was at least prepared to follow his assumption of atheism to its inevitable conclusion. More concerning is that the New Atheism has a social agenda, supposing that the eradication of all religion will lead to a more moral and enlightened civilization. The militant and intemperate tone of this agenda has alarmed many, not just believers. The philosopher Michael Ruse has famously stated, *"The God Delusion* makes me embarrassed to be an atheist".[7] Stephen Jay Gould, the evolutionary biologist, has written that scientists who claim, "Darwinism disproves God", should have their knuckles rapped by his third-grade teacher.[8] There have been a number of well-reasoned demolitions of Dawkins' *The God Delusion,* in particular *The Dawkins Delusion* by the theologian Alister McGrath (with his wife Joanna) and *Why There Almost Certainly Is a God* by the philosopher Keith Ward, which aptly demonstrate the many fallacies Dawkins commits. Rather than engage in a negative and reductionist argument with the New Atheists, this volume will consider real and positive evidence for belief.

What these evangelical atheists are symptomatic of is a popularist dismissal of religion. The real challenge to Christianity in the modern age is not atheism but apathy; genuine religious feeling is dismissed with a wave of the hand and sarcastic retort – evangelical atheists simply provide excuses for not taking God seriously. It is significant that all these New Atheists point to examples of bad religious people to justify the claim that religion should be done away with. Though this is clearly unreasonable (no-one would propose scrapping the dictionary just because some people spell badly), it is the case that one of the biggest detriments to Christianity has been the abject failure of Christians to live up to its calling. The danger is that these examples of hypocrisy and weakness will lead to some societies abandoning religion altogether.

Faith – A Misunderstood Term

Faith is a much-maligned term in the modern world. Dawkins has chosen to define faith as "blind trust, in the absence of evidence, even in the teeth of evidence".[9] Though I know of no major religion that defines faith in

---

[7] Printed on the cover of Alister McGrath's *The Dawkins Delusion.*
[8] S. J. Gould, "Impreaching a Self-Appointed Judge", *Scientific American* 267 (1992): 119.
[9] R. Dawkins, *The Selfish Gene* (2nd ed; Oxford University Press, 1989), 198.

such way, this conception of faith remains popular. Claims that all religious faith is irrational or delusional are demonstrably false.[10]

The term 'faith' can be used in two different, though connected, ways; as belief about something and trust in something. [11] Faith as belief is not blind; you must have reasons for belief such as evidence. Religious belief is no different from any other sort of belief. Some of the evidence is of a different sort but the process is essentially the same: you weigh the evidence and you form a conclusion.[12] And religious belief is not free from doubt – how could it be? Belief without doubt is meaningless. If you believe something and never question whether you have reached the right conclusion, your belief in that conclusion is arbitrary and thus worthless.

Often when people talk about religious faith, what they are really talking about is trust. Trust is a different sort of thing to belief. Trust is usually about other people and usually it is not so easy to test. For example, I trust my wife. I trust that she wants what is best for me and will never try to harm me. However, I cannot test the proposition "my wife will never harm me" because it is do with the future, and about her free choice. Trust is not blind – I have good reasons for trusting my wife – but it is difficult to test. Some aspects of religion are based upon trust. In the Bible God promises rewards for those who trust him, but as these are propositions about the future, they cannot be tested and need to be accepted on trust. There is nothing irrational about this; if someone is trustworthy then there is nothing irrational about believing what they say is true. In the same way, if the Bible is trustworthy, then we can accept on trust those statements that cannot be tested in any other way.

Neither faith as belief, nor faith as trust, is blind. You should not believe in something, nor should you put your trust in something, without sufficient reason. Sufficient reason is not the same as absolute proof.

---

[10] P. McNamara, *The Neuroscience of Religious Experience,* (Cambridge University Press, 2009), 18-20.

[11] In the New Testament the word translated "faith" in English Bibles is the Greek word *pistis,* which can be used for either meaning. In Latin these two meanings are expressed using the words *credo,* which is about belief about something, and *fide,* which is about trust in something.

[12] In the New Testament people are presented with evidence, such as miracles, and so they decide to believe (e.g. John 2:23). Whenever the Apostles are writing to potential converts they always supply reasons to believe (John 20:31; Romans 16:26; 2 Peter 1:16); no-one ever says "ignore the evidence, just believe". The apostle John specifically instructs Christians not to believe everything their told (1 John 4:1).

When I drive over a bridge I trust that the structure of the bridge is sufficiently secure to hold the weight of the car. I do not have absolute proof – perhaps there is a hairline fracture in the key bridge support that nobody can see – but the weight of evidence gives me sufficient reason to trust that it is safe to drive over the bridge. Fortunately, the human mind is not constrained to wait for absolute proof before it forms a conclusion, and so we are able to go about our daily lives forming beliefs about things and trusting in things. Religious belief functions in the same way – we examine the evidence, we judge whether there is sufficient reason for belief and if there is, we believe. This is the only way we can operate.

The purpose of this book is to outline **the reasons for belief in God, in Jesus and in the Bible**. This is not absolute proof and no single argument is sufficient. We believe that the weight of evidence gives us sufficient reason to believe that there is a God and that he has revealed himself through Jesus and through the Bible.

Faith and Science

Another popular myth is that science and religion are fundamentally opposed. Particularly popular are tales such as that of Galileo, the astronomer condemned by an ignorant and authoritarian Church. The truth is somewhat more complicated. Galileo had support for his views within the Catholic Church, and his *Dialogue concerning the Two Chief World Systems* received the imprimatur from censors in Florence. It was primarily political problems that prompted Pope Urban to move against Galileo. Though put under house arrest, Galileo was never tortured or imprisoned, and was allowed to continue to write about science. Most historians consider that Galileo remained a believer all his life.

Yet, whatever the case about specific instances of Church interference in the pursuit of knowledge, this does not touch on the question of whether science and religion *per se* are fundamentally opposed. Many scientists, both historically and in the present day, find no contradiction between their scientific research and their belief in a personal God. Indeed, many academics find that religious belief is proportionally higher amongst their scientific colleagues than their colleagues in Humanities. Elaine Ecklund, after a four-year survey of 1700 scientists, concluded:

> The 'insurmountable hostility' between science and religion is a caricature, a thought-cliché, perhaps useful as a satire on groupthink, but hardly representative of reality.

15

More worrying is Ecklund's discovery that many scientists with religious beliefs keep their beliefs secret from their colleagues because of the stigma attached to religion.[13]

Why do people continue to believe that science and religion are opposed? Part of the reason is to do with the assumption of naturalism.

Modern science has its origins in the seventeenth century, when a shift was made away from scholasticism (where conclusions are based on what other people previously wrote) towards natural philosophy (where conclusions are based upon observation and experiment). The principles of natural philosophy were laid out by individuals like Robert Boyle, himself a believer and early member of the Royal Society. One of the key principles of this new approach was methodological naturalism, which meant that natural philosophers (later "scientists") should only consider natural causes. This is a useful way of working as it forces scientists to perform experiments and make observations rather than, say, suppose that invisible gremlins did it. The point to remember is that methodological naturalism is an assumption, not a proven fact. In making this assumption, Boyle hoped to draw the distinction between natural philosophy and metaphysics as separate disciplines. Strangely, some modern scientists (and plenty of laymen) have concluded that because science does not consider God in its investigations, science has somehow disproved God. It is not possible for science to do this, because, according to methodological naturalism, God is beyond the remit of science.

What many modern atheists are actually advocating is materialism; the view that all that exists is matter. This may seem scientific, because matter is one of the things scientists deal with, but materialism is as much a metaphysical position as theism. Followed to its logical conclusion, materialism requires that even the human mind does not really exist in any meaningful sense. Throughout this book, we will see many reasons to challenge this materialist dogma. Can matter alone explain the origins of the universe? If all that exists is matter, why is it ordered in a regular and meaningful way? Can information be understood in purely materialist terms? How do we explain the existence of the human mind with all its complexities with reference only to matter?

---

[13] E. H. Ecklund, *Science vs Religion: What Scientists Really Think* (Oxford University Press, 2010).

The Purpose of Religion

If the New Atheists had their way then all religion would be exorcised from society, but would society really be better off without religion? There is extensive, and growing, medical literature which indicates that religious adherence can contribute to greater mental well-being, better quality of life, higher resilience to pain and illness, and ultimately longer life.[14] Some of these results may be explained by higher levels of care experienced by those with support of a congregation or community, but there are also psychological factors that cannot be ignored. Though it is premature to draw definite conclusions, one probable explanation is that humans are inherently spiritual beings – to deny or ignore our spiritual needs may have negative consequences upon our well-being. This proposal – that we are naturally religiously inclined – is supported by research into the neuroscience of religiosity:

> Very carefully designed experiments with children of various ages have consistently shown that children naturally suppose that a world of objects and forces is governed by teleological entities and that God exists and is watching over them.[15]

Similar conclusions have been reached by 'The Cognition, Religion and Theology Project' led by Dr Justin Barrett at Oxford University:

> This project suggests that religion is not just something for a peculiar few to do on Sundays instead of playing golf. We have gathered a body of evidence that suggests that religion is a common fact of human nature across different societies. This suggests that attempts to suppress religion are likely to be short-lived as human thought seems to be rooted to religious concepts[16]

Banishing all religion runs the risk of denying some of our most basic inclinations. So whilst it is right to expose religious hypocrisy and to

---

[14] P. D. Morgan *et al*, "Spiritual well-being, religious coping, and the quality of life of African American breast cancer treatment: a pilot study", *ABNF J* 17:2 (2006); D. E. Hall, "Religious attendance: more cost-effective than Lipitor?", *J Am Board Fam Med* 19:2 (2006); R. A. Hummer *et al*, "Religious involvement and adult mortality in the United States", *South Med J* 97:12 (2004); P. S. Mueller *et al*, "Religious involvement, spirituality, and medicine: implications for clinical practice", *Mayo Clin Proc* 76:12 (2001); etc. etc.
[15] P. McNamara, *The Neuroscience of Religious Experience*, (Cambridge University Press, 2009), 233.
[16] Roger Trigg quoted: www.ox.ac.uk/media/news_stories/2011/110513.html.

remove the veil of religiosity that shields abusers, it is imperative to encourage good religion and not to inhibit a very real and meaningful part of human experience.

At its most basic, religion is the quest for meaning. The philosopher Ludwig Wittgenstein wrote in his notebook on 8 July 1916:

> To believe in a god means to see that the facts of the world are not the end of the matter. To believe in God means to see that life has a meaning.[17]

If matter is all there is, then the world and life in the world is essentially without meaning, but if prior to matter there is a mind, then the world is essentially meaningful. Religion, inasmuch as it seeks to understand that Mind, is a search for meaning in the world. If there is indeed a Mind at the base and centre of all that exists then we ignore religion at our peril. This is not to imply that all religion is correct or that religious people have all the answers, but it is important to recognize that the contemplation of our place in the universe is a religious contemplation. It is not surprising therefore that some form of religion has been almost universally practised by mankind far back into pre-history. To dismiss all religion is to abandon the most fundamental questions of human nature.

The more scientists understand about the relation between religious experience and the psyche, the more we find that religion has performed a most valuable role in the function of human beings. Patrick McNamara explains:

> A unified sense of Self, a unified consciousness, is quite an achievement for human beings. It freed us from slavery to impulse and from ineffective and divided goal states. That does not mean that we never experience divided and conflicting desires. It merely means that we have the ability to take conflicting desires and states and synthesize them into a new unity that benefits the individual.[18]

By assisting human beings in positioning themselves within the universe in relation to a supreme Mind, religion has helped human beings transcend the chaos of our various whims and desires and create a unified sense of Self (i.e. a complete sense of being who we are). This is not to

---

[17] L. Wittgenstein, *Notebooks* (eds. G. H. Von Wright & G. E. M. Anscombe; Oxford: Basil Blackwell, 1961), 94.
[18] McNamara, *Neuroscience of Religious Experience*, 258.

claim that there are not other strategies for assisting human beings become mentally well-adjusted, but it certainly seems that religion has performed that role for mankind.

This decentring and unifying of the Self is seen practically in our moral capacities. Religion and morality have been linked throughout man's history, and modern attempts to construct secular moralities have not proved particularly successful. Religion is falsely characterised as a set of restrictions ("thou shalt not ...") when in reality proper religion provides a moral framework which allows human beings to freely operate, providing direction and value to their actions. Of course, a non-religious person may perform good actions and a religious person may perform bad actions. Nevertheless, for the religious person, their morality will be set within the context of a meaningful framework; the non-religious need to question in what sense their morality is meaningful.

Thus far we have talked generally about religion and the positive functions it serves. Yet it should be clear that, despite some positive benefits, not all religion is true (and not all religion is positive). Different religions make different, and often conflicting, claims; though they may be symptomatic of our innate religious needs, these different religions cannot all be true. So it would be as well to put our cards on the table, because the greatest and most specific benefit of "religion" is not temporary benefits in this life, but the hope of life to come. Perhaps some will think it irrational to talk of life after death, but why should it be thought impossible that the Creator of the universe should recreate a person who has died? And why should it be thought strange that the God of love should wish to do so? This hope is powerfully confirmed by the historical resurrection of Jesus Christ from the dead.

Why isn't God obvious?

Before proceeding, it is important that we tackle perhaps the most common objection that people, either consciously or subconsciously, raise against belief in God: why isn't God obvious? Believing in trees and tables is easy - they're obvious. You don't need any special skills to believe in them; you don't even need to think about believing in them, and it is almost trivial to ask whether such things exist. So why can't God be like that? Why can't God be just so obvious that it would be silly even to question his existence?

There are two aspects to the question, a philosophical and a moral part. The former is, why is it impossible for human beings to directly perceive God – to see him or to touch him? The latter is, how is it fair that God doesn't make his existence more obvious, so that everyone can believe in him?

In answer to the philosophical part of the question, it is a necessary implication of God's very nature that he should be beyond human perception. If God created the world, then he cannot be part of that world – so we should not expect God to be like created things such as trees and tables. As C. S. Lewis writes:

> If there was a controlling power outside the universe, it could not show itself to us as one of the facts inside the universe – no more than the architect of a house could actually be a wall or staircase or fireplace in that house.[19]

This is also the consistent testimony of the Bible: God cannot be directly perceived (Exod 33:20; Job 9:11; John 1:18; 1 Tim 6:16). This does mean, regrettably, that it is hard for humans to come to know of God, but that says nothing about God's existence. Consider black holes. They are very difficult to perceive; not only are they far away in distant space, but also, because light does not escape them, they are almost undetectable. The fact that black holes are less obvious than trees and tables does not mean they do not exist.

The difficulty does not just rest on our inability to directly perceive God, but also our inability to fully comprehend the nature of God. However, our inability to grapple with the idea of God is not a good reason for dismissing his existence, as the philosopher Keith Ward explains:

> When we are dealing with God, it is to be expected that the nature of God far surpasses any possibility of complete comprehension by human minds. So it is just not good enough to claim that, since I seem to be able to picture a world without God, there could actually be one. How could I possibly know that I have coherently conceived of such a world, when its ultimate structure is not known to me?[20]

If God is, as theists claim, the cause of all things, the ultimate reality behind everything, then it is not surprising that we cannot begin to

---

[19] C. S. Lewis, *Mere Christianity* (London: Fount Paperbacks, 1997), 20.
[20] K. Ward, *Why there almost certainly is a God* (Oxford: Lion, 2008), 110.

fathom the nature of God. It is difficult to grapple with the size of our own galaxy, let alone the universe – how much more difficult, then, to conceive of the being that caused this universe. If the existence of God does not appear obvious, it is because we are dealing with concepts that are, in some sense, beyond our imagination. Ward is probably correct when he says, "if we could understand God truly, we would see that it is impossible for God not to exist".[21]

Yet someone may object that, even though God cannot be directly perceived, there are ways in which God could make his existence more obvious. For instance, in the Bible a number of individuals receive a miraculous revelation from God. Surely God could just give everyone this kind of revelation and so make his existence known. But there are reasons why God might not choose to reveal himself in this universal way. One commentator, Alan Hayward, gives a useful analogy.

> Suppose for a moment that God made His presence felt all the time – that every action of ours, good or bad, brought an immediate response from Him in the form of reward or punishment. What sort of a world would this be then?

> It would resemble, on a grander scale, the dining room of a hotel in Africa where I once stayed for a few days. The European owner evidently did not trust his African waiters. He would sit on a raised platform at one end of the room, constantly watching every movement. Goods that might possibly be pilfered, such as tea bags, sugar knobs and even pats of butter or margarine, were doled out by him in quantities just sufficient for the needs of the moment ... The results of all this supervision were painfully obvious ... Their master's total lack of trust in them had warped their personalities. As long as he was watching they acted discreetly, but the moment they thought his guard was down they would seize the opportunity to misbehave.[22]

God could make his presence felt all the time and it would undoubtedly force human beings to behave themselves. But in this circumstance, people would be acting out of fear, not out of a genuine desire to perform good acts or to love God. It is reasonable that God should choose not to make his presence felt in such an obvious way, so that humans do have

---

[21] Ward, *Why there almost certainly is a God,* 122.
[22] A. Hayward, *God Is: A scientist shows why it makes sense to believe in God* (Nashville: Thomas Nelson, 1978), 134.

the freedom to ignore God, if they wish, and to misbehave, if they choose.

Reasons for seeking

This book starts with a blank slate; we do not presuppose that there is a god or what sort of god he might be. The successive chapters of the book build up a picture that, we believe, brings us to the God of the Bible.

In the first chapter, **Thomas Gaston** presents some of the philosophical arguments for the existence of God, showing that there are good reasons for expecting there to be a God. With this expectation, we look at some of the evidence coming from modern science. **Peter Jeavons**, a computer scientist from Oxford University, describes some remarkable "coincidences" in the structure of our universe that point to the careful design of a transcendent Mind. Then we turn to life itself with **Paul Boyd**, a biochemist, who demonstrates that life could not have originated without a Creator.

In the next chapter we encounter the problem of consciousness. **John Launchbury** brings his experience as a computer scientist to bear on the problem and presents an alternative to the materialist dogma. We then take a look at morality. Like other values, such as beauty, morality is effectively meaningless under a materialist worldview and yet we continue to believe morality to be meaningful. **Thomas Gaston** argues that this is another indication that there is a God.

Finally, we close this section with a look at the problem of evil as one of the most significant philosophical challenges to God. **David Levin** steers his way through the various claims to the core issue of evil and how this can be reconciled with the existence of God.

Some people would be content to stop here. For instance, some people, often called "deists", believe that there is a god who caused the universe with its ordered laws but do not think that this god intervenes in the world. But we would urge you to go further. If there is a god, a divine creator, then surely you would want to know more about him. If human life was intended – created for a purpose – then surely you would want to know what that purpose is. Isn't it reasonable to suppose that if God went to all the effort of creating intelligent, conscious, moral people, then he would want to be known by them and even enter into a relationship with them? These are reasons for seeking.

Reasons for believing

In the second section of the book we move towards the God of the Bible.

Since some have called into question the textual basis of the Bible, we begin with a chapter by **Jonathan Burke** reaffirming the reasons for trusting the integrity of the text. Then **Andrew Perry** explores the historical reliability of the Old Testament.

The next two chapters present evidence that the Bible is the Word of God. **David Alexander** uses his training in statistics to help us assess the value of biblical prophecy, demonstrating that it is a strong witness to the divine origin of the Bible. Then **Reg Carr** traces the history of God's interaction with the people of Israel, explaining how this relationship is a witness to God.

Finally, we turn to Jesus. After **Andrew Perry** has established the historical credentials of Jesus and his witnesses, **Simon Dean** describes the evidence of the resurrection of Jesus from the dead – the cornerstone of the Christian faith.

These arguments take us from the god of philosophy and science to the revealed God of the Bible – a God not just of intellectual curiosity but of life-changing significance.

We close the book with an epilogue from **Alan Eyre**, who has been a follower of Christ for many decades. He moves us from arguments and evidence to the conviction that comes through a living relationship with God.

Further Reading

For a general introduction to some of the issues considered in this book, you might like to read *The Thinker's Guide to God* by Peter Vardy & Julie Arliss, or for something more philosophical, see Richard Swinburne's *Is There A God?*

On the popular myth of the conflict between science and religion, see *God's Undertaker: Has Science Buried God?* by John Lennox, and *The Bible & Science* by John Bilello. Alan Hayward's *God Is: A scientist shows why it makes sense to believe in God* is older but still worth reading.

There have been numerous responses to the New Atheism, in particular Dawkins' *The God Delusion*. See particularly Alastair McGrath's *The Dawkins Delusion* and Keith Ward's *Why There Almost Certainly Is A God*. Other responses include *Deluded by Dawkins?* by Andrew Wilson and *The Dawkins Letters* by David Robertson.

Part One:
Reasons for Seeking

Philosophical Arguments

Thomas Gaston

"Good logic does convince sometimes. Other times, something else is needed" – R. E. Maydole[1]

Introduction

The philosophical arguments for the existence of God were developed by the ancient Greek philosophers and have been adopted and developed in each of the monotheistic faiths: Judaism, Christianity, and Islam. These arguments may be unfamiliar to many. Those who are familiar with the arguments may think that they have long ago been discredited (though this is far from the case). Others may feel that the appeal to philosophy is unnecessary or even inappropriate, feeling that revelation alone should be sufficient. However, why should it surprise anyone that the existence of God should be supported by reason and logic? Also, since philosophical arguments are raised against God, it is useful to respond in kind. These arguments are still relevant and powerful today and worth considering.

It is generally considered that there are three classic philosophical arguments for the existence of God. We will explore each of these in detail in this chapter:

- The **cosmological** argument states that the universe must have a cause outside itself and that that cause is God.

- The **ontological** argument states that necessary existence is implied by our concept of a supreme perfect being, and so God exists.

---

[1] R. E. Maydole, "The Ontological Argument" in *The Blackwell Companion to Natural Theology* (ed. W. L. Craig & J. P. Moreland; Oxford: Blackwell, 2009), 586.

- The **teleological** (or design) argument states that the universe appears to be designed and so is likely to be the product of a designer.

However, this list is not exhaustive. There are many other arguments for God, which include:

- The **noological** (or consciousness) argument states that human consciousness cannot be explained on purely materialistic grounds, and so there must be some non-material explanation for this. This argument will be explored in a later chapter.

- The **moral** argument states that our sense of right and wrong entails the existence of a supremely moral being. This argument will be explored in a later chapter.

- The argument from **reason** states that the intelligibility of our universe cannot be explained on purely materialistic grounds and is the product of an intelligence.

- The argument from **transcendent desire** states that given our innate desire for the divine, there is likely to be something that corresponds to that desire (i.e. God).

- The argument from **religious experience** states that individual experience of the divine increases the probability that there is a God.

- The argument from **revelation** states that God provides witness to his existence through his revelation in the Bible and in Jesus Christ. This argument will be explored throughout the second half of the book.

In contrast, there are not many arguments for atheism. Those that there are fall under three main types:

X   The argument from **insufficient evidence** states that there simply isn't enough evidence to justify belief in God. The readers will judge for themselves whether this is the case.

X   The argument from **incoherence** states that the concept of God isn't coherent and therefore it is impossible that God exists. We will respond to this argument in the next section.

X   The argument from **evil** states that the existence of evil in the world is inconsistent with the existence of a loving God. We will respond to this argument in another chapter.

We should not be tempted to dismiss these arguments out of hand. The claim that there is a God would not be convincing were the evidence for God lacking or the concept of God incoherent. However, we should be cautious about how we determine what is sufficient evidence, or what we consider to be coherent. It is the third argument that presents the most significant challenge to belief.

The Concept of God

As a starting position, we may define God as an unlimited personal being.

We can understand the concept of a personal being because we are all persons. We can also understand the concept of something being eternal. To be eternal is simply to be without beginning and without end; to always be. Though we might struggle to imagine what it would be like to be eternal, we can recognize that it is possible that there might be an eternal person.

We can also understand the concept of something being unlimited. For example, though we are limited by gravity, we can conceive of something being unlimited by gravity. Though we are limited by our knowledge, we can conceive of something with unlimited knowledge. And so on.

The concept of God as an unlimited personal being seems coherent and conceivable. There is nothing intrinsically impossible about the existence of such a being.

Some attempt to create paradoxes in order to demonstrate that the concept of God is incoherent. For example, the question is posed: could God create a stone so heavy that he was unable to lift it? The paradox is designed to show that the concept of an all-powerful (omnipotent) being is incoherent, because either way there is something God could not do. Such objections are based on a false definition of God. We do not define God as being able to do logically impossible things; we define God as being unlimited and thus able to do anything that it is possible to do.

Since the concept of God seems coherent, it is possible that such a being might exist. We now consider arguments that point to the existence of such a being.

The Cosmological Argument

The cosmological argument is a deduction from the existence of the universe (Greek: *kosmos*) to a first cause. **Deduction** is a form of argument where the conclusion necessarily follows from the premises, if the argument is valid and sound. The classic example is as follows:

Premise 1:	Socrates is a man
Premise 2:	All men are mortal
Conclusion:	Socrates is mortal

The argument is valid, because there are no contradictions or circular reasoning, and the argument is sound, because both premises are true. Therefore the conclusion is true.

The cosmological argument is conventionally stated as follows:

Premise 1:	The universe has a beginning
Premise 2:	Everything that has a beginning has a cause
Conclusion:	The universe has a cause

This argument is valid. It is exactly the same form as the Socrates example. But is the argument sound? Are the premises true?

The first premise is currently almost universally accepted amongst both philosophers and scientists. This was not always the case. Many of the ancient philosophers, such as the Platonists, held that the universe is eternal, and so did not have a beginning. The idea of an eternal universe was also the dominant view amongst scientists at the beginning of the twentieth century. However, astronomical observations indicated that the universe is expanding. Physicists made calculations tracing the expansion of the universe back to the initial moment of creation, commonly known as the "Big Bang". This confirmed that the universe had a beginning. Modern cosmology has begun to qualify the Big Bang within larger cosmological framework, such as multiverse theories. Yet we need not wed ourselves to any scientific theory, as the general point remains the same: the universe had a beginning in time.[2]

The second premise is also generally accepted. It is our experience that things do not come into existence without a prior cause. In fact, the whole scientific enterprise is based upon the principle that things have causes. It has been objected that electrons can disappear and reappear in another location. However, it seems that these electron fluctuations are not uncaused but depend on fluctuations in the surrounding vacuum.[3] It would certainly seem implausible that there should be no uniform causality on the micro level when this is exactly what we find on the macro level.

Both premises appear to be true, so the argument is sound. Therefore the conclusion is true; the universe has a cause.

Can we say anything about what sort of thing this cause might be? The cause of the universe must also be something that preceded the universe, so it cannot be any part of the universe. When we talk about the universe we mean both space and time; according to physicists, both of these came into existence at the Big Bang. Therefore the cause of the universe must be something outside space (i.e. immaterial) and outside time (i.e. eternal). The only known things that we know are immaterial and/or eternal are minds or abstract objects (e.g. numbers). Abstract objects do not have any causal power, but minds do have causal power. Therefore it is probable that the cause of the universe is an immaterial and eternal mind. This cause corresponds with our concept of God.

---

[2] See particularly, B. Gordon, "Inflationary Cosmology and the String Multiverse", in *New Proofs for the Existence of God*, (Robery Spitzer; Eerdmans, 2010).
[3] Vardy & Arliss, *The Thinker's Guide to God*, 81.

Possible Objections

Why can't the cause of the universe be matter?
The cause of the universe must be something prior to the universe, but matter came into being at the Big Bang. Therefore, matter cannot be the cause of the universe.

Why can't the cause of the universe be the laws of nature?
The cause of the universe must have causal power. Whilst the laws of nature are immaterial and (arguably) could be eternal, they do not have causal power. Consider the rules of chess; they govern the way the pieces move, but they do not explain why chess exists.

Why can't the universe have just winked itself into existence?
If we deny premise 2 ("everything that has a beginning has a cause") then the universe does not require a cause but few would be willing to accept the consequences of this. If things can just appear out of nothing without any cause whatsoever, then we have no justification for scientific enquiry, or even expecting the world to still be there in the next moment.

What caused God?
Only things that have a beginning have a cause. God, by definition, is eternal and so does not require a cause.

The Ontological Argument

The ontological argument is a deduction from the concept of God, involving existence (Greek: *ontos*). The argument came from the Christian theologian Anselm and may be stated as follows:

> We can understand the concept of something such that it is not possible to conceive of anything greater. Because we understand the concept, the concept exists in our minds. This thing could exist only as a concept in our minds or could also exist in reality. If this thing only existed in our minds then we could conceive of something greater (i.e. something existing in reality). Therefore that thing, which it is not possible to conceive of anything greater, exists.[4]

The essential argument may be stated more simply as follows:

---

[4] Anselm, *Proslogion* 2.

31

Premise 1:	The greatest possible being is defined as having all great-making properties
Premise 2:	Existence-in-reality is a great-making property
Conclusion:	The greatest possible being exists

It has been objected that this argument is invalid because it is circular (i.e. it assumes the thing it is trying to demonstrate). It is argued that assuming that it is possible for God to necessarily exist is the same as the conclusion that God necessarily exists. However, it seems that there is an important difference between saying something is possible and saying something is reality. Therefore this objection from circularity fails.

It has also been objected that the argument isn't sound because the premises are not true. It is objected that existence is not a property (against premise 2). Properties tell you about the concept of a thing such as its shape or weight; existence tells you whether there is something that corresponds to that concept in reality or not. If something does not exist it is not because it lacks the supposed property of existence, it is because there is nothing in reality that corresponds to that concept. Whilst this objection is valid as far is it goes, intuitively it seems as though a being that exists is greater than a being that does not exist. So it seems we can avoid this criticism by approaching this argument from a different angle:

Premise 1:	The greatest possible being is defined as one that necessarily exists
Premise 2:	It is possible that the greatest possible being exists
Conclusion:	The greatest possible being exists

Premise 1 is based upon Anselm's principle that we cannot conceive of a greater being than one that necessarily exists. Assuming that the concept of the greatest possible being is not self-contradictory then it is possible that the greatest possible being exists, so Premise 2 is true. If it is possible that the greatest possible being necessarily exists then the greatest possible being necessarily exists. This then brings us to our final problem: is the concept of a necessarily existent being coherent?

Something can be said to have contingent existence if its existence is dependent upon something else. Something can be said to have necessary existence if its existence is not contingent, i.e. if it doesn't depend on anything else for its existence. Most things have contingent existence. As we saw with the cosmological argument, there must be a first cause to explain the existence of contingent things. This first cause cannot be contingent otherwise it cannot be the first cause. Therefore we can talk coherently about something having necessary existence, that is, the first cause. So Anselm's original intuition, that there could be a necessarily existent being, seems correct. And because it is possible that there could be a necessarily existent being, therefore, there is a necessarily existent being.

Discussion

Many people consider that this argument is just playing with words. As the philosopher Richard Swinburne has said, "I think that ontological arguments for the existence of God are very much mere philosophers' arguments and do not codify any of the reasons which ordinary men have for believing that there is a God".[5] The readers will have to judge for themselves whether they feel that it is a convincing argument.

If the ontological argument is valid, then what can we say about this necessarily existent being? Anselm approached the ontological argument by thinking about that than which nothing greater can be conceived. This approach seems valid. Contingent beings are limited by their dependence on other things. For example, I am limited by my dependence on my body, my need for food and air, and my short lifespan. A necessary being, by definition, is not limited in any way because a necessary being does not depend on any other thing. Therefore, contingent things - things such as space or time, could not limit a necessary being.

Also there could only be one necessary being. Imagine there were two necessary beings: what would distinguish them? Not location (because not limited by space) and not chronology (because not limited by time). Since there is nothing that could possibly distinguish two necessary beings, there can only be one necessary being.

If we accept the ontological argument, we would conclude that there necessarily exists one Supreme Being that is not limited by space or time. This being corresponds with our concept of God.

The Teleological Argument

Often known as the design argument, the teleological argument is an inductive argument from certain features of the universe. **Induction** is the inference from the particular to the general. For example, if we observe that every time I drop an object it falls to the ground (particular) I might

---

[5] R. Swinburne, *The Existence of God* (Oxford University Press, 2004), 10.

infer that there is some universal force, gravity, which makes this happen (general). Science depends on inductive reasoning, using observation and experimentation to infer the laws of nature.

The teleological argument points to certain features of the universe that appear to have come about from some purpose or end (Greek: *telos*) and this implies the existence of a designer. The argument may be stated as follows:

Premise 1:	Certain features of the universe appear to be designed
Premise 2:	Things that appear designed are usually the product of a designer
Conclusion:	There is a designer of the universe

This argument is not deductive, because we cannot say that Premise 2 holds universally; the most we can say is that it holds for many things that we observe. This does not mean that the argument is invalid; it means that we must consider alternatives to design that might falsify the conclusion.

Premise 1 is uncontroversial. Everyone concedes that there are features of the universe that *appear* to be designed; examples of these will be considered in subsequent chapters. The question is, is the design just apparent or is it actual?

There are two alternatives to design, which are necessity and chance. If you unplug your bath and let the water run out down the plughole then interesting and complex patterns will form in the water. Depending on how dirty your bath water is, there may also be interesting and complex patterns left in the residue on the bottom of the bath. These are not designed; you did not intend to make them when you released the plug. A mixture of necessity (e.g. gravitational force) and chance condition these patterns. If every instance of apparent design in the universe can be explained by either necessity or chance then they cannot be unequivocally be assigned to the actions of a designer.

However, defining more closely our criteria for detecting design can strengthen the design argument. After all, there is a difference between patterns in bath scum and a finely crafted watch. The basis of these criteria is specified complexity. By specified we mean that there were many possible options, but a specific option was chosen; this would rule out necessity. By complexity we mean that the final outcome is sufficiently detailed to rule out chance. Where we find specified complexity, then we have a strong argument for design. A good example of this is a piece of writing, say, this chapter. For every letter that I type, there are 26 possible options, but each letter is specifically chosen to arrive at a complex arrangement. Here there is demonstrably specified complexity, and so we can reasonably conclude that this chapter is a product of an intelligence, not chance or necessity. If we can find features of the universe that exhibit specified complexity, then we have a strong argument for design.

The design argument does not, of itself, identify who or what this designer might be. From our experience of human designers, we can draw out some analogies that might apply to the designer of the universe. Human designers are intelligent and have intentions, so we should be looking for these qualities in our universe-designer. Also, human designers are a different thing to the thing they design (architects aren't houses; engineers aren't cars, etc.), so we should be looking outside the universe for our universe-designer. Our universe-designer then should be an immaterial, eternal being that is also an intelligence, and has intentions. Lastly, if one of the purposes of this universe-designer turns out to be the creation of intelligent human life, then it would seem that this universe-designer is interested in human beings. The universe-designer corresponds with our concept of God.

Possible Objections

Given enough time, anything that is possible will happen; how can you ever rule out chance?
Extending your timeframe increases your probabilistic resources by allowing for a greater number of "trials" to reach the desired outcome. If you roll three dice just once, it is fairly unlikely that you will get three sixes, but the more times you roll the dice, the greater your chances of getting that outcome. If you had an infinite amount of time, then you are certain to get that outcome. However, as we have seen, the universe is not infinite – it had a beginning in time. Therefore it is possible to calculate the probabilistic resources available, and it is possible to rule out chance for very low probability phenomena.

What about multiverse theories? If there are an infinite number of universes, any possible universe exists. You can never rule out chance.
If there were more than one universe, then this would increase your probabilistic resources by allowing a greater number of "trials" to reach the desired universe. If there were an infinite number of universes, then the existence of a universe like ours is certain. However, multiverse

theories are still just theories – there is no evidence for any universe other than our own.

Also, the multiverse theory is in danger of rendering all explanation obsolete. Imagine you are examining the impact crater in the aftermath of a battle. The most likely explanation is that a missile from one of the opposing armies caused it. But it is also remotely possible that during the middle of the battle, a team of highly intelligent alien engineers came and carefully crafted the crater to look just like an impact crater. This scenario, though laughably improbable, is also certain to have occurred somewhere if there are an infinite number of universes and so, regrettably, you could never rule it out as an explanation (multiverse theories are discussed in greater detail in the next chapter).

If the world is designed, why is there so much pain and suffering in the world?
The problem of suffering is an important issue, and is covered in greater detail in a later chapter. However, it is not an argument against design. Once chance and necessity are ruled out, then the appearance of design in the universe requires a designer. The question is, what does the existence of suffering tell us about the designer? One possibility is that the designer is malevolent and only interested in causing pain and suffering. But if that were the case, why would there also be goodness and beauty in the world? Another possibility is that the designer is indifferent to the fate of mankind and happy to let both good and evil happen. But if that were the case, why would the designer go to the trouble of producing mankind at all? The third possibility is that the designer is good and cares about mankind, but has others purposes than just making men and women blissfully happy.

The Best Explanation

The arguments presented in this chapter are the "classic" arguments for the existence of God; none of them is new or original, though recent developments in philosophy and science have given new perspectives on them. But how do we decide to what extent these and other arguments support the conclusion that there is a God?

One approach is to consider each argument in turn, find some objection to the argument, and so conclude that no argument supports the conclusion. Swinburne writes "sometimes ... philosophers consider the arguments for the existence of God in isolation from each other, reasoning as follows: the cosmological argument does not prove the conclusion, the teleological argument does not prove the conclusion, etc.,

etc., therefore the arguments do not prove the conclusion. But this 'divide and rule' technique with the arguments is inadmissible."[6] He correctly reasons that arguments may strengthen or weaken one another and so the right approach is to consider whether the arguments taken *as a whole* support the conclusion or not.

In this chapter, we have considered both deductive and inductive arguments for God. There is a third type of inference called **abduction,** where the conclusion is accepted on the basis that it is the best explanation of the available evidence. For example, in the case of a murder, if only one suspect had a motive, the means and the opportunity, then he is probably the murderer. Abduction does not exclude other possibilities, but infers the conclusion from the explanation most consistent with the evidence. It is the cumulative weight of evidence that establishes the conclusion; the more evidence, the stronger the argument. Finding some objection to each argument in turn does not undermine the conclusion, whilst the existence of God remains the best explanation for the available evidence.

In this chapter, we have considered three arguments in detail. From the cosmological argument we saw that there must be a cause of the universe. It seems most probable that this cause is an immaterial and eternal mind. We saw that if we accept the ontological argument then there must be one being that is not limited by space or time. From the teleological argument we saw that there is likely to be a designer of the universe, who has intelligence and intentions, and who is likely to have created humans for some purpose. These arguments all converge on the concept of God.

Other arguments could be added to these that add to the cumulative weight of our abductive argument. The world, and particularly our experience of the world, does not submit easily to materialist explanations. Humans are not mere biological machines but are discrete units of consciousness with a conception of self and with free will. We experience the world as a logical and intelligible place. We experience the world as a place where beauty, truth and goodness matter. None of these things would be expected on a materialist worldview, but are entirely consistent with the concept of God. Added to these arguments are more subjective experiences, like the desire for something transcendent, and individuals' experiences of God acting in peoples' lives. The best explanation for this variety of arguments and experiences is that God does exist.

---

[6] Swinburne, *The Existence of God,* 12.

However, whilst all these arguments are strong evidence for the existence of God, they do not give us specific information about him or his purposes. If God intended to give men and women specific information about himself and his purposes he would need to reveal himself in specific ways. In later chapters we will argue that God has done just this through the Bible.

Summary

- The concept of God is logically coherent – it is possible that such a being exists.
- If the universe had a beginning then there must have been a supernatural cause (cosmological argument).
- A necessarily existent being would not be limited by space and time (cf. ontological argument).
- If there is strong evidence of design in the natural world then there must have been a supernatural designer (teleological argument).
- The concept of God provides the best explanation for the available evidence.

Further Reading

For academic level explorations of the cosmological, ontological and teleological arguments see *The Blackwell Companion to Natural Theology*, edited by William Lane Craig and J. P. Moreland. For contemporary philosophical arguments see *New Proofs for the Existence of God* by Robert J. Spitzer.

For non-academic treatments of the "classic" arguments, then a college textbook such as *The Thinker's Guide to God* (chapter 6), will provide adequate introduction.

For the general reader, these arguments are considered in Timothy Keller's bestseller *The Reason for God* (chapters 8 & 9).

Fine-Tuning

Peter Jeavons

"Everyone agrees that the universe looks as if it was designed for life." – Paul Davies[1]

Introduction

Recent scientific advances in our understanding of the origin and development of the universe are raising some very profound questions.

We live on a planet we call Earth, that orbits a star we call the Sun; the Sun is one of a very large number of stars forming the Milky Way galaxy; that galaxy, in turn, is one of a very large number of galaxies, spread out across vast regions of space. Discoveries in physics, chemistry and cosmology suggest that the existence of a stable universe of this kind, providing an environment that can sustain complex life, is a remarkably delicate phenomenon. It is becoming increasingly clear from mathematical models and computer simulations that the formation of galaxies, stars, and planets depends on many physical constants having very precise and carefully co-ordinated values. The astrophysicist Paul Davies puts it like this: "If almost any of the basic features of the universe, from the properties of atoms, to the distributions of the galaxies, were different, life would very probably be impossible."[2]

The idea that many aspects of physics and chemistry seem to be required to take a very particular form in order to allow a universe to exist where life can develop has become known as the "anthropic principle".[3] The fact that so many apparent coincidences are required to account for the universe existing in a way that is capable of supporting life has become a

---

[1] P. Davies, *The Goldilocks Enigma: Why is the Universe Just Right for Life* (Penguin Books, 2007), 217.

[2] Davies, *The Goldilocks Enigma*, 3.

[3] The term "anthropic principle" seems to have been first used by the British astrophysicist Brendan Carter in 1974, and now has a very large literature. For an early comprehensive treatment with many references see J. Barrow & F. Tipler, *The Anthropic Cosmological Principle* (Oxford University Press, Oxford, 1986).

major puzzle in theoretical physics, which is sometimes referred to as the issue of "fine tuning".

Many physicists and astronomers have been struck by the surprising nature of these findings. The Nobel prize-winning physicist Arno Penzias, one of the discoverers of the cosmic microwave background radiation, reacted like this:

> Astronomy leads us to a unique event, a universe which was created out of nothing, and delicately balanced to provide exactly the conditions required to support life. In the absence of an absurdly improbable accident, the observations of modern science seem to suggest an underlying, one might say, supernatural plan.[4]

The theoretical physicist and mathematician, Freeman Dyson, famous for his work in quantum field theory, solid-state physics, astronomy and nuclear engineering, stated that:

> As we look out into the universe and identify the many accidents of physics and astronomy that have worked together to our benefit, it almost seems as if the universe must in some sense have known that we were coming.[5]

In this chapter we will first give some examples of the apparent coincidences that are raising such profound questions, and then we will go on to consider how such coincidences could possibly be accounted for.

Some Examples of Fine-Tuning

The examples we will consider are not about the nature of our particular local environment on planet Earth, which make it ideally suited for life forms such as ourselves (that is another story). Instead, we will focus on much more fundamental considerations relating to the possibility of life of any kind existing anywhere at all. Paul Davies sets out very clearly some of the necessary conditions for any kind of life to exist:

> To permit life in at least one place in the universe, three basic requirements must be satisfied:

---

[4] Quoted in W. Bradley, "The 'Just-so' Universe: The Fine-Tuning of Constants and Conditions in the Cosmos," in *Signs of Intelligence* (eds. W. Dembski and J. Kushiner; Grand Rapids: Brazos Press, 2001), 168.
[5] F. Dyson, *Disturbing the Universe* (New York: Harper and Row, 1979), 250.

1. The laws of physics should permit stable complex structures to form.
2. The universe should possess the sort of substances, such as carbon, that biology uses.
3. An appropriate setting must exist in which the vital components come together in the appropriate way.[6]

In other words, life requires suitable laws, suitable substances, and a suitable setting. We will consider each of these in turn.

Suitable Laws

The laws of physics are currently understood in terms of four fundamental forces: gravity, electromagnetism, and the strong and weak nuclear forces. All of these forces, working together in a delicate balance, seem to be necessary for stable complex structures to form. "If gravity did not exist, masses would not clump together to form stars or planets..... If the strong force didn't exist, protons and neutrons could not bind together and hence no atoms with atomic number greater than hydrogen would exist. If the electromagnetic force didn't exist, there would be no chemistry."[7]

As we begin to develop our understanding of these fundamental aspects of nature, we can get a clearer and clearer picture of what would happen if the strengths of these forces or the relationships between them were very slightly different. For example, it is now thought that the process of nuclear fusion going on in the inside of stars is reasonably well understood. Stars are held together by gravity, and the pressure exerted by gravity on the interior leads to the production of energy by the breakdown of the atoms. The force of gravity is extremely weak, compared to the electrical forces that bind atoms together and keep them from collapsing, which is why stars have to be enormously large in order to begin to exert enough pressure on the atoms at their centre to start the nuclear furnaces burning.

However, the formation of a stable nuclear furnace, such as our own Sun that is able to burn for billions of years and supply the constant source of

[6] Davies, *The Goldilocks Enigma*, 151.

[7] R. Collins, "The Teleological Argument: An Exploration of the Fine-Tuning of the Universe" in *The Blackwell Companion to Natural Theology* (eds. W. L. Craig & J. P. Moreland; Oxford: Blackwell publishers, 2009).

energy that sustains all life on Earth, requires a remarkable coincidence between the strengths of the forces involved. Paul Davies puts it like this:

> An alteration in say, the strengths of the gravitational force by a mere one part in 10^{40} would be sufficient to throw out this numerical coincidence. In such a world all stars would then either be blue giants or red dwarfs. Stars like the Sun would not exist, nor, one might argue, would any form of life that depends on solar-type stars for its sustenance.[8]

The number that Davies gives, 10^{40}, is scientific notation for a 1 followed by 40 zeroes, or in other words, ten thousand billion billion billion billion. It is the discovery of this astonishing level of precision[9] in the balance of the forces that is needed to form such fundamental structures as stars that has raised such a puzzle for scientists to explain.

The laws of physics also attempt to describe the properties and behaviour of the fundamental particles that make up the material world. All of the matter that we have been able to directly detect and investigate, including the matter that makes up the Earth and ourselves, consists of atoms of a few dozen different types, known as the chemical elements. These atoms in their turn are made up of more fundamental particles known as protons, neutrons and electrons. Each of these fundamental particles has a property called mass, which determines how the force of gravity affects it, and how it will react with other particles. Protons and neutrons each have around 2000 times as much mass as electrons, but have roughly the same mass as each other.

It is becoming clear that the exact values of the masses for different fundamental particles, and the relationships between them are crucial in determining the overall composition and properties of the matter in the universe.[10] For example, there is a very slight difference between the mass of a proton and the mass of a neutron – a neutron has around 0.1% more mass than a proton. Remarkably, it seems that this small difference needs

---

[8] P. Davies, *God and the New Physics* (Penguin Books, 1984), 188.

[9] Some authors have questioned whether such extreme precision is really necessary to achieve long-lived stars, notably Victor Stenger in "Natural Explanations for the Anthropic Coincidences", *Philo* 3 (2000). However, Stenger relies on a single simplified equation for estimating stellar lifetimes which does not take into account features such as size and mode of energy transport. For a more detailed response to Stenger see Collins, "The Teleological Argument".

[10] For an extensive early list of examples see Barrow and Tipler, *The Anthropic Cosmological Principle*.

to be very precisely set in order to allow the universe to develop a complex material structure at all. If the mass of a neutron was 0.2% higher than a proton, then protons could not fuse together to produce deuterium, so stars would not be able to burn hydrogen to release energy. On the other hand, if the mass of a neutron was slightly closer to the mass of the proton, then almost all hydrogen would be rapidly converted to helium, and the lifetime of stars would be drastically curtailed.

Suitable Substances

Stars play a significant role in the second basic requirement for any form of life that we listed above: the production of the sort of material substances that can be used to build complex life.[11] In the current scientific models of the universe, all of the chemical elements, apart from hydrogen and helium, are thought to have been formed in the nuclear furnaces of stars. Hydrogen atoms are fused together in these reactions to form helium, and helium atoms are then fused together in processes that lead to all of the heavier elements, including all those that make up planets such as the Earth, and complex life-forms such as ourselves.

However, there is a major problem with forming elements in this way: when two helium atoms fuse together to form beryllium, the result is extremely unstable, and will fall apart almost as soon as it is formed. This seems to allow little opportunity for a third helium atom to also become fused in order to form carbon before the beryllium decays. In fact, nobody could see how to make the process of nuclear fusion in stars create any significant quantities of the heavier elements such as carbon and oxygen until the physicist Fred Hoyle suggested in 1954 that there might be a remarkable coincidence in the properties of carbon and oxygen[12]. He suggested that the nuclei of carbon atoms might have a special excited state at a very specific energy level that corresponds to the energy of a beryllium nucleus plus a helium nucleus. He also suggested that oxygen would fail to have the same kind of excited state, at the

---

[11] Life on Earth is built largely out of chemical compounds of carbon, together with hydrogen, oxygen, nitrogen, phosphorus and sulphur, and traces of many other elements. It seems possible (but much less convenient) that complex life-forms could be built out of other chemical elements, but it is hard to imagine complex life-forms of any kind consisting entirely of hydrogen and helium. These elements simply do not sustain the required level of chemical complexity.

[12] The story of Hoyle's predictions and subsequent discoveries is told in more detail in a number of books, including *Cosmic Coincidences* by John Gribbin and Martin Rees (Black Swan 1991). It is a particularly interesting example because the remarkable physical coincidence was predicted before being discovered.

43

relevant energy level, which would explain why all the carbon that was produced was not converted to oxygen.

Hoyle suggested that these strange coincidences in the atomic properties of carbon and oxygen must hold, simply because they seem to provide the only way that carbon and oxygen can be formed in large quantities in nuclear reactions. When his predictions were borne out by experiments, they became one of the first examples of the use of the "anthropic principle" to understand the properties of the natural world. A more recent study in the journal *Science* has confirmed that small changes in the strengths of the electromagnetic force or the strong nuclear force would eliminate the delicate balance and result in virtually no carbon or oxygen production in stars.[13] The popular science writer John Gribbin, and the Astronomer Royal Martin Rees comment that "This combination of coincidences, just right for resonance in carbon-12, just wrong in oxygen-16, is indeed remarkable. There is no better evidence to support the argument that the universe has been designed for our benefit – tailor-made for man."[14] Although he remained a firm atheist all his life, Hoyle himself said that "I do not believe that any scientist who examined the evidence would fail to draw the inference that the laws of nuclear physics have been deliberately designed with regard to the consequences they produce inside stars."[15]

A Suitable Setting

Finally we consider the third basic requirement that we listed above for any form of complex life: the requirement for an appropriate setting to exist in which the vital components come together. The current scientific account of the universe proposes that it began in a very hot and dense fireball some 14 billion years ago – the so-called "Big Bang" – and has been expanding ever since. Initially, some atheist scientists resisted this description of the formation of the universe, partially on the grounds that it appeared to give too much justification to belief in a creator![16] However, the evidence for this scientific model has been steadily growing, and most scientists currently accept this as being a reasonable description of the

---

[13] H. Oberhummer, A. Csótó, and H. Schlattl, "Fine-Tuning of Carbon Based Life in the Universe by Triple-Alpha Process in Red Giants", *Science* 289:5476 (2000): 88-90.

[14] Gribben & Rees, *Cosmic Coincidences*. These authors go on to discuss alternative explanations which we will consider later in this chapter.

[15] Barrow and Tipler, *The Anthropic Cosmological Principle*, 22.

[16] See, for example, J. Maddox, "Down with the Big Bang", *Nature*, 340, (1989): 425.

history of the universe. (The atheists amongst them have had to make the necessary adjustments to their worldview to accommodate the idea.)

The idea of the whole universe expanding from a tiny beginning several billion years ago, and developing as it expands so that stars and planets come to be formed, and life comes to emerge on at least one planet, is now widely presented in popular scientific accounts. What is *not* often stressed, but is becoming steadily more appreciated by cosmologists and astronomers studying these phenomena, is the fact that this model only works if we introduce some remarkable "fine-tuning" in the basic constituents and the initial conditions.

For example, the density of the universe, a figure that cosmologists refer to as Ω, is absolutely crucial. If the universe emerged from the Big Bang with a density that was just a little too high, then it would be pulled together too strongly by gravity, and would collapse on itself in a "Big Crunch". On the other hand, if the density were just a little too low, then the expansion would spread the material of the universe too thinly for galaxies and stars to form, or for any interactions at all. Both of these are runaway processes – if the density is too large it rapidly gets larger and larger as the universe collapses; if the density is too small, it rapidly gets smaller and smaller. However, the Big Bang model suggests that we are now 13.7 billion years away from the Big Bang, and the universe clearly contains very many stars and galaxies. This implies that the value of the density at the beginning must have been very close indeed to the critical, "just-right" value, which is denoted by setting Ω to 1. John Gribbin puts it like this:

> In order for the Universe to have lasted that long, but not to have spread itself so thin that stars and galaxies could not form at all, the value of Ω in the first second after the beginning must have been very close indeed to 1. In fact, any deviation from 1 must have been smaller than 1 part in 10^{15} (one in a million billion).[17]

Incidentally, although the Big bang model requires the density of the universe to have a value which is exceedingly close to the critical value,

[17] J. Gribben, *In Search of the Multiverse* (Penguin Books, 2010), 53. Gribbin discusses inflation (a hypothetical period of extremely rapid expansion within the first fraction of a second) as a possible explanation for the value of Ω being so close to 1. However he points out that, even if inflation has taken place, one still has to explain why it should stop at precisely the right point.

the value that we obtain by adding up all of the matter in the stars and galaxies that we can observe is only around 4% of this critical value. By observing the way that galaxies move, astronomers conclude that there must be another form of matter in the universe, poetically known as "dark matter", which is estimated to make up another 23% of the critical density. This so-called dark matter is thought to be a form of matter that has not yet been identified on Earth, so very little is known about it. The remaining 73% of the critical density is completely unaccounted for; it is presumed to exist in an unknown form known as "dark energy". As Paul Davies remarks, "it seems that dark energy constitutes most of the mass of the universe, yet nobody knows what it is."[18]

Another remarkable feature of the universe is that it is very nearly, but not quite, uniform. Wherever we look in the universe, in all directions, we see galaxies containing hundreds of billions of stars, and those galaxies occur in clusters, containing thousands of galaxies. By estimating how much mass these clusters contain, and how tightly bound they are by gravity, astronomers can calculate the overall "lumpiness" of the universe - the deviation from the average density. In every cluster that has been investigated, this deviation comes out to around one part in a hundred thousand. This ties in very neatly with observations that have been made recently of the cosmic microwave background radiation that reaches the Earth from all regions of space and is thought to be left over from the radiation emitted by the Big Bang itself:

> One of the great triumphs of observational cosmology in the first decade of the twenty-first century has been the detection of irregularities exactly this size, one part in a hundred thousand, in the cosmic background radiation. This means that the irregularities, the seeds from which clusters of galaxies grew, were indeed imprinted long ago when the universe was young.[19]

But then the question arises of why the irregularities, now thought to be imprinted very early in the history of the universe, were that size and not a different size. Computer simulations suggest that if they were one tenth of this size, then stars and galaxies would not have been able to form at all. On the other hand, if the irregularities had been bigger, then massive concentrations of matter would have been brought together and collapsed into black holes. Indeed, if the deviations had been one part in a thousand, rather than one part in a hundred thousand, then the

---

[18] Davies, *The Goldilocks Enigma*, 140.
[19] Gribbin, *In Search of the Multiverse*, 56.

simulations suggest that all the matter of the universe would have collapsed into black holes. At present there is no clear reason why the universe should have emerged from the Big Bang with irregularities of just the right size to allow the formation of galaxies, stars and planets. It seems to be just another convenient fact, and another example of the fine-tuning required to generate a universe that allows any form of life.

To summarise all the examples given in this chapter: the best current scientific theories of the universe seem to require the strengths of the fundamental forces and the properties of the fundamental particles to be very precisely chosen in order to allow a complex stable universe to exist at all. Moreover, the Big Bang model only describes a universe with complex structure such as ours if the initial conditions, including the overall amount of matter and its distribution are specified with enormous precision.

Many of these examples, and others, are surveyed in a recent book called *The Grand Design*, by Stephen Hawking and Leonard Mlodinow – both atheists. In a chapter called "The Apparent Miracle", they state:

> Our universe and its laws appear to have a design that both is tailor-made to support us and, if we are to exist, leaves little room for alteration. This is not easily explained, and raises the natural question of why it is that way.[20]

Explanations for Fine-Tuning

There are very many scientists throughout the scientific community today who believe in some form of God, and simply regard these recent scientific findings as further confirmation and demonstration of the wisdom of the Creator, strengthening and deepening the statement of the Psalmist that "the heavens declare the glory of God."

However, some scientists, including Hawking and Mlodinow, are reluctant to accept any notion of a transcendent Creator,[21] and hence look for some

---

[20] S. Hawking & L. Mlodinow, *The Grand Design: New Answers to the Ultimate Questions of Life* (Bantam Press, 2010), 162.

[21] Indeed some authors, such as cosmologist Edward Harrison and science writer John Gribbin are so reluctant to contemplate a transcendent Creator outside of the physical world that they prefer to invoke the possibility of a designing intelligence within the physical world. In other words, they propose that our entire universe may be an artefact designed and brought into being by some advanced technological civilization, that somehow itself arose by chance (see E.W. Harrison, "The natural selection of universes containing intelligent life",

alternative way to account for the many examples of fine-tuning that are increasingly forming part of the scientific description of nature. What possible explanations are available?

A Unifying Theory?

An approach that was common in the latter part of the twentieth century was to assume that all of the remarkable coincidences found in nature would one day be shown to be consequences of some deeper underlying theory. However, this approach has now fallen somewhat out of favour. The very wide range of different fine-tuning coincidences, from the strength of gravity, to the energy levels of carbon, to the total amount of matter, seems to make such a hope rather ambitious. Certainly there are no theories currently envisaged that would account for all of these things, but it is of course possible that such a theory will one day be devised. What effect would devising such a marvellous theoretical unification have on our view of the universe? The existence of such a marvellously creative law of nature, that somehow entailed the development of a universe with all the right properties, would surely cry out for an explanation of its own. Hence this attempt at explaining fine-tuning only shifts the problem to another level. In other words, "even if all apparently anthropic coincidences could be explained [in terms of some grand unified theory], it would still be remarkable that the relationships dictated by physical theory happened also to be those propitious for life." [22]

Another issue, of course, is that no mathematical theory, no matter how elegant and profound, could ever, of itself, bring a universe into being. As Stephen Hawking puts it, "The usual approach of science of constructing a mathematical model cannot answer the questions of why there should

---

Quarterly Journal of the Royal Astronomical Society 36:3 (1995), 193, and Gribbin , *In Search of the Multiverse*, 197). Paul Davies comments rather wryly on such speculations: "If it were not for the fact that the speculators include some scientists of great distinction, the discussion could probably be dismissed without further ado. The fact that some great minds have been driven to explore such wild ideas is testimony to the intractable nature of the problems being confronted." (Davies, *The Goldilocks Enigma*, 230.) Paul Davies himself goes on to speculate that the universe might perhaps have been brought into being by the conscious minds that arise within it, as a result of some mysterious process of "backwards causation".
[22] B. J. Carr & M. J. Rees, "The Anthropic Cosmological Principle and the Structure of the Physical World", *Nature* 278 (1979): 605 -612.

be a universe for the model to describe. Why does the universe go to all the bother of existing? Is the unified theory so compelling that it brings about its own existence?"[23] Believing that an elegant theoretical description is a sufficient explanation for the universe is rather like believing that the rules of chess are sufficient on their own to manufacture the pieces and to play a thrilling game. More is needed to bring about a universe than elegant theories or laws.[24]

A lucky accident?

Another possibility is that the universe is simply a fluke, a remarkably lucky accident. This explanation alone seems somewhat unsatisfactory. For one thing, it can lead to the rather odd claim that everything within nature is intelligible, but nature itself is not: it just happened for no reason.

Some have attempted to make the accident hypothesis more palatable by invoking the anthropic principle in a particular way – they argue that we should not be surprised to find that the universe has the properties necessary to sustain complex life, because if it did not, then we would not be here to observe it. This argument has some rhetorical appeal, but *on its own* it doesn't actually take us very much further than the accident hypothesis. It still claims that something very unlikely has happened, for no apparent reason, but just tries to persuade us that we should not be surprised by it. The philosopher, John Leslie, gives a helpful analogy: If you found yourself sentenced to be executed by firing squad, 50 trained marksmen aimed their guns at you and fired, but you somehow escaped unhurt, you would doubtless be surprised and seek some sort of explanation. It would be unlikely to satisfy you if someone simply said that you shouldn't be surprised at this happy outcome, because if they had not all missed, you would be dead, and hence not around to observe it.

---

[23] S. Hawking, *A Brief History of Time. From the Big Bang to Black Holes*, (London, Bantam Press, 1988).

[24] As William Paley wrote in 1802 "It is a perversion of language to assign any law, as the efficient, operative cause of any thing. A law presupposes an agent; for it is only the mode, according to which an agent proceeds: it implies a power; for it is the order, according to which that power acts. Without this agent, without this power, which are both distinct from itself, the law does nothing; is nothing" (William Paley, *Natural Theology*, chap 1.VII).

49

One of many?

If we combine the anthropic principle with another hypothesis, that the entire universe we inhabit is part of a very large collection of universes, then it may begin to provide a certain kind of probabilistic explanation for fine-tuning.[25] This hypothesis, known as the multiverse hypothesis, is highly speculative, but it does at least attempt to deal with the issue of how it comes about that our particular universe has so many remarkably fortuitous properties – the idea is that, if we assume there are enough universes to choose from,[26] then it seems plausible that there will simply be some that get lucky, and we happen to find ourselves in one of them.

In fact several versions of the multiverse idea are currently being proposed, not all of which are compatible with each other. Some notions of the multiverse propose that everything that can possibly exist does in fact exist.[27] Although this is mathematically rather neat, it seems an extravagant hypothesis, and seems to lead to some rather absurd conclusions. It would appear to imply, for example, that in the vast majority of universes there would be no predictability at all, since every possible sequence of occurrences, no matter how bizarre, actually occurs somewhere.

Other versions of the multiverse hypothesis link it to the equally speculative "many worlds" interpretation of quantum mechanics, although this link needs to be viewed with caution. The many worlds interpretation of quantum mechanics postulates the existence of a large number of branching universes that split off from each other whenever certain quantum phenomena take place. These hypothetical universes

---

[25] Of course there are cases where such an argument, known as the *observer-selection effect* is perfectly valid, and makes a seemingly improbable outcome much more likely, or even inevitable. For example, it might initially seem very unlikely that not a single one of your ancestors died childless. However, the fact that you have been born actually makes it not just likely but absolutely certain that all your ancestors had children! However, observer-selection effects only apply in situations where there is a large collection of trials from which we have selected one with a particular outcome. Hence this form of argument can only be applied to explain fine-tuning if we are proposing that there exists a very large collection of universes to choose from.

[26] The number of separate universes required to make fine-tuning unremarkable is clearly very large indeed. Much larger, for example, than the number of stars in the observable universe (which is estimated to be around 10^{24}) or even the number of atoms in the observable universe (estimated to be around 10^{80}).

[27] See, for example, "Is 'the theory of everything' merely the ultimate ensemble theory?" *Annals of Physics* 270 (1998): 1-51.

share the same physical laws, and the same initial conditions, so they have no relevance to the issue of fine-tuning of these laws and conditions. The collection of universes required to address the problem of fine-tuning is rather different: these universes must have varying physical laws, and varying initial conditions, so that the right ones show up by sheer chance.

The most common form of the multiverse hypothesis is to assume some form of "universe-generating mechanism" that spits out universes continually, with appropriately varying laws and conditions.[28] One source of speculation about a universe-generating mechanism comes from the area of theoretical physics known as string theory. It was originally hoped that string theory would provide a unifying underlying theory accounting for the specific values of the various physical constants and predicting the laws of physics. However, it now seems that there are very many possible versions of string theory, each of which predicts different values for the physical constants and different forms for the laws. Some have attempted to turn this vice into a virtue, and proposed that somehow all of the different possibilities are actualised by some mechanism that, presumably randomly, brings into being vast numbers of separate universes covering the entire range of possibilities.

Although the idea of a multiverse is currently gaining popularity in some circles, it is important to remember that it is not yet supported in any direct way by experimental or observational evidence.

> …if we cannot visit the other universes, or experience them directly, their possible existence must remain just as much a matter of faith as belief in God. Perhaps future developments in science will lead to more direct evidence for other universes, but until then, the seemingly miraculous concurrence of numerical values that nature has assigned to her fundamental constants must remain the most compelling evidence for an element of cosmic design.[29]

The absence of empirical evidence obviously raises the question of whether such speculative ideas can count as a scientific theory at all. As Paul Davies says

> It is hard to see how such a purely theoretical construct can ever be used as an *explanation* in the scientific sense, of a

---

[28] For example, the chaotic inflationary multiverse proposed by Linde in "The self-reproducing inflationary universe", *Scientific American* (Spring 1998): 98-104.
[29] Davies, *God and the New Physics,* 189.

feature of nature. Of course, one might find it easier to believe in an infinite array of universes than in an infinite Deity, but such a belief must rest on faith rather than observation.[30]

As well as the complete lack of evidence, there is also the philosophical difficulty that once we assume a sufficiently large number of universes, then we can argue that any observation at all becomes possible, and hence unsurprising.[31] This completely undermines the scientific enterprise: "By providing an all-too-easy explanation for *anything* that has happened or may happen, the multiverse ends up explaining *nothing* at all."[32]

Most significantly of all, for our purposes here, we note that all of the mechanisms that have been proposed to generate multiple universes seem to require their own fine-tuning in order to achieve the desired properties in a stable and sustainable form[33]. Hence this approach again seems to simply move the problem of fine-tuning from the universe that we know something about, to a hypothetical universe-generating mechanism, that we know nothing about and cannot observe.

In the beginning, God

The existence of many exquisitely fine-tuned coincidences in the nature of physical laws, and in the initial conditions of the universe, is clearly consistent with the existence of a supremely wise Creator who brought the universe into being in a very particular, carefully-chosen form in order to bring about the existence of life. Historically, this has probably been the dominant view amongst Western scientists – certainly it was the view of many of the scientific pioneers, who established the scientific method, including Galileo, Kepler and Newton. These early scientists viewed their scientific work as an attempt to discover more about the creative works of God. They would not have been at all surprised to learn of the extreme delicacy and precision required to make a universe where life can exist.

---

[30] Davies, *God and the New Physics,* 174.

[31] Indeed, the idea of a multiverse has already been used in this way by one author to account for the extremely improbable event of the origin of life, see E. Koonin, "The cosmological model of eternal inflation and the transition from chance to biological evolution in the history of life," *Biology Direct*: www.biology-direct.com/content/2/1/15, published 31/05/2007, accessed 31/12/2010.

[32] B. Gordon, "Inflationary Cosmology and the String Multiverse", in *New Proofs for the Existence of God,* (Robery Spitzer; Eerdmans, 2010), 101.

[33] The original formulation of the inflationary multiverse had to be revised by introducing considerable fine-tuning of the initial conditions so that the universes generated did not bump into each other. See Alabidi and Lyth "Inflation models and observation", *Journal of Cosmology and Astroparticle Physics* (2006).

In the twenty-first century, as the examples of fine-tuning we discover become ever more remarkable, the most satisfying and economical explanation seems to be that we live in a unique universe[34] of remarkable delicacy and precision, fashioned by its Creator for his good purposes.

> For this is what the LORD says,
>> the one who created the sky – he is the true God,
>> the one who formed the earth and made it;
>> he established it,
>> he did not create it without order, he formed it to be
>> inhabited (Isaiah 45:18)

Summary

- The universe appears to be fine-tuned for the existence of life.
- This fine-tuning is apparent in many aspects, including:
    - the laws of nature
    - the formation of the chemical elements
    - the existence of complex stable structures such as galaxies, stars and planets.
- Attempts to explain away these "coincidences" by appeal to speculations about a multiverse are unconvincing.
- The remarkable complexity evident in the fine-tuning of the universe speaks of a Creator.

Further Reading

For more examples of fine-tuning, and more details on the examples given here, see Paul Davies, *The Goldilocks Enigma: Why is the Universe Just Right for Life* or Martin Rees, *Just Six Numbers: The Deep Forces that Shape the Universe.*

---

[34] Of course, there is no reason why a Creator capable of creating our universe should not have created a carefully-designed universe-generating mechanism, or some other form of multiverse. Believers in God can be perfectly happy to adopt an open mind on the whole question of the multiverse, and to wait and see whether any of the current ideas can be developed into a truly workable and coherent theory with evidential support. The historical precedents suggest we should beware of underestimating the power of God or the extravagance of his creative activity.

For a philosophical treatment of the fine-tuning argument see John Leslie, *Universes* or the chapter by Robin Collins, in *The Blackwell Companion to Natural Theology*.

For a discussion of the implications of these scientific discoveries for belief in God see John Lennox, *God's Undertaker: Has Science Buried God?* (chapter 4), or Alister McGrath, *A Fine-Tuned Universe: the Quest for God in Science and Theology*.

The Origin of Life

Paul Boyd

"knowledge of the physical, chemical, and biological conditions that life requires makes it extremely implausible that life simply arose by chance" – Roger White[1]

Introduction

Few things excite the passions of debate more than a discussion over the origin of life. The stakes are high. If a supreme being is credited with creation, then there are obligations to that creator. If life can be explained away by purely natural phenomena, then the consequence is freedom to live however one pleases and hope that life will gradually and naturally get better.

Science is building a knowledge base of truth about life based on the facts. In this chapter we will also be dealing with facts. Even the Bible asks us to "examine all things" (1 Thess 5:21). So we have a common mechanism of establishing truth – it must be based on facts.

It *almost* goes without saying that no man saw the origin of life. No man can tell us what happened – so we must look at what facts are available from other sources. This is what we do for many other things in life. We do not see most of what we know, but we do form conclusions based on information from other sources. Our justice system is based on this approach. When there is reasonable evidence, then the judge and/or jury make their decisions. In the same way, we can form opinions about the origin of life from the evidence around.

At different times, scientists have tried to replicate the early conditions that are thought to have existed on the primitive earth. They have done

---

[1] R. White, "Does Origins of Life Research Rest on a Mistake?", *Noûs* 41:3 (2007): 475.

this in an attempt to repeat the formation of life. Particularly famous is the work of Stanley Miller at the University of Chicago.[2] He established this 'primitive atmosphere' in the laboratory. Nitrogen, hydrogen, carbon dioxide, water and ammonia were subjected to stimulations of lightning, and the products measured. After two days, he discovered the mixture was about 2% amino acids. Further experiments were able to produce 19 out of the 20 amino acids that are necessary for life. They also found other simple biochemicals had occurred, including some of the chemicals found in DNA. Science hailed this experiment as the answer to the origin of life.

But since those early experiments, things have become less clear. The primitive conditions of the earth are now thought to be very different from what was used in those early experiments.[3] The new conditions are much less likely to make amino acids. In particular, it is now known that the early atmosphere contained oxygen, and oxygen is known to cause the breakdown of amino acids. Scientific attempts to replicate the formation of life in experimental conditions have not shed light on how life could have occurred by natural means.

Francis Crick, the co-discoverer of the structure of DNA, when commenting on this problem in *Life Itself*, said;

> The origin of life seems almost to be a miracle, so many are the conditions which would have had to have been satisfied to get it going[4]

Klaus Dose describes the position:

> More than thirty years of experimentation on the origin of life in the fields of chemical and molecular evolution have led to a better perception of the immensity of the problem of the origin of life on earth rather than to its solution. At present all discussions on principal theories and experiments in the field either end in stalemate or in a confession of ignorance[5]

---

[2] S. L. Miller, "A production of amino acids under possible primitive earth conditions", *Science* 117 (1953): 528-9.
[3] C. F. Chyba, "Rethinking Earth's early atmosphere", *Science* 308 (2005): 962-3; M. Hoashi et al. "Deep sea rocks point to early oxygen on earth", *Nature Geoscience* 2 (4) (2009): 301-306.
[4] F. Crick, *Life Itself: Its Origin and Nature* (Simon and Schuster, 1981), 88.
[5] K. Dose, "The Origin of Life; More Questions than Answers", *Interdisciplinary Science Reviews* 13(4) (1988): 348-356.

Since the time these words were spoken, our increased knowledge has only reinforced this view.

The Origin of the First Protein

The first and greatest step in the origin of life is the formation of the simplest self-replicating life form. This is the cell. There are many types of cells, from the large and very complex to the "simple". We will not debate about what might have been the first cell; we will assume that we need to look at the simplest. Before we look at the simplest cell, we will look at the formation of some of the basic chemicals that make up the cell. Firstly, we will look at the formation of a protein. Proteins are essential parts of cells that must have existed prior to the formation of a complete cell.

Proteins are the 'doing' chemicals in the cell. They are like the skilled workmen who perform the majority of tasks. Without proteins, we simply do not know how life could work. A protein is like a necklace made out of beads, but without the ends joined. The single chain of beads is then twisted and bent into a complex 3D structure, with certain repetitive units and with certain units working together to make specific 3D shapes. This is no haphazard shape, for the resulting shape has exactly the right beads in the right place. This allows the protein to link to other proteins and other chemicals and perform its job.

Each bead of a protein is an amino acid, and a typical protein has more than 100 of them in a specific sequence. There are twenty types of beads that are used in any specific protein. Further complexity comes from linkages that are made within the sequence to make the 3D structure tough, but we will ignore this for the sake of simplicity. Generally, each bead must be in the right place on the necklace for the protein to work. There are some substitutions that can be made, and generally these are substitutions with beads of similar properties.[6]

For life to occur by natural means, a protein needs to be able to form naturally. That is, the amino acids need to come together randomly to form this 100-amino acid protein. We are able to model the likelihood of this happening. Using probabilities, we are able to calculate the likelihood

---

[6] Amino acids may be hydrophilic, hydrophobic, acidic, basic, simple, aromatic and cysteine. For the sake of this discussion, we will assume substitutions can be made within each of these seven groups. In reality this is not always the case.

of getting the correct sequence of amino acids (or rather the correct sequence of groups). This is a simple calculation, and is $(1/7)^{100}$. This is one chance in 10^{84} (1 with 84 noughts after). This theoretical calculation is not far off experimental studies,[7] which put the chance formation of a functional protein as ranging from 1 in 10^{63} to 1 in 10^{75}.

So what does this number mean? To put it in perspective, the chances of winning the UK National Lottery in a given week are approximately 1 in 10^{7} (1 with 7 noughts after). This is so unlikely that many people do not bother with the lottery. These odds are remote, but they are huge compared to the possibility of a single protein randomly forming.

Now probabilities are easy to misunderstand. Part of this is the use of the word "probable". It sounds like the event *is* probable. But one can put a probability value on almost anything and say that, given enough time, something is bound to occur. What is the probability of a pig flying? What is the probability of trees sprouting dollar bills? The fact that there is a probability does not mean that it can really happen. A man may take 10 hours to swim the English Channel, but what time will he take to swim the Atlantic? The reality is that man will never swim the Atlantic, and asking the question in the first place makes loads of assumptions that are not true. For example, it is assumed that the man has enough fitness; that he will have food on the way, that the weather will be kind, that he is not eaten by sharks, etc.

In the same way, the question around the "Probability of life forming by chance" invokes many assumptions and misconceptions. Firstly, this event is not "probable" at all. Secondly, there are a whole host of assumptions that are made around this argument. Let us look at *some* of them:

1. That all 20 beads are present in the same place, in approximately equal amounts and in sufficient concentrations to be available to combine randomly.

---

[7] B. J. Strait & G. T. Dewey, "The Shannon information entropy of protein sequences", *Biophysical Journal* 71 (1996): 148-55; J. U. Bowie, J. F. Reidhaar-Olson, W. A. Lim & R. T. Sauer, "Deciphering the message in protein sequences: Tolerance to amino acid substitution", *Science* 247 (1990): 1306-10; cf. H. Yockey, *Information Theory in Molecular Biology* (Cambridge: Cambridge University Press, 1992): 242-258; cf. W. L. Bradley, "Information, Entropy, and the Origin of Life" in *Debating Design* (eds. W. A. Dembski & M. Ruse; Cambridge: Cambridge University Press, 2006): 336-8.

2. That the beads were all the right mirror image variety, and not a natural mix of left and right hand images (this is a technical reality that exists with amino acids in cells).

3. That the temperature and conditions in which the amino acids might react together to form a protein are optimal.[8]

4. That the conditions are stable over the billions of years to allow chance to operate in this optimal way.

5. That the protein, when formed, is stable and does not change. That it is not destroyed by the heat of the day or the cold of the winter (in reality, they are highly likely to be destroyed).

6. That the proteins are not dispersed by wind, rain or immediately diluted by diffusion in water.

7. That the protein is able to replicate, and that the other proteins are also stable (proteins do not replicate).

8. Most proteins are actually made of many more amino acids than 100, and a number are made up of combinations of several proteins linked together. We assume that a simple protein is enough to get things going!

Now none of these assumptions is likely to hold when we consider the possibility of life occurring by natural means. All of these assumptions will make the possibility of a protein forming by natural means less likely. To get a sense of how unlikely it is, let us consider the number of particles in the universe. By particles we mean protons, electrons and neutrons: the small particles that make atoms (our elements). It is estimated[9] that the number of particles in the universe is 10^{80}. This number is similar to the 1 in 10^{84} that we calculated for the formation of a single protein. It means that if every particle in the universe were a random sequence of 100 amino acids, there would only be enough particles in the universe to make a single protein by natural means.

The Origin of the Genetic Code

We can look at the problems of the origin of existing life forms from a different angle. The discoveries of the workings of the genetic code allow us to consider the possibilities of the genetic code occurring by natural means. Within each cell, it is the DNA that has the information to make

---

[8] Amino acids can be linked together in the laboratory by multiple steps of complex chemical reactions. Each of these steps requires different optimal conditions and different chemicals at each step

[9] W. A. Dembski, *The Design Inference: Eliminating Chance through Small Probabilities* (Cambridge: Cambridge University Press, 1998).

the proteins. This information can be compared to a series of technical manuals as to how to make life. The manuals are written using different chemicals that are able to spell out a language based on four letters. The origin of this information must be explained in any discussion on the origin of life. If we had "Which came first?" discussion, rather like the chicken or the egg, we could argue that maybe the DNA came before the protein. In fact, no one seriously believes the DNA came first, because the problems with this theory are far greater than if the protein came first. Nevertheless, a discussion of the DNA does provide us with a fresh look at the origin of life by natural means.

DNA (DeoxyriboNucleic Acid) is a complex yet beautiful chemical. It consists of two chemical chains closely linked together and then twisted round each other, making a single long twisted strand. The chemical chains themselves can be made up of different components. It is the order of the components in the chains that makes up the chemical letters. In reality, things are a little more complex. Sets of three components (bases) define what the chemical letter actually is, and other biochemicals recognise these triplets as different. As a result, and via a complex but elegant chemical pathway, a triplet determines which amino acid goes into a protein. As the chain of amino acids grow, it is crafted into a complex 3D molecule.

The genetic code is, simply stated, a sequence of information. It functions in a similar way that by which software controls a computer. Bill Gates, the founder of the Microsoft computer company, compared DNA with a computer program:

> DNA is like a computer program, but far, far more advanced
> than any software we've ever created."[10]

If DNA is like a complex computer program, then it begs a huge question: where did the genetic code come from? Did someone write it, or did it just happen?

Let us consider the possibility of the DNA code occurring by natural (random) means. Although human DNA has 3 billion letters, we will look at the formation of something much simpler. Let us consider the possibility of getting a single sonnet of Shakespeare by random means. A sonnet has a typical length of 488 letters. Since there are 26 letters in the English alphabet, then the possibility of a sonnet occurring by chance is

---

[10] Bill Gates, *The Road Ahead* (Viking, Penguin Group, 1995), 188.

26 times itself 488 times (26^{488}). This is one chance in 10^{690}. As we said before, the number of particles in the universe is 10^{80}. So even if all the particles in the universe were random sequences of 488 letters of the English alphabet, there are not enough particles for a single sonnet to occur naturally. Or to put it another way simply – it is impossible.

It is not just the sequence of DNA that makes the formation and functioning of DNA by natural means unlikely. The complexity involved in controlling and copying the DNA is very great. In order for a single gene (a small part of the DNA) to be used to make a protein, somehow the cell must know which gene and where to find it. Like an index to an encyclopaedia, it must locate the right volume, then unravel the right part of the DNA as if taking out a volume, turn to the right page and then photocopy the right section of the page. The complexity in the cell is even greater than this. Many genes are made up of bits from about 30 pages from different parts of the encyclopaedia. These bits are then sown together in a process called "splicing", to make a full gene. The control around this process is simply amazing. It requires the DNA to be unwound and unzipped at high speed (100 "letters" a second). The cell has its own unwinding mechanism, and errors in this unwinding mechanism give rise to disease (Werner's syndrome or premature aging).

The DNA has to be perfectly copied otherwise the errors give rise to further diseases. It has been estimated that an error rate of 1 in 100,000 bases in cells would result in inactive proteins that would lead to cell death.[11] Experiments show that the enzyme that copies DNA do gives rise to one error every 100,000 bases. Although this is amazingly accurate, it would spell disaster for the cell. In a human this would mean 120,000 mistakes every time a cell replicated. Fortunately the cell has proofreading proteins that correct 99% of these errors. Even then that is not good enough for normal replication. Fortunately, there is another mismatch correction protein that reduces copying errors down to acceptable levels. In some bacteria, self-correcting mechanisms give rise to error rates of only one error in 3 billion letters![12] This is mind-blowingly accurate copying, even inside simple bacteria. Without such correcting mechanisms, DNA replication by natural means is prone to error.

[11] M Voliotis et al, "Backtracking and Proofreading in DNA Transcription", *Physical Review Letters* (2009): 102(2).
[12] L. Pray, "DNA replication and causes of mutation", *Nature Education* (2008): 1.

The Third Way – RNA

We have seen the significant barriers to life arising from either proteins or DNA. Consequently, scientists have looked for another molecule. There is one other obvious alternative – RNA. RNA is like DNA but more flexible. It occurs within cells in many different forms. Significantly, it is the intermediate between proteins and DNA in the cell – DNA is copied by RNA, which is then used to make proteins. Two properties of RNA make some scientists consider RNA as the viable first life chemical. Firstly, it stores information much as DNA can. Secondly, it is able to speed up chemical reactions (like enzymes). This happens because the shapes of RNA are more versatile than DNA.

Despite the advantages of RNA, there are also disadvantages. One of the problems with RNA is that it has been very difficult to make in the laboratory. It is only recently that a simple RNA molecule has been made under 'natural' conditions.[13] In order for this molecule to be made, a precise sequence of events and conditions was required in the laboratory. Another disadvantage is that RNA can be easily broken down. This means that its potential as a long term store of information in limited. Finally, RNA is also prone to sequence changes (mutations) when it is copied, caused by ultraviolet radiation.[14]

RNA, like DNA, has a chain of different nucleotides, so that it contains the information of DNA. RNA, like proteins, has complexity coming from its 3D structure. This means that similar probability calculations done on proteins and DNA can also be done on RNA. The likelihood of RNA being the starting molecule for life is as likely as that of proteins or DNA – that is, impossible.

Other Alternatives for Starting Molecules

The difficulties with the origin of life from protein, DNA or RNA molecules have led scientists to look elsewhere for the molecules that started life. The Iron-Sulphur World Theory[15] suggests that replicating

---

[13] M W Powner, B Gerland & J D Sutherland. "Synthesis of activated pyrimidine ribonucleotides in prebiotically plausible conditions", *Nature* 460 (2009).

[14] T. Lindahl, "Instability and decay of the primary structure of DNA". *Nature* 362 (1993): 709–15.

[15] G. Wächtershäuser, "From volcanic origins of chemoautotrophic life to Bacteria, Archaea and Eukarya", *Philosophical Transactions of the Royal Society B: Biological Sciences* 361 (2006): 1787–1808.

biochemicals commenced in volcanic vents at high temperature and pressure. Here, simple carbon molecules are converted into more complex carbon molecules. The presence of mineral surfaces like iron sulphide is postulated to make these reactions more likely. Alternative theories for the origin of life suggest that clays or deep-sea vents were potential locations for primeval chemicals to get started. Any situation where a biochemical could form is considered a potential source of life getting started.

None of these chemical theories has got to the end of the first step – the generation of replicating molecules of sufficient complexity. There are many ideas and many successful elementary experiments on how to get simple biochemicals. But none of these can get us to the first step of complex biochemicals that can replicate on their own. This means that there is currently no workable theory that has shown how life could get started. The next step for chemicals is how to sustain what was started, and how to make the chemicals even more complicated. These steps have not been addressed and there is little understanding as to how they can have taken place. We have not yet discussed how groups of different types of molecules can be made in different places and then come together to form simple groups of chemicals. There is no point in discussing these steps unless the first step can be explained.

The Origin of the First Cell

The simplest cell is thought to be a bacterial cell. A cell is a vast array of simple and complex chemicals bound together and working together somehow (we do not know how) to make the cell living. The composition of a typical cell has been estimated below:[16]

- Metabolites, cofactors, ions – many millions (>800 types)
- Glycogen – 4,300
- Lipids – 22 million
- Lipopolysaccharides – 1.4 million
- Peptidoglycan – 1
- Polyamines – 6.7 million (2 types)
- Proteins – 1 million (1850 types)

---

[16] F, Neidhardt et al. *Escherichia coli and Salmonella typhimurium: Cellular and Molecular Biology* (ASM Press, Washington, DC, 1996).

- DNA – 1 (very long)
- RNA – 250,000 (663 types)

Among bacteria, the simplest bacterial cells are from a group called mycoplasma. It should be noted that even the mycoplasma is not as simple as first thought, and has many similarities with the more complex bacterial cells.[17] We will take the mycoplasma as the simplest bacterial cell.

It is thought that, under certain situations, mycoplasma may not require all its complex machinery. It has been estimated that only 382 of the genes of a mycoplasma are critical for the simplest type of life.[18] If we assume that each gene is the simplest type and gives rise to a single protein (of 100 amino acids), then each cell requires 382 different types of proteins. If each protein has a probability of occurring by chance as 1 in 10^{84} (see before), then the probability of the proteins in the cell forming by chance is 1 in $10^{84 \times 382}$ (10^{32088}). And we have not considered anything apart from the appearance of proteins. It is clear that the probability of the proteins forming is far far less than any probability figure we have so far considered. If the probability of a single protein occurring by chance is impossible, then we can easily see that the formation of a cell by chance is (if it were scientific to say it) even more impossible.

We need to try and put these figures into context. What if we consider all the particles and all the time in the universe?

The total amount of material and time in the universe has been used in calculations to estimate what could be achieved by nature:

- There are estimated to be around 10^{80} particles in the universe.
- The universe is estimated to be about 10^{25} seconds old.
- It is estimated that chemicals transition from one physical state to another cannot occur faster than 10^{45} times a second. This is even under the most favourable conditions.

If one combines all these factors into what is possible, we have:

$$10^{80} \times 10^{25} \times 10^{45} = 10^{150}$$

[17] A. Christiansson & P. Mårdh , "Chemical composition and ultrastructure of Mycoplasma hominis", *Sex Transm Dis.* 10(4 Suppl) (1983): 240-3.
[18] Glass et al, PNAS, (2005).

This value of 10^{150} is the limit of all chemical reactions within the universe. If the entire universe were committed to forming life, and all the time for which the universe existed was spent on this activity, then there was not enough time available by a long way. 10^{150} is far short of 10^{32088}.

Fred Hoyle, when discussing the probabilities of the formation of a cell, put it in a famous and graphic way:

> The chance that higher life forms might have emerged in this way is comparable with the chance that 'a tornado sweeping through a junk-yard might assemble a Boeing 747 from the materials therein'.[19]

All the (Available) Time in the World

The standard argument against the "unlikelihood of life" discussion above is that there is "all the time in the world" for chance to run its course and nature to come up with a winner. This is not true. We have considered the age of the universe in the calculation above. Here we will consider the age of the earth.

The date of the origin of the earth comes from rocks. The age of the earth is generally agreed to be 4.5 billion years.[20] The earth was thought to be inhospitable for the first 500 million years. This was a time when the earth was under attack from meteorites – one of which is thought to have caused the moon to break off.[21] Rocks dated 150 million years later are being found with single-celled life.[22] This means current science says that the first single-celled life arose within a 150 million year period. In the whole scheme of things, this time period is very small indeed. Time does not explain the occurrence of life by natural means.

Alternative Theories for the Origin of Life

We have examined the possibility of life on earth occurring by natural means. The formation of a single cell has been found to be impossible.

---

[19] F. Hoyle, quoted in "Hoyle on evolution," *Nature* 294 (1981): 105.
[20] G. Dalrymple, "The age of the Earth in the twentieth century: a problem (mostly) solved", *Special Publications Geological Society of London* 190 (2001): 205–221.
[21] S. Gould, "The Evolution of Life on Earth", *Scientific American* (1994).
[22] S. J. Mojzis *et al.*, "Evidence for life on earth before 3,800 million years ago", *Nature* 384 (1996): 55–9.

The formation of just a single protein, RNA or DNA – three of the most likely starting molecules – by natural means, is impossible. When faced with such calculations, some scientists argue that they may be true, but that there must have been different molecules or conditions that were used, and even simpler life forms as starting points.

Of course, we can break down any journey from one form to another into smaller and smaller steps, so that the intermediate steps start to seem possible. We could draw an evolutionary sequence of how a child's tricycle changed into a sports car. Each step could be made smaller and smaller so that the first step starts to seem possible. This does not mean that the full evolutionary journey happened. It just means we can imagine it.

There would undoubtedly be more likelihood of simple chemicals occurring by chance. But what is the value of an amino acid sequence of 5 amino acids? It cannot perform any function, it cannot replicate, and getting to a more complex form is very difficult. And of what value is a DNA sequence just spelling the first "word"? It does not have any biological meaning, and it must somehow get to a more complex form in order to be useful. We may have reduced the chances of getting to the first step, but then the first step is not particularly helpful. Simple chemicals must get to the next step or the one after in order to be functional and useful.

There are many scientists who understand the enormity of this problem. This is why many, including Francis Crick, proposed that life did not occur on earth, but must have occurred in outer space and then come to earth on meteorites or by some other means.[23] This is the theory of panspermia. Now, this does not solve the problem of the origin of life. It simply moves it to another place. In fact, it makes the concept of the origin of life more difficult, since life must survive re-entry into the earth's atmosphere and collision with the earth's surface. Wherever the problem of the origin of life is moved to, the problem still remains. There may be more time, because the age of the universe is thought to be greater than the age of the earth, but the time element is not that different. The age of the universe is thought to be 14 billion years,[24] as opposed to the 4.5 billion year age of the earth. And there are still no more particles in the

[23] F. H. Crick, & L. E. Orgel, (1973). "Directed Panspermia", *Icarus* 19 (1973): 341–348.
[24] "Seven-Year Wilson Microwave Anisotropy Probe (WMAP) Observations: Sky Maps, Systematic Errors, and Basic Results", (NASA, US Government).

universe to make even a simple protein by natural means. The probability gets a bit larger, but not significantly.

Summary of the Materialist Position Based on Facts

All the above theories struggle with getting much beyond the basics. Single chemicals can be formed under natural conditions, but not much is achieved beyond that. In none of these theories is there the ability to move to the more complex sustainable and replicating chemicals that might be associated with life. This leaves all existing materialistic explanations without proof of a workable theory.

This in turn leads the materialist into a difficult position. Without a workable theory for the origin of life, the materialist must make some assumptions. He must assume that nature alone found a way to make life. Somewhere, somehow, it must have happened. He does not know how, but there must have been a way that has not yet been discovered by science. This, then, is a belief. It is a belief that science will one day explain the origin of life by natural means. In some ways, this belief is like a position of faith, as is sometimes acknowledged within the scientific community[25] – faith that life arose naturally and that science will one day prove this.

We started this investigation with a desire to follow the facts. The facts seem to rule out a materialistic explanation of the origins of life on this planet.

A Creator

If life could not have occurred by natural (i.e. random) means, then it leaves us with the alternative – that there must have been an intelligent creator. Only creative intervention can explain the formation of a protein, or the simplest cell, or the 100-trillion-cell human body. All other theories are impossible.

We must deal with the facts, as a scientist should. Unfortunately, scientists are human too, and allow non-scientific attitudes to get in the way of the facts. The Greek philosopher Socrates said, "*We must follow the argument wherever it leads*." We too should follow the argument wherever it leads. It is rare to see this spirit of bravery among scientists on the subject

---

[25] J. T. Trevors & D. L. Abel, "Chance and necessity do not explain the origin of life", *Cell Biology International* (2004): 736.

of the origin of life, but it does happen. Consider the comments of the British physicist and atheist Chandra Wickramasinghe:

> It is quite a shock. From my earliest training as a scientist I was very strongly brainwashed to believe that science cannot be consistent with any kind of deliberate creation. That notion has had to be very painfully shed. I am quite uncomfortable in the situation, the state of mind I now find myself in. But there is no logical way out of it.

> Once we see that the probability of life originating at random is so utterly miniscule as to make it absurd, it becomes sensible to think that the favourable properties of physics on which life depends are in every respect 'deliberate'.[26]

The analogy of software is helpful and challenging when considering the origin of DNA. All software has a programmer. The code can be copied, corrupted and destroyed, but new chapters do not just happen unless a programmer makes an upgrade. No new DNA software chapters are known to have occurred in nature. It must be admitted that this would be difficult to detect and prove, but it is true nonetheless. However, errors and corruption of the code do occur naturally (when we are speaking about DNA, these are called mutations). They give rise to genetic diseases, deformities and natural variation. The DNA instruction manual of life needs an author. It makes sense that this is an intelligent creator.

Summary

These are the things we have learnt in this study:

1. It is impossible for even a single small protein to occur by chance.
2. It is impossible for the genetic code to occur by chance.
3. It is impossible for a single cell to occur by chance.
4. Current scientific theories of the origin of life are not workable.
5. All the evidence points to a designer.

There is a principle in science. This is the principle that one should not invent complex explanations when there is a simpler one. It is the simplest explanation that is usually the right one. This principle is attributed to William of Ockham, and is known as Occam's Razor. The

---

[26] Quoted in "Hoyle on Evolution", *Nature* (Nov 1981): 105.

reference to the razor is a reference to the need to shave away unnecessary complexity, in order to get to the simplest explanation. This is what must be done when dealing with complex arguments in this debate.

We should use the principle of Occam's Razor when considering the origin of life. Does it make more sense to believe in the impossibilities of a natural origin of life? Or does it make sense to believe in a designer to which all the evidence points? We must follow the argument wherever it leads.

Further Reading

There are a number of accessible treatments of the issue of the origins of life. Some recommendations are John Lennox's *God's Undertaker* (chapters 7-11), John Bilello's *Bible and Science* (chapter 10) and Alan Hayward's *God Is* (chapter 5).

Consciousness

John Launchbury

"Idealists would say that what the materialist argument is missing is consciousness" – Keith Ward[1]

This chapter is about *consciousness*. It is hard to define consciousness precisely—it's that part of us that is aware of being aware—but it's easy to experience it. Just stop reading for a moment and be aware of how it feels to be sitting, the feeling of your breath entering and leaving your body, what your toes and fingers feel like. Okay, do it now.

In this moment of mindfulness, you are fully conscious. That's what we're talking about.

We will use the phenomenon of consciousness to counter a view that's quite prevalent in the western world, namely that everything in the universe—including us—is made up of physical stuff and nothing more. We will explore implications for arguments against the existence of God.

Our line of argument will entail four steps:

1. Review what science is, and distinguish it from *physicalism*;
2. Explore what consciousness is, and how it might be measured;
3. Tie into ideas of quantum physics and time;
4. And draw some conclusions.

Science and Physicalism

Let us start by asking, "What is science?" Science is the development of predictive models of observed events, as seen from the vantage point of an objective, external observer. Hmm. That's pretty dry so let's expand it a little.

---

[1] K. Ward, "Debunking Simplicity", *EerdWord* (March 2011). Online at: eerdword.wordpress.com/2011/03/09/debunking-simplicity-by-keith-ward.

The process of science starts with cataloguing observations. It amasses descriptions, like stamp collecting. Then, on the basis of recognizing patterns, scientists build simple models of behaviour and may begin to make some predictions. As the discipline matures, the models gain a more mathematical flavour and the predictions become more precise.

The theory of gravity is an excellent example of this. The events themselves were well known for thousands of years: "things tend to fall downward". By Newton's time, it was also well known that planets orbited the sun, and moons orbited the planets. What Newton, Kepler and others realized is that if gravity exerts a force of attraction that depends only on the masses and distance (inverse square law), everything is perfectly explained! Stunning discovery.

In time, and with very detailed observations, scientists discovered that even Newton's law was not quite right. Einstein reformulated gravity, not as a force, but as curvature of space, and now the new model matched observations even more closely.

This is the strength of science — the willingness to revisit old ideas and reformulate them when discrepancies arise. This is how science corrects itself from delusion and error – like the "discovery" of canals on Mars, which were later shown to be an optical illusion.

However, the very success of science at explaining so many phenomena in terms of *physical behaviours* has led many people to go further. Because physical explanations have been so good, many people have come to believe they will always suffice — that everything in the universe will be explicable in terms of matter and forces and so on. Variations on this perspective are called "Metaphysical Naturalism", or "Scientific Materialism", or just "Physicalism". They state that there is nothing but natural things, such as forces and causes, of the kind studied by the natural sciences, and of the kind that have mechanical properties amenable to mathematical modelling.[2]

Scientists generally, both believers and unbelievers, adhere to 'methodological naturalism'; that when conducting experiments or observations, they only focus on the natural world. However, in practice, methodological naturalism has been taken by some to imply physicalism,

[2] D. Stoljar, "Physicalism" in *The Stanford Encyclopedia of Philosophy* (ed. E. Zalta; Fall 2009 Edition). Online at: plato.stanford.edu/archives/fall2009/entries/physicalism.

in such a way that physicalism is the unstated assumption of many contemporary scientists, and the prevailing "acceptable view" in large parts of western society. Anything else is looked down upon as superstition, or blind and misguided faith that may be okay for children, along with Santa and the Easter bunny.

But note this. *Physicalism* is a philosophical position. It is not actually science. Why? Because it is not established by any empirical experiment. Rather, it is an application of philosophical induction: "because so many things have physical explanations, then everything will have a physical explanation." Physicalism is an expectation. It is a belief or an assumption.

This technique of philosophical induction is often very helpful. Because the sun has always risen in the morning, then tomorrow I again expect the sun to rise. But other times it may not be helpful. Just because I have found many treasures using my metal detector, this does not mean I should expect to find *all* treasures using my metal detector. It seems to me that the induction behind physicalism is more the latter kind than the former.

The power of physicalism is that it drives people towards finding physical explanations whenever and wherever they may be found. This motivator has borne fruit in the past. Lightning is a natural electrical discharge (not the wrath of the gods), diseases have organic origin (not malevolent spirits), and so on. Imagine a world without antibiotics, where any infection is cause for serious concern, without long distance communication, or where a round trip to the village five miles away occupies an entire day. Such profound impacts!

The weakness of physicalism, however, is that it rules out anything but natural explanations *a priori*. Even before looking at any specific evidence, it rejects all non-physical or supernatural explanations. In particular, the tenets of physicalism prohibit the idea of God in just about any form. No proof is required. A non-physical being is impossible and thus inconceivable.

In the rest of this chapter, we will use the phenomenon of consciousness to argue that *physicalism* is insufficient and that there are aspects of the universe that appear to be outside its explanatory power. In doing so, we will walk in areas that resonate with things described in the Bible; these will be noted in the conclusion.

The nature of consciousness

Perhaps the most famous slogan of philosophy is about consciousness: "Cogito, ergo sum," the phrase often used to express Descartes' remarkable insight, "I think, therefore I exist." He identified consciousness as the one foundational experience we have. Everything that we know is mediated through the experience of consciousness. The conscious awareness of the present moment seems to be the one thing that we can absolutely rely on. All else could be imaginary, a dream, or dim guesses—like prisoners in Plato's cave experiencing shadows on the wall. Or to put it in a modern setting, maybe we are brains in vats in some laboratory, all our experiences being fed directly into our brains by a computer.

Understanding consciousness is a very hard problem, so we need to tread carefully. As Chalmers attests after many years of researching the topic, anyone who claims to have it all sorted out is likely to have fallen into one or more of the innumerable traps for the unwary.[3] Consciousness is also a huge subject. A current bibliography of work in the philosophy of mind, cognitive science, and consciousness consists of 28,490 entries![4]

To make matters worse, western scientific study is ill suited for some of the fundamental explorations into consciousness. As we said earlier, (western) science takes an objective view. It concerns itself with what can be called *Third Person* phenomena. Whether we study chemical interactions or social structures, we do so from the perspective of an *external* observer. This objective view takes the item of study as an object distinct from the observer. The challenge with making consciousness the subject of this kind of scientific investigation is that there appear to be no third-person methods that can determine the presence or absence of consciousness.

Already I hear you object: Of course we can tell whether someone else is conscious! He will be moving, or breathing. She will be talking, calculating or hearing.

Indeed, there is a well-established medical scale of consciousness used by practitioners who are trained to assess patients. Yet all of these indicators and measures are proxies, established by analogy: "I know that I am

---

[3] D. J. Chalmers, *The Conscious Mind: In Search of a Fundamental Theory*, (Oxford: OUP, 1996).
[4] *MindPapers* (eds. D. J. Chalmers & D. Bourget; Australian National University). Online at: consc.net/mindpapers.

conscious, so I presume that another creature who shows corresponding physical attributes and behaviour is also conscious." But this statement is a presumption. In all the time since the Greeks, no one has come up with a third-person objective test that definitively demonstrates consciousness in others.

Consider the following case. Neuroscientist Adrian Owen at Cambridge University had a patient in a persistent vegetative state.[5] In this state, a person will have lost cognitive neurological function and awareness of the environment, but may retain non-cognitive function, including things like a sleep-wake cycle. Their eyes might even move around, but as far as we can tell, the person is just not there anymore.

As an experiment, Dr Owen placed his patient in an MRI and asked her to imagine playing tennis. Immediately, her brain lit up just like the brain of a conscious person. When he asked her to stop, her brain activity quietened down. So is she conscious or not? It is still impossible to know. This experiment has now been performed many times on many other patients,[6] and doctors debate whether the test is definitive or not. Even with an MRI machine able to watch neural activity directly, we cannot actually tell whether another human being is conscious or not.

So the challenge with testing or determining the existence of consciousness is that we have no way to observe it externally. Medical professionals can measure how tall you are, how likable your personality is, your IQ or EQ, and so on. But they cannot measure the state and nature of your consciousness, other than by measuring proxies and extrapolating from that.

Would it be possible to build an artificial being that appeared to be conscious but was not? Or are there consciousnesses that exist in forms so different from us that we have no idea that they are there at all? We have no way to know.

This leaves us in a bit of a conundrum. The *one* phenomenon we can be sure of from a philosophical perspective is largely outside the reach of our current scientific techniques.

---

[5] A. M. Owen, "Detecting Awareness in the Vegetative State", *Science* (September 2006).
[6] M. M. Monti et al., "Willful Modulation of Brain Activity in Disorders of Consciousness", *The New England Journal of Medicine* (2010).

First person science

Consciousness appears to be a phenomenon that has to be studied from the *inside*, from a *first person perspective*. Nagel, one of the earlier western researchers to wake up to this perspective, states:

> While an account of the physical basis of mind must explain many things, this appears to be the most difficult. It is impossible to exclude the phenomenological features of experience from a reduction in the same way that one excludes the phenomenal features of an ordinary substance from a physical or chemical reduction of it—namely, by explaining them as effects on the minds of human observers. If physicalism is to be defended, the phenomenological features must themselves be given a physical account. But when we examine their subjective character it seems that such a result is impossible. The reason is that every subjective phenomenon is essentially connected with a single point of view, and it seems inevitable that an objective, physical theory will abandon that point of view.[7]

His argument is that physics is *objective*, but the phenomenological features of experience are fundamentally *subjective*, and cannot be reduced to objective analysis without losing their fundamental attribute. It is something tangible to see colour, or to feel pain, or to experience sadness. These individual subjective elements of the mind are called *qualia*. The essences of qualia seem to get lost if ever we try to move to a third person perspective of pure physicality. Chalmers cites Nagel's work and expands on the individual subjective elements of the mind.

> The really hard problem of consciousness is the problem of experience. When we think and perceive, there is a whir of information-processing, but there is also a subjective aspect... This subjective aspect is experience. When we see, for example, we experience visual sensations: the felt quality of redness, the experience of dark and light, the quality of depth in a visual field. Other experiences go along with perception in different modalities: the sound of a clarinet, the smell of mothballs. Then there are bodily sensations, from pains to orgasms; mental images that are conjured up internally; the felt quality of emotion, and the experience of a stream of conscious thought. What unites all of these states is that there

---

[7] Thomas Nagel, "What is it like to be a bat?", *The Philosophical Review* 83 (1974).

is 'something it is like to be in them'. All of them are states of experience.[8]

This "subjective experience" is very real, but is only experienced by the individual, not by someone else. We cannot understand this component of consciousness by looking from the outside, by external measurements, because external methods lose the essence of the phenomenon being explored.

Consider an illustration from the movie *Groundhog Day*.[9] Phil, the weatherman, finds himself trapped in Punxsutawney reliving Groundhog Day over and over again, and again and again. Everything else around him happens exactly as before, so over "time", he is able to learn and predict everything that will happen. Phil attempts to explain to Rita, his producer, that he has relived the day hundreds of times. She asks him to prove it, so he describes everyone in the restaurant, their lives, their histories, their characteristics, what is just about to happen, and so on. Everyone is amazed that he knows so much about them, because they have no memory or experience of having any interaction with him. From the perspective of the movie viewer, we know his explanation is correct. Yet Rita rejects his explanation. It is outside her experience and conception. And—this is the point—he has no way to convince her of what was a purely first person experience.

While clearly fiction, the movie story reveals a core problem of understanding and appreciating consciousness. Just imagine you were Phil—or Rita—and consider how difficult it would be to take on the other's perspective.

To really get to grips with consciousness, we need a *first-person* science. Here is how the Dalai Lama puts it:

> Consciousness is a very elusive object, and in this sense, it is quite unlike the focus on a material object, such as biochemical processes... Whatever our philosophical views about the nature of consciousness, whether it is ultimately material or not, through a rigorous first-person method we can learn to observe the phenomena, including their characteristics and causal dynamics. On this basis, I envisage the possibility of broadening the scope of the science of

---

[8] D. J. Chalmers, "Facing Up to the Problem of Consciousness", *Journal of Consciousness Studies* (1995).
[9] H. Ramis, <u>Groundhog Day</u> (Columbia Pictures, 1993).

consciousness and enriching our understanding of the human mind in scientific terms.[10]

For the past 2500 years, investigations within Buddhism have focused on the study of consciousness. Every scientific discipline needs to be able to hone its instruments so that the observations are real and repeatable; so too does a first-person science. The practices of mindfulness and insight meditation[11] have been developed to permit exactly this kind of study. They have been designed to avoid self-delusion, which is a great risk when using the human mind to study itself. Reliable insight observations are repeatable not only on multiple occasions by an individual researcher, but by multiple researchers. These techniques enable the discipline of first person science.

> Indeed, I would agree with Varela that if the scientific study of consciousness is ever to grow to full maturity – given that subjectivity is a primary element of consciousness – it will have to incorporate a fully developed and rigorous methodology of first-person empiricism.[12]

The prominent computer scientist Henk Barendregt, now fully trained in insight meditation, devotes his research efforts to understanding the mind from the perspective of its computational processes and components. I find it interesting to hear how he addresses the question as to whether consciousness might arise as a manifestation of the computing infrastructure of the brain. He says:

> No matter how many levels of cognition and feedback we place on top of sensory input in a model of the mind, it a priori seems not able to account for experiences. We always could simulate these processes on an old fashioned computer consisting of relays, or even play it as a social game with cards. It is not that I object to basing our consciousness on outer agents like the card players (we depend on nature in a similar way). It is the claimed emergence of consciousness as a side effect of the card game that seems absurd.[13]

---

[10] Dalai Lama, *The Universe in a Single Atom* (Three Rivers Press, 2006).
[11] See for example, B. H. Gunaratana, *Mindfulness in Plain English* (Wisdom Publications, 2002).
[12] Dalai Lama, *Single Atom.*
[13] H. Barendregt, *Reflection and its Use: From Science to Meditation*, (Templeton Foundation Press, 2003).

As a computer scientist myself, I share Barendregt's views. I can envision software producing all the cognitive processing functionality involved in making sense of visual and auditory signals, and so on. But I know nothing in computer science that could build *experience* into software. How would you program the felt experience of *pain*? Even if the software were reflective and able to cognitively process its own state, I see no reason why it should make the leap to experiential consciousness, i.e., individual subjective *qualia*.

Quantum Physics

So where does consciousness come from? What is it—this apparently non-physical part of our being?

Quantum physicist Henry Stapp argues that consciousness has been built into the universe at a fundamental level, and that any understanding of physics that ignores it is doomed to failure.

> The 'Hard Problem' is the problem of conscious experience: What is it? Why is it present at all? Why is it so different from the other part of Nature, namely the objective aspect of reality? Chalmers asks these questions, and says that right now we have no candidate theory that answers these questions. But we do!
>
> Chalmers suggests that perhaps there is a small loop-hole in quantum theory that might provide an opening for consciousness. But there is not just a small loop-hole: there is a gigantic lacuna, which consists of fully half of the theory, and this hole provides an ideal home for consciousness.[14]

Stapp did his postdoctoral work with Pauli, and then worked with Heisenberg, so he's been in the field a while! Quantum physics, he says, is fundamentally about the *interaction* of consciousness with the quantum potential. The originators of quantum mechanics understood this clearly:

> In our description of nature the purpose is not to disclose the real essence of phenomena but only to track down as far as possible relations between the multifold aspect of our experience.[15]

---

[14] H. P. Stapp, "The Hard Problem: A Quantum Approach", *Journal of Consciousness Studies* (August 1996).
[15] N. Bohr, *Atomic Physics and Human Knowledge* (Wiley, 1958).

Quantum theory has led the physicists far away from the simple materialistic views that prevailed in the natural science of the nineteenth century.[16]

These are powerful statements whose implications still haven't really entered the collective scientific narrative. Perhaps the reason is that we still don't *get* quantum physics. Indeed, some objectors have pointed out that quantum mechanics is just mathematics, that it is only when the mathematics is interpreted that consciousness comes into play. As there are five major and distinct interpretations, how can we know which is correct? Stapp says we don't need to know:

> Searle, when, confronted by the suggestion that quantum theory, with its inherent dualistic ontology, is important to the resolution of the mind-brain problem, says that he will wait until quantum theorists come into agreement among themselves about the interpretation of the theory. But that misses the point completely.

> All interpretations agree on the need for a dualistic ontology, with one aspect being the quantum analog of matter, and the other aspect pertaining to experiences. Thus the whole debate among quantum theorists is essentially a debate about the mind-matter connection.[17]

Quantum mechanics, *in every one of its interpretations*, holds consciousness as just as fundamental as the physical aspects of reality. It is the interaction of the quantum potential with consciousness—the collapse of the wave function[18]—that defines and creates the components of the universe around us.

No wonder the implications are hard to take on board. Perhaps it would be simpler and more comfortable to work with purely physical models of the universe, and return to "the simple materialistic views" to which Heisenberg referred. And yet we don't get to choose whether to accept quantum physics or not. There are repeatable experiments that demonstrate decisively that Newtonian models of reality are insufficient.

---

[16] Werner Heisenberg, *Physics and Philosophy*, (Harper & Row Publishers, 1962).

[17] Stapp, "Hard Problem".

[18] The collapse of the wave function is when the probability amplitude appears to reduce to a single state after interaction with an observer, or, more simply, when many possibilities for, say, the position of a particle, are reduced to a single actual position when the particle is observed.

The quantum view is here to stay.

At this point, no one knows how consciousness, the brain and quantum mechanics all interact. Some suggest that the interaction is at the level of individual chemical reactions within the brain, providing some element of randomness within our psyches. Stapp's own conjecture is that the collapse of the wave function takes place in a holistic and coordinated fashion at the level of the organism, as conscious thoughts. I have no idea which is correct, but what I find intriguing about this idea is that it neatly allows for quantum mechanics to introduce elements of freewill that are not simply manifestations of pure randomness.

Here's Barendregt again:

> Spiritual reflection introduces us to awareness beyond ordinary consciousness, which is without content, but nevertheless conscious. It is called pure consciousness. This phenomenon may be explained by comparing our personality to the images on a celluloid film, in which we are playing the title role of our life. Although everything that is familiar to us is depicted on the film, it is in the dark. We need light to see the film as a movie. It may be the case that this pure consciousness is the missing explanatory link between the purely neurophysiological activity of our brain and the conscious mind that we (at least think to) possess. This pure light is believed to transcend the person. The difference between you and me is in the matter (cf. the celluloid of the film). That which gives us awareness is said to come from a common source: the pure consciousness acting as the necessary 'light'.[19]

Again, I don't fully get everything Barendregt is saying—which points to the difficulties in communicating experiences from first person investigations—but I am struck by the correspondence between this and Stapp's perspectives on consciousness and quantum mechanics.

A thought experiment

So far, all of our analysis has been done by quoting the understanding of others, but in the spirit of first person science, let's run a thought experiment in which we can all participate.

---

[19] Barendregt, *Reflection and Its Use.*

What in the world defines "Now"?

Let's separate a number of distinct time-like ideas.

1. We start with time itself. Leibniz's reductionist view is that time is simply the progression of the states that make up the universe,[20] and that there is no distinction finer than the change of state of the matter or energy within the universe. This is very appealing, as it seems to be as simple a theory as it could be. From Einstein, we now know that time is not global, so we would have to interpret Leibniz's theory within each frame of reference, which each have their own way of assessing state of change.

   With this perspective, the equations of physics map out what physical and energy changes occur within the universe. The equations hold across all time (we believe) and, interestingly, they may be run forwards or backwards—the laws of physics are reversible on the small scale.

   So we have a theory of time, and equations in physics to describe how particles and forces interact. But none of this structure has anything in it that identifies a designated moment called "Now".

2. On a larger scale, entropy comes into play. Entropy is the measure of disorder in the universe. In one direction, the laws of physics increase the amount of disorder. In the other direction they decrease. Our experience of time is that it moves in the direction of increasing entropy, disorder. So this gives us the direction of time's arrow, at least in so far as we experience it.

   But again, time direction does not give us a designated moment "Now".

3. Then there's simultaneity. How do we determine when two events happen at the same time? Again, Einstein taught us that this depends on the frame of reference. In any frame of reference, one can develop a global notion of time, and determine (within this frame of reference) when two events take place at the same moment. In a different frame of reference, these two events (that had happened at

---

[20] D. Burnham, "Leibniz: Metaphysics" in *Internet Encyclopedia of Philosophy* (2001).

the same time in the first frame of reference) might have happened at different times in the second! One event happens before the other. Strange it may be, but it is also demonstrable through experiment.

But here's our point: even though simultaneity is related to the notion of "Now", it does not define it. It may say whether a "Now" in one place occurs at the same time as a "Now" in another place, but it does not define what "Now" is.

I find all this fascinating: none of the physical/mathematical aspects of time identify a concept of "Now". They describe how one moment in time and space is related to another in time and space, but nothing in the equations of physics defines the moment "Now".

Instead, "Now" appears to be uniquely an experience of consciousness. Pause for a moment to experience it. Close your eyes, note your breathing, and be aware of this moment, "Now". It is our conscious experience that defines the moment "Now".

We can go further. Not only is "Now" uniquely an experience of consciousness, but "Now" is also the *only* experience of consciousness. Again, you may object. Our consciousness has experienced the past and will experience the future! But think about it some more. Our consciousness actually experiences the *memory sense* of our brains. This memory sense has a particular configuration that we interpret as describing previous events (to some varying degrees of accuracy). When does our consciousness experience the memory sense? It does so now!

For consciousness, "Now" is the only moment. It is the only reality.

What about my experience of "Now" and your experience of "Now"? Are they the same thing? Do they occur at the same time? I don't even know if the question makes sense.

However, if we are correct in concluding that "Now" is uniquely the experience of consciousness, and that nothing else in the world can define or determine it, then we have just gained further evidence that the core of consciousness is an additional component of the universe – additional to the particles and energy states of the physical models. It cannot arise by combinations of physical elements by themselves, because nothing in those models defines or determines a privileged moment of observation called "Now".

Some Conclusions

So where are we? We started by considering the philosophy of *physicalism*, noting that although it has grown out of the success of science in describing the physical world, physicalism is actually a philosophical position, not a scientific one. Now, after a journey through consciousness, quantum mechanics, and time, we have ended up with evidence that the essence of our being – our experience of consciousness – is distinct from the physical world of atoms, forces, energies and so on. Consciousness and physicality are connected together in the collapse of quantum potentiality – perhaps they even co-define each other – but they are ontologically distinct. In other words, there are two realms – the physical, and the conscious – and neither can be reduced to the other.

Does this suggest anything about God? I think so.

We are in the very early days of taking first person science seriously, but what we know about pure consciousness seems to relate to descriptions of the presence of the divine in the universe. Obviously we are in the realm of speculation here, so take all this with a pinch of salt. But I find it fascinating that the Apostle Paul describes our nature with respect to the divine in essentially this way. When he is talking with the philosophers in Athens, Paul says,

> God did this so that they would seek him and perhaps reach out for him and find him, though he is not far from any one of us. 'For in him we live and move and have our being.' (Acts 17-27-28 [NIV])

God is all around us, he says. And that last sentence – likely a quotation from the poet Epimenides – is very powerful. In the divine, he says, we live and move and have our being. I don't know of a better description of my current understanding of the nature of consciousness and its role in defining the world in which I live.

Other biblical writers wrestle with similar concepts. Nothing exists, according to an anonymous Psalmist, without the spirit of the divine.

> When you send your life-giving breath [or spirit], they are created, and you replenish the surface of the ground. (Psalm 104:30)

In a purely physical universe, this would make no sense. Under the

83

physics of the nineteenth century, we could view the universe as a mechanistic process. But under quantum physics, we have to recognize the additional fundamental dimension of consciousness that is indeed involved in the very definition of all physical states. As I say, this is speculation, but perhaps the Psalmist sees this as the spirit of God at the core of our being, which forms and maintains the universe in its present form. At death, according to the teacher in Ecclesiastes, that life-giving element is relinquished:

> The dust returns to the earth as it was, and the life's breath returns to God who gave it. (Ecclesiastes 12:7)

There are many other passages like these. In biblical language, the spirit of the divine pervades and sustains the universe. I find it remarkable how similar it is to the role consciousness plays in quantum physics. Are they related? I don't know, but am struck by the parallels.

So has our study of consciousness *proved* the existence of God?

No. At least, not as far as the revealed God of the Bible is concerned. But we actually set out to do something much less ambitious. We set out to show that *physicalism*, the popular philosophical position that would automatically deny his existence, is flawed. And I think we did that.

We saw a number of reasons that indicate that there is more to the universe than just the purely physical states of matter and energy. The phenomenon of consciousness that we each experience gives us an excellent reason to look further and deeper, and discover spiritual dimensions too.

Summary

- Consciousness cannot be explained as a material composite and is unlikely ever to be replicable by a machine.
- Physicalism is insufficient; there is more to the universe than matter.
- Quantum mechanics has dispelled previous mechanistic views of the universe and has opened the possibility that consciousness and matter interact in ways currently beyond our understanding.
- This allows us to speculate that the base of the universe is a divine consciousness.

Further Reading

For more on the issue of human consciousness and its relationship to the human body, see *The Soul Hypothesis* (edited by M. C. Baker and S. Goetz).

For more on the concept of consciousness (or mind) as the basis of reality, see Keith Ward's *More than Matter?*

Morality

Thomas Gaston

"One still hopes to get along with a moralism without religious background: but that necessarily leads to nihilism" – Friedrich Nietzsche[1]

Introduction

The moral argument for God has been expressed in a number of different ways. These approaches share the basic idea that the existence of morality presupposes the existence of a supreme moral being.

The moral argument is most frequently associated with the German philosopher, Immanuel Kant (1724-1804). Kant had concluded in his *Critique of Pure Reason*[2] that God was essentially unknowable – that many of the traditional arguments for the existence of God were not conclusive – yet Kant still believed in God. In his *Critique of Practical Reason*[3], Kant proposed that, although God was unknowable by pure reason, God was a postulate of practical reason. This means that the outworking of practical reason assumes the existence of God – morality was the key example. For Kant, morality is teleological; it is directed towards a certain end or purpose. Kant proposed that the end of morality is the highest good: complete moral virtue and complete happiness. However, complete moral virtue cannot be achieved in a human lifespan and present moral action is not always followed by happiness. Therefore, Kant proposed that the existence of morality and this journey towards the highest good entails both immortality (during which humans can achieve moral perfection) and God (to ensure the achievement of perfect happiness).

A second approach to the argument from morality was popularised by C. S. Lewis in his book *Mere Christianity*.[4] Lewis argues that all humans intuitively know that certain things are right and certain things are wrong. This intuitive knowing is, according to Lewis, a result of a moral law in

[1] F. Nietzsche, *Nachlass,* in *Werke* III, 881.
[2] I. Kant, *Critique of Pure Reason* (1781).
[3] I. Kant, *Critique of Practical Reason* (1788).
[4] C. S. Lewis, *Mere Christianity* (London: Fount, 1997), 3-26.

the universe. This moral law is objective and universal (i.e. the same for all humankind), but unlike the laws of nature it can be ignored or broken. The moral law is a different kind of law: it is not a description of how things are, but of how things should be. Though humans are not slaves to the moral law, Lewis argues that humans feel an impulse to obey it. For Lewis, this impulse requires the existence of a supreme lawgiver who imprints this moral impulse within us.

Neither Kant's nor Lewis' approach is without criticism. Many people would baulk at the idea of an objective morality.[5] For example, one person believes abortion is permissible, another person believes it to be wrong; why do we disagree if morality is universal and intuitive? More generally, some would question whether morality exists at all: is morality anything more than a social contract or even personal taste? Most importantly, the role of God in morality is frequently called into question; an atheist can act in good and moral ways, so is God necessary for morality?

In this chapter I wish to approach the question from the opposite perspective, considering various attempts to explain morality without God. This will lead us to develop the view that morality is not reducible to natural causes, but that it is best explained as coming from God. Our own awareness of moral values will be shown to be a powerful indication of God's existence.

Morality without God

For many people, Friedrich Nietzsche (1844-1900), the German philologist, is the archetypal atheist; he is famous for the quote, "God is dead". Nietzsche lost his faith aged twenty and spent much of the rest of his life trying to come to terms with the philosophical implications of his atheism – "facing into the abyss", as he described it. The "death" of God signified that God could no longer serve as a basis of meaning and value in the world; objective truth was now impossible. The implications for morality were immense. Right and wrong, as independent values, were no longer meaningful and were understood by Nietzsche as symptoms of the 'will to power'. Nietzsche interprets the Judeo-Christian values of Western

---

[5] It is interesting to note that Richard Dawkins acknowledges the existence of objective moral standards, though he supposes there must be an evolutionary explanation for this universality (*Dawkins Interview with Justin Brierley* www.premierradio.org.uk/shows/saturday/unbelievable/Features.aspx [cited: 22 February 2011]).

Europe as a consequence of slave-morality, where "good" is assigned to the restriction of power and the virtues of slaves, whilst master-virtues, such as aggression and selfish behaviour, are identified as "evil". For Nietzsche, our pretensions of morality are simply attempts to restrict the strong and the powerful.

Many modern scholars would reject Nietzsche's attempts at a genealogy of morality, but his realisation of the nihilistic consequences of the "death" of God has been extremely influential in Western thought. However, his amorality has not been widely adopted; indeed the Nietzchesque mantra, "there is no good or evil, there is only power", has been put into the mouth of every Hollywood villain from Voldemort (*Harry Potter*) to the Green Goblin (*Spiderman*). Contrary to Nietzsche's prediction, morality has, as yet, failed to die; even the "New Atheists" find Nietzsche's bleak amorality rather unsettling and strive instead to create a godless morality.

The existentialist philosopher Jean-Paul Sartre (1905–1980) is another who saw the moral implications of the "death" of God. Without a creator there is no purpose to human existence, no essence. He wrote that "existence precedes essence", that is, we have no innate purpose (essence) to our existence – our essence, our purpose, is something we give ourselves. Sartre concluded that we are "condemned to be free". Our actions are entirely our own, there is no guidance and there is no moral framework. There are no objective rights and wrongs, only choices. Without God, without purpose, morality was impossible.

Sartre, however, did not regard himself in practice as absolutely free or without morality. He famously acknowledged on French television that he was not free to kick an Algerian beggar in the street. But on what basis could Sartre say that kicking a beggar was wrong? That is a moral judgment. Sartre did not return to a belief in God, choosing instead to interpret his morality along Marxist lines. Nevertheless, it is an interesting lesson that someone who proclaimed that without God objective morals were impossible nevertheless came to regard certain things as being objectively right or objectively wrong. He could not help but describe actions in moral terms.

Morality and Meaning

Another influential philosophical movement in the twentieth century was Logical Positivism. The central tenet of this movement was that only scientifically verifiable statements about the world and truths of logic are meaningful. All other statements are nonsense. This has obvious implications for morality as explained by A. J. Ayer, a major proponent of Logical Positivism:

> If now I ... say, 'Stealing money is wrong,' I produce a sentence which has no factual meaning – that is, expresses no proposition which can be either true of false. It is as if I had written 'Stealing money!!' ... in saying that a certain type of action is right or wrong, I am not making any factual statement.[6]

Ayer proposes that when we use moral language, we are not describing anything about the world or making a genuine proposition about the way things are. For Ayer, moral language is just a way of expressing or provoking emotional responses; morality itself is meaningless.

Ludwig Wittgenstein, a philosopher of language, makes a similar argument. He writes:

> I believe the tendency of all men who ever tried to write or talk Ethics or Religion was to run against the boundaries of language. This running against the walls of our cage is perfectly, absolutely hopeless. Ethics so far as it springs from the desire to say something about the ultimate meaning of life, the absolute good, the absolutely valuable, can be no science.[7]

Wittgenstein regarded philosophy primarily as the analysis of language; the way we use language reveals the way we think. He reasoned that people couldn't talk about religion or ethics without similes. When we say, "he is a (morally) good man", we mean something *like* "he is a good footballer", but, unlike talk about football, we cannot identify something about the world to which "(morally) good" refers. For Wittgenstein, we are forced to talk about ethics in similes because there is no reality to talk about; moral statements are meaningless.

We can see similarities between Ayer and Wittgenstein; indeed, Wittgenstein was strongly influenced by Logical Positivism at this time. However, both Ayer and Wittgenstein changed their minds on these issues and Logical Positivism has largely been rejected. Ayer later wrote, "Logical positivism died a long time ago. I don't think much of *Language,*

---

[6] A. J. Ayer, *Language, Truth and Logic* (Victor Gollancz: London, 1967), 106.
[7] L. Wittgenstein, "A Lecture on Ethics", *Philosophical Review* 74:1 (1965; delivered at Cambridge University 1929).

Truth and Logic is true".[8] Wittgenstein later rejected the idea of a uniform language that depicts the world. In *Philosophical Investigations* (1951) he describes how language varies according to the different areas of life; language is meaningful within its particular "language game". Religious and ethical language is not meaningless, though it refers to things that are different from other types of language. The change in both Ayer and Wittgenstein can be ascribed to the rejection of the verification principle, i.e. the idea that the only meaningful statements are those verifiable by scientific enquiry.

This leads us to an important conclusion. Moral statements are meaningful but do not refer to things in the world like trees or tables. You cannot point to something and say "look, goodness", or "there is badness", nor are moral laws like the laws of nature that we can test by experiments. Moral statements refer to our choices and the value we place upon them, but this does not make them any less meaningful. When we say, "he is a (morally) good man", we know what we mean – no simile is needed – good means good, evil means evil. The fallacy of Logical Positivism (and of the New Atheists) is the attempt to reduce morality to material things.

Morality and Evolution

The theory of evolution has become one of the most influential paradigms in modern thought. Its influence is felt far beyond the biological sciences, in philosophy and social sciences, and is now central to the way human behaviours are explained. Once it is assumed that man evolved from primitive forms of life, then it becomes viable and attractive to explain every aspect of humanity with reference to evolution. The philosopher Daniel Dennett has used the analogy of cranes and skyhooks to describe the situation. Cranes suspend things in the air but are founded firmly on the ground. In the same way, our explanations of human behaviours, though they may appear far removed from biological considerations, must be rooted in natural processes. Alternative forms of explanation are like skyhooks – suspended from nothing and thus impossible. Of course, behind Dennett's analogy is the assumption that God does not exist. Dennett, like others, is unwilling to consider the possibility that anything can be explained by God – for him, these explanations are just skyhooks.

---

[8] A. J. Ayer, "The Existence of the Soul" in *Great Thinkers on Great Questions* (ed. R. A. Varghese; Oxford: One World, 1998), 49.

Morality is one type of human behaviour that requires an explanation. If we set aside for a moment the God explanation (a "skyhook"), then we are required to find some explanation rooted in evolution (a "crane"). There are two basic types of evolutionary explanation for something: either that thing confers a genetic advantage, or that thing is a side effect of some other mutation. For example, super-strong teeth would confer a genetic advantage to certain animals because it would give them a better chance of survival. However, natural selection does not only preserve advantageous traits; natural selection preserves any trait that does not confer a genetic disadvantage. Imagine that the mutation that gave the animal super-strong teeth also gave that animal's teeth a blue tinge. This blue tinge would confer no genetic advantage, but neither would it significantly disadvantage the animal, and so natural selection would preserve this trait as well. An evolutionary explanation of morality must either demonstrate that morality confers a genetic advantage (like super-strong teeth) or that it is a side effect of other developments (like blue teeth). If, on the other hand, a moral sense conferred a genetic *dis*advantage, then it would not be preserved by natural selection.

Some actions that are generally deemed to be morally virtuous would confer some genetic advantage. For example, sharing food and other benefits with family members would, all other things being equal, result in that family grouping being better able to face difficulties, such as food shortages, than a selfish and divided family grouping. This is particularly evident with regard to a parent's care for its offspring. A parent that looks after its children, even to its own disadvantage, is more likely to preserve its genes (i.e. in its progeny) than a parent that is neglectful. To this extent, natural selection would not necessarily produce selfish character traits (if natural selection can produce character traits at all). If evolution were the sole explanation, then we would expect animals (including humans) to be kind and even altruistic (selfless) with regard to their children and close relatives. However, what we would not expect is for animals to assist non-relatives (non-kin related altruism) but amongst humans, we do see examples of people assisting other people regardless of their genetic similarities. If I see someone injured in the street I stop to see if I can help, and I call an ambulance. I do not first examine their hair colour or facial features, let alone their genetic code. This compassion is not contingent on any sense of relationship, but is universal; I may feel greater attachment to my own kin, but I have compassion for all mankind. Yet such forms of non-kin related altruism do not confer any advantages to my own genes; rather they run the risk of conferring a disadvantage to my genes, as it may result in my disadvantaging myself in favour of another genetic grouping. Even as a side effect of some other evolutionary

91

development, non-kin related altruism is unlikely to have been preserved by natural selection, since it confers a disadvantage in terms of genetic survival.

Many thinkers have proposed that morality is not a direct product of evolution, but a result of the development of reason. The capacity for practical reason, it is argued, would confer a genetic advantage because it enables humans to think about their actions based upon a wide range of information rather than acting purely on instinct. The philosopher Colin McGinn writes:

> Rationality and the capacity to apprehend how the world works (what it is intrinsically like) are themselves tremendously advantageous characteristics for an individual, and hence a species, to possess: they are powerful aids to survival ... Now what I want to suggest is that morality is an inevitable corollary of evolutionarily useful intelligence: in becoming rational animals human beings, *eo ipso*, became creatures endowed with moral sense.[9]

There is some element of truth in the association between our capacity for reason and our capacity for moral action. After all, moral decisions are rarely based upon immediate impulses, but are based upon reasoned analysis of available information. For example, in one circumstance you might judge it moral to give someone money (e.g., if they were starving) and in another circumstance you might judge it immoral to give someone money (e.g., if you thought it likely that they would spend it on drugs). Reason does assist us in making moral decisions, however, reason does not explain the existence of morality, nor does it explain our impulse to do moral things. Reason cannot create desires; it only helps us choose which desire to act upon. For example, taking the medicine prescribed by the doctor is usually the most reasonable course of action, but it is only reasonable if our desire is to get well; if our desire is to remain ill, then it is would be irrational to take the medicine. For reason to function as a guide to moral actions there must be some substance, some desired end, which reason will help us achieve – reason alone is without intention.

It might be proposed that our desire is for survival – a good evolutionary trait – and that reason has guided us to form moral societies, where we curb our selfish desires for the good of all. So far so good, but it is

---

[9] C. McGinn, "Evolution, Animals, and the Basis of Morality", *Inquiry* 22 (1979): 93.

difficult to explain moral impulses. If my desire were for survival, then it would be perfectly reasonable for me to act immorally for my own advantage, assuming it doesn't impact negatively on society. If everyone else is behaving morally, it is perfectly reasonable for me to take advantage of that situation to further my own survival.

> If the moral code can be violated, without detection (or at least without consequences) for some significant benefit, then why not do it? What precisely is wrong with the perfect murder? Or, more likely, if one has enormous power (as Stalin had), then why not eliminate your opponents ruthlessly and personally enjoy the resources of the state? ... Why not support the moral code for the sake of social order, while searching for opportunities to enjoy the benefits of periodically violating that code?[10]

Nietzsche may have supported, or at least seen the inevitability, of such a way of thinking – the strong rising above the herd – but I think most people would find such a way of thinking rather unsettling. This is the problem with an evolutionary morality – or any godless morality – it does not reflect the morality that most of us hold. Though there may be, on occasion, evolutionary reasons for altruistic actions, this should ultimately serve our selfish interests. Evolution can provide us with no moral inclination greater than the desire for the survival of our genes. Even if, through reason and our other mental faculties, we can "overcome the tyranny of our genes", as Dawkins would put it, we are still left with no inclination towards moral action.

Our Moral Capacity

The position I have taken in this chapter is that moral questions are meaningful – they are something you can get right or get wrong. To me this seems an inevitable conclusion of the human condition; when we think about what we do we are concerned to get it right. Moral language is not just a cipher for something else. When I say, "this is the right thing to do", I do not necessarily mean, "this is what I want to do", because sometimes what we consider to be right is different from what we desire. And I do not mean, "this is what society tells me is right", else how would social morals change (e.g., attitudes towards slavery). And I certainly don't mean, "This is best for my genes". I mean something different, something meaningful.

---

[10] I. S. Markham, *Against Atheism* (Chichester: Wiley-Blackwell, 2010), 36.

This is the real point. It is not just that we do good things, like helping others; it is that we *believe* that certain things are good. It may be possible to formulate naturalistic explanations for creatures (including humans) doing things that we consider to be good, or possessing character traits that we consider to be moral. It is even possible that evolutionary psychologists might arrive at a plausible explanation for non-kin related altruism. But there does not seem to be any reason why these survival traits should be accompanied by moral beliefs. Our moral awareness is completely superfluous to a naturalistic explanation, as the philosopher Richard Swinburne explains:

> If genetic mutations produce creatures naturally inclined to behave altruistically towards others of their community (though there does not seem to be any particular reason why animal biochemistry should be of such a kind that these mutations would occur), then there may well be a good Darwinian explanation for their survival ... But having the understanding of these actions as morally good (even when we do not desire to do them) is something beyond mere altruistic behaviour. And there seems no particular reason why any mechanisms of mind–body interaction that cause creatures to have beliefs should produce moral beliefs.[11]

As we noted above, our moral beliefs are something different from our natural inclinations. We are often faced with situations where there is some action that we believe to be good, but we are not naturally inclined to perform that action, for instance, when it will result in our being disadvantaged. Moral beliefs are not empty, like reason, but are accompanied by a moral desire that moves us to action even when the natural inclination is lacking:

> While having a desire to do an action that is in fact morally good does not require the belief that it is morally good, the belief that some action is morally good does require a desire, however weak, to do that action ... You could not really believe that it is morally good to comfort someone in distress unless you had some minimal desire to help them, even if you have stronger desires to do other things instead ... Moral choice requires moral awareness and desires both good and bad.[12]

---

[11] R. Swinburne, *The Existence of God* (Oxford University Press, 2004), 216-7.
[12] Swinburne, *The Existence of God*, 217-8.

These moral desires do not determine that we should act in a certain way – often we do not – but they present us with a choice: to do what we believe to be good or to do what we believe to be more advantageous to ourselves. If then we believe that we have moral choices, if we believe that they are meaningful, it follows that we must have some moral awareness accompanied by desires to do both good and bad things. The question then becomes, where did this moral awareness come from?

The God Hypothesis

As we have seen, there is no particular reason to suppose that morality would exist in a godless universe. For an atheist like Nietzsche, no God meant no morality either; Sartre too, although he ultimately could not deny his moral capacity, he saw the absence of God as an absence of morality. A materialist world, that is, a world made purely of matter, should not contain morality – moral statements do not refer to objects in the world like trees and tables; so in a materialist world moral statements should have no meaning at all. Even evolutionary theory, which may have explanations for why animals are inclined to help each other, cannot provide us with a reason to take morality seriously, or an explanation as to why we *do* take morality seriously.

Let us now turn and examine the God hypothesis. My proposition is that there exists a God who wanted to create conscious beings with free will. God could have chosen to create beings that automatically do what is good all the time, but such beings would not have had free will. For free will to operate, these conscious beings need to be presented with a choice, and choice requires both the awareness of different actions *and* the desire to do them. Therefore, if God wanted to create conscious beings with free will, then he would endow these beings with a moral awareness.

Humans have a moral awareness; we believe that some actions are good and some actions are evil. On the one hand, there is no reason to suppose that such a moral awareness would exist if there were no God. On the other hand, if God exists, then we would expect him to endow humans with a moral awareness. So the existence of our moral capacity – our beliefs that some things are right and some things are wrong – is a strong indication that there is in fact a God.

95

Objections

Before concluding, it would be useful to consider some common objections to the moral argument to God, as this will help clarify the argument I am making.

Atheists can and do do good things, like giving to charity and helping others. God isn't necessary for morality.

In proposing that our moral awareness points towards the existence of God, I am not claiming that it is impossible for people to do good things unless they believe in God. A moral capacity is a feature of the human experience, and is not contingent on the beliefs you might hold. This very fact – that morality is real for atheists, as well as theists – supports my claim that a moral capacity is a universal feature of the human experience. That being said, for theists, morality does take on an additional quality as moral behaviour is influenced by a relationship with God. On the other hand, we may legitimately question in what way morality is meaningful to an atheist.

Nature is harsh and cruel. Animals are violent and cannibalistic. There is no morality in nature.

It is important to emphasize that I am not claiming that the world is a moral place. Animals do not have a moral capacity – they do not form or act upon moral beliefs. They may act in ways that we consider to be good. They may also act in ways that we consider to be evil. But these moral judgments have no power over animals because they have no awareness of what it is to be moral. It is only humans that have this moral awareness. The very fact that humans are different from animals is another strong indication that morality is something special, different from natural inclinations.

Human beings are not naturally good. Many people are bad, and everyone does bad things at some point. There is no innate impulse that makes us behave morally.

The obligations of morality are not automatic. Our moral capacity does not force us to act in a certain way; it presents us with a choice. Many people choose to do what is more pleasurable or of greater benefit to themselves rather than doing what is right. It is our awareness of the moral significance of these judgments that makes the existence of God likely. The fact that some people choose to act in immoral ways is due to free will, and is entirely consistent with the God hypothesis.

People disagree about what is right and what is wrong. For example, some people say abortion is always wrong, some say it is sometimes permissible, whilst others say it is up to the individual. There is no objective and universal moral code.

It would be very difficult to claim that there is an objective moral code imprinted on the human brain that tells us what to do in every circumstance. Not only does this seem unlikely given the number of moral disagreements, but additionally, it is difficult to conceive of what that moral code would be. However, the very fact that people continue to disagree once again demonstrates that people have a moral awareness they take seriously. We continue to argue about moral issues because we are moral creatures. Although there will be a degree of universality in human morality to the degree that moral decisions are determined by reason, as discussed earlier, reason is empty and without substance unless it is provided with some direction. We need some principles to get going.[13] The important point is that the continued disagreement with regard to moral questions is another demonstration of the reality of our moral capacity.

Conclusion

There is a moral dimension to human existence. It is both meaningful and powerful, and continues to influence the decisions that we make from day to day. We may not agree about which actions are right and which are wrong, but we experience the world in these terms. This moral dimension is difficult to explain without God. Even if we could provide evolutionary explanations for what we consider to be morally good actions, this would not explain why we consider them to be moral. But if we presuppose the existence of a supremely moral being (i.e., God) then our awareness of morality is explainable.

Without God we may still choose to be moral, but our morality lacks meaning. With God, morality becomes meaningful and purposeful – a journey overcoming our selfish ego and conforming ourselves to the will of God.

---

[13] As a Christian, I believe that many of those principles are provided by God in the Bible – but that's another story.

97

Summary

- Atheist philosophers, like Nietzsche, saw that the absence of belief in God should lead to a denial of morality, but moral beliefs persist, even in the absence of theistic beliefs.
- Attempts of atheist philosophers to explain away moral statements as nonsensical lack plausibility.
- The human moral capacity is real and meaningful.
- The emergence of a moral capacity would not be expected on a naturalistic world view, but would be expected under the God hypothesis.

Further Reading

For more on the argument from morality see Alan Hayward's *God Is*, chapter 10, and C. S. Lewis' *Mere Christianity*, book 1.

For a philosophical treatment of the arguments see Richard Swinburne's, *The Existence of God*, chapter 9.

For a reasonably accessible treatment of the philosophers covered in the chapter see Roger Trigg's, *Ideas of Human Nature*.

The Problem of Evil

David Levin

"I can't believe in an all-powerful God in a world so filled
with evil and suffering."

Is it Really a Problem?

Among the chief reasons people give for denying the existence of God (or
abdicating their faith if they were once believers), is the issue generally
known as "the problem of evil." The formal statement looks like this:

Premise 1:	God is all-powerful (omnipotent).
Premise 2:	God is all-good and loving (omnibenevolent).[1]
Premise 3:	Evil and suffering exist in the world.
Conclusion:	God is either limited in power (against premise 1), limited in goodness (against premise 2), or both – or non-existent.

To the sceptic, the first three statements above cannot co-exist. Premise 3
looks unassailable; that leaves the first two vulnerable. David Hume, the
famous empiricist philosopher of the Scottish Enlightenment put it this
way:

> Is he willing to prevent, but not able? Then he is impotent. Is
> he able, but not willing? Then he is malevolent. Is he both
> willing and able? Whence then is evil?[2]

An impotent or malevolent God is no God at all, so the most likely
outcome of the above thinking is atheism. However, many people choose
an intermediate position, generally some form of deism, which posits an

---

[1] I use "omnibenevolent" in the popular sense where that which is good is
understood in terms of our personal freedom from any discomfort, pain,
hardship, etc. It discounts that the goodness of God might involve human
suffering.

[2] David Hume, *Dialogues Concerning Natural Religion* (orig. pub. 1776. Richard
Popkin, ed., 2nd. ed. Indianapolis: Hackett, 1998), 63.

impersonal God who created the universe and then left it to run on its own. This position is essentially the one advocated by Rabbi Harold Kushner in his popular book, *When Bad Things Happen to Good People*, which promoted an impotent God.

The syllogism as stated above appears impenetrable. Who could deny any of the premises or the conclusion? How does a theist, one who believes in the traditional God of Christianity, or any monotheist for that matter, begin to get any traction in defending his or her belief in a personal God? Do we believe in an impotent or malevolent God? No – we affirm the God of the first two statements. How do we conform that belief to a world so rife with evil and suffering? Where do we find an opening to begin our defence?

This topic, known technically as theodicy, or the justification of God in the light of evil, is of great age and generates an enormous amount of debate in lay, religious, and academic arenas. Philosopher Daniel Howard-Snyder tabulated some 4,200 items published on the problem of evil between 1960 and 1990.[3] A current Google search on the "problem of evil" yields over half-a-million entries! Theodicy appears to be a consuming issue, one resistant to any quick or simple resolution.

This chapter divides the problem into smaller questions and topics to achieve some clarity on this vital question. In the end the problem of evil does not say anything about God at all, but it does say a lot about people who think that it is a theological issue. The problem of evil is a "people problem", rife with human limitations, misunderstandings, emotionality, and fuzzy thinking.

Evil as Reality and as Theory

The problem of evil and suffering has two faces; one personal and real, the other impersonal and theoretical. The human face of evil and suffering is the reality of experience; anyone who has had a personal encounter with tragedy or severe trauma or illness knows how little comfort philosophical and theological explanations of suffering provide. Job learned this from his three friends, who exacerbated his misery when they abandoned emotional support and ventured into theology – dismal theology at that. The human face of suffering asks perpetually, "Why?"

---

[3] Cited by G. Ganssle "God and Evil" in *The Rationality of Theism* (eds. P. Copan & P. K. Moser; New York: Routledge, 2003), 274.

The other face of evil and suffering is abstract and arbitrary, highly relative, contextual, and subjective. Philosophers and theologians knock it back and forth like a tennis ball, unconnected to any human experience. We can treat evil as a philosophical object like beauty, and wonder whether or not evil and suffering have any ontological status at all.

For those who suffer, pain is real. For dilettantes of philosophical speculation, pain and suffering are merely abstract notions based on some human experience. Always remember that it is *people* who suffer, even if we sunder the human experience of pain and suffering from our purview. Suffering is excruciatingly real for those engulfed by it. Without recognizing this dual perspective of evil and suffering, some of the arguments later in this chapter might sound crass and insensitive. Let's acknowledge the reality of suffering as a human experience, but not let the accompanying emotionality of that suffering become an argument against God.

Parsing the Problem

Theodicy has so many facets that even clarifying the issues is a laudable achievement. To do so, this chapter addresses the sub-issues individually as follows:

1. Issues related to the acknowledged presence of evil and suffering
    a. The amount and distribution of suffering
    b. Specific instances of "God allowing" evil
2. Types of suffering and evil
    a. Evil and human involvement
    b. Natural disasters
3. The nature of suffering
    a. Can we define suffering and evil?
    b. The value of suffering
4. The real problem and the real answer

This chapter will still leave much unsaid. For a more complete account, see a series of articles by this author under the titles of "The Theodicy Enigma", and "Is God Fair?"[4]

---

[4] Christadelphian *Tidings* v.67, no.1 (Sept.2004)-v.68 no.3 (Mar., 2005). Available online at www.tidings.org/past.htm (search using these titles).

How Much is Enough?

Major catastrophes often precipitate a renewed outcry against God such as, "So much suffering—how could there be a good and wise God?" However, let's ask instead: what would be the threshold that would cease to elicit such a response? Is there some number of fatalities lying within acceptable limits that allows for theism? Even if direct "acts of God" are relatively rare, how many earthquakes and hurricanes does it take to show that God cannot be all-loving and all-powerful?

Let us borrow the Abrahamic approach,[5] and wonder just how few casualties it would take to allow belief in God. If a person denies the existence of God because, say, five million people perish in natural disasters every year, what number does it take to restore belief? Is God reinstalled as the omnipotent, all-loving Supreme Being if that figure drops to only two million? Two hundred thousand? Twenty thousand? Two thousand? When is God exonerated?

This is a ridiculous pursuit. Belief in the existence of God cannot depend on any given number of casualties, some standard that held "Five million dead—God cannot exist; 50,000—I can live with that figure; five thousand, now that's a reasonable number of people to die and still let me believe in God." Could anyone find satisfaction on the "amount of evil" issue following this protocol?

The argument must come down to the *presence* of evil, period, and not any given *amount* of evil. Theodicy is not, as popularly conceived, a quantitative issue. The amount of evil generates human emotion, but that has no currency as an argument.

Our Perception of Evil is Relative

Our perception of the amount of evil is relative to our experience. Extreme mass tragedies, such as the 2004 Indian Ocean tsunami, the 2010 Haitian earthquake, and the 2011 Japanese tsunami stand out because of their rarity. The Haitian earthquake struck a densely populated area with exceptionally poor infrastructure integrity, resulting in approximately the same death toll as the much more widespread tsunami, each in excess of 300,000 souls. We think of these as rare occurrences, but that is relative to our "frequency expectation." What we experience in our world shapes our perception. If we lived in a world where natural disasters occurred much

---

[5] Gen. 18:22-33

less frequently and seldom killed people, then we might have outcries against God if twenty perished in a typhoon. On the other hand, if we lived in a world where every year on average a geophysical event claimed over 300,000 lives, we would expect that, and there wouldn't be any more or any less outcry against God. Whether we lived in a world of extremely rare disaster, daily disasters, or the in-between world that we do have, we would attribute the same relative causality to God.

Suppose, though, that we lived in a world of even more rare tragedy and suffering, a hypothetical world. Suppose there were no natural disasters (even though this is physically impossible on our living earth), and everyone lived to be 100. In this make-believe world, *anything* that went wrong would have the same emotional impact as the mass tragedies we experience. An outbreak of bedbugs would raise a hue and cry against God. How could the Almighty allow this! I speak tongue-in-cheek, of course, but the point is that no conceivable world free enough from tragedy and disaster would appease the sceptic. Arguments from "the amount of suffering" are relative to our experience, and there is no threshold that would quell all gainsayers.

In these times of expanding life span, access to abundant food, water, shelter, and health care for many (but by no means all), much of the world actually has a pretty good time of it. No Westerner living today would want to trade places with an inhabitant of medieval Europe, with its miserable living conditions, life expectancy less than half of what we have today, continual wars and plagues, almost no opportunity for education for the vast majority, and essentially no health care at all. Those who complain most against God are probably those who are the most well off.

Instances of God's Intervention

This point is similar to the above in that it shows how we can lose our rationality due to the emotional impact of a particularly vile evil. I refer here to the iconic evil, the Holocaust, which has enormously influenced discussions of theodicy. First, let me make clear that I do not mean to minimize the Holocaust, or what its memory means today. I'm only referring to the inappropriate use of the Holocaust as an instance of evil. Let's look at just two examples:

> One interesting fact to emerge from recent discussion of the problem of evil is that the paradigm evil event to which virtually all theodicists now refer—including all the contributors of this book—is the Holocaust. ... Let me pose

this question for the authors and readers of this book: are there any theodicies, represented here or elsewhere, which are credible when they try to account for the Holocaust?[6]

If he [God] could bring Jesus back from total lifelessness to life, I believe that God could have changed the minds of the Nazi leaders, thereby preventing Auschwitz.[7]

The first statement, a rhetorical question, implies that no theodicy can account for the Holocaust. The second inculpates God for failing to prevent the Nazi leaders from carrying out the Holocaust, represented by Auschwitz, one of the major Nazi death camps.

The Holocaust accounted for on the order of ten percent of World War II casualties; total civilian death estimates are in the forty to fifty million range, and another twenty to twenty five million military deaths.[8] So let's say that God did change the Nazi leaders' minds and prevented Auschwitz, but allowed World War II to proceed on a more civil basis. Would this author be a satisfied theist without a Holocaust? Would the other sixty to seventy five million people who died not bother his faith? Is he willing to say that God should have changed the U.S. leaders' minds about incinerating Hiroshima and Nagasaki?

Assertions that attack theism on the grounds of a specific event in history have a converse—if that event didn't happen, then it removes the objection to theism. In other words, if you say that you can't accept theism because of the Holocaust, does that mean that you would accept theism if the Holocaust had not happened? Consistency demands that you use the Holocaust only as an example, not as the defining event. God didn't cease to exist when the Nazis started killing Jews. Either God exists and existed before the Holocaust, or God never existed.

Let's assume that the example about the Holocaust extends at least to the other civilian deaths. That is, instead of using the Holocaust as the only part of WWII that justifies a rejection of God, we will give those who seem to promote that view a reprieve from their emotionally based reasoning. We will credit them with believing that any of the other 20 million plus civilians who perished (including most of the extended families of my grandparents) would suffice for the same argument.

---

[6] *Encountering Evil* (ed. S. T. Davies; Atlanta: John Knox Press, 1981), 6.
[7] J. K. Roth, "A Theodicy of Protest", in *Encountering Evil,* 33.
[8] en.wikipedia.org/wiki/World_War_II_casualties (cited: 28/02/2011).

The systematic attempt to exterminate European Jewry may have differed in scope, but did it differ epistemologically from any other civilian deaths, such as the million or so who perished in the siege of Leningrad? Can you use one group as a reason for atheism but say that other ethnic groups' horrible sufferings don't bother your faith? From this standpoint, you must accept that even though it might have been the chief of all atrocities in our memory, the Holocaust has no greater weight than any other tragedy.

What of the two Japanese cities levelled by nuclear devices? The military account ran along utilitarian lines; that fewer lives would be lost than in a conventional invasion of Japan, which was apparently the only other viable option to end the war in the Pacific. Were the residents of Hiroshima and Nagasaki exempt from theodicy arguments because the writers are Westerners? Does anybody want to draw *that* distinction?

Let's say that the entirety of WWII offends your sentiments the same as the Holocaust, and you can't draw any line that says the deaths on one side are okay but the deaths on the other side of the line put God out of existence. Logically all WWII casualties should be in the same category as the Holocaust; they *all* argue against the conventional monotheistic view of God. What then of WWI? What about any war? Where *do* we put that line that says, "I can live with this instance of evil, but not that one?" One might as well say that God could have prevented Cain from slaying Abel.

Even relatively small instances of evil, suffering, or injustice will lead us to the same conclusion: there is no minimum amount of evil at which you can say, "The presence of this much evil is consistent with belief in God, but more than this, then atheism must be true." Citing a specific instance of evil is an emotional expression of outrage and a sense of helplessness, but it carries no weight as an anti-theist argument. Like the "amount of evil" argument, the "specific instance of evil" argument is pure vapour.

Whatever was true about God in 1945 was true in 1200 A.D. and 1200 B.C. Yet how many times have we encountered words such as "I can't believe in God after the Holocaust"? Is this not a posthumous slap in the face of every victim of any evil before the Holocaust? There is no "post-Holocaust" theodicy that need differ from what anyone might have proposed in 1920, or might yet propose in 2050 should the world cook itself with nuclear weapons and global warming.

The 1755 Lisbon earthquake presented a similar challenge to theologians and philosophers. This event has particular significance in the history of the problem of evil. Lisbon, then the fourth largest city in Europe, and one of the wealthiest and most splendidly constructed, was nearly entirely destroyed on 1 November 1755, by a massive earthquake followed by widespread fires and flooding from a tsunami. Loss of life was in the many tens of thousands. The French philosopher, author, and poet Voltaire wrote two major works in response to this event, taking to task prevailing philosophical and theological ideas. His lengthy poem, "The Lisbon Earthquake," along with its preface, reveal his emptiness and inability to account for any plausible explanation why God should allow such an occurrence, and his distaste for those who could overlook the monumental human suffering and dish out philosophical musings to explain evil.[9] Much of the poem is a reply to the philosophical position first advanced by the German philosopher and mathematician Gottfried Wilhelm Leibniz, the coiner of the word "theodicy." Leibniz said that we live in the best possible of all worlds, because God could, of course, not make anything less. Any evil that was present had to be subsumed under a larger picture that all worked for an ultimate greater good. Voltaire continued his attack on this position a few years later with his greatest work, the short satirical novel *Candide*.[10] The hero, Candide, encounters an absurd series of disasters, but he is repeatedly reminded that, nonetheless, this is the best of all possible worlds we inhabit. It is indeed a great piece of writing by a master of humour and satire, but it is sad to see how constrained and feeble is even a great wit without knowledge of God's purpose. Ultimately, Voltaire, and the rest of his ilk, have nothing to offer but perplexity. More recently, the great 2004 tsunami that struck Indonesia and Southeast Asia supplanted Krakatoa as the iconic natural ("act of God") disaster. It's necessary to use examples when discussing the problem of evil, but no single form, amount, or instance of evil on its own requires a special theodicy.

Types of Causation

Does it matter if an evil is human caused or if it results from a force of nature, oft-times pejoratively described as an "act of God"?

The following is one way to classify the sources of evil:

---

[9] *The Portable Voltaire* (ed. B. R. Redman; New York: Viking, 1968), 556-569. Voltaire observed, "All things are doubtless arranged and set in order by Providence, but it has long been too evident, that its superintending power has not disposed them in such a manner as to promote our temporal happiness."
[10] *The Portable Voltaire*, 229-238.

- **Social evils** are entirely of human origin. Injustice, prejudice, oppression, greed, war, fraud, hatred, violence, abuse, persecution, and such like all form a detestable catalogue of the nefarious exercise of human free will.

- **Accidents** are also of human origin, but they result from carelessness, recklessness, and a disregard for safety, not from purposeful ill will. This category includes vehicle crashes, falls, fires, drownings, accidents with machines, and other mishaps that spell loss of life, health, and property.

- **Natural disasters,** often known as "acts of God," are distinguished by their tremendous, rapid devastation and their origin in nature, with no known human causality.[11] This category includes severe weather and geophysical events such as earthquakes, storms, avalanches, and floods. These are but the forces of nature in their ongoing process of shaping and reshaping the earth—until humans get in their path. When they occur in populated areas, the damage, in human terms, is stunning.[12]

- **Disease** includes every sort of health-related problem, such as infection, pain, cancer, bodily dysfunction, etc. These have multi-factorial causation: genetics, personal health habits, and environment. This category is distinguished by its unremitting and relentless attack on humanity. Seldom does it affect large numbers in a very short time, even during epidemics, but its pervasiveness makes it the leading cause of morbidity and mortality. Preventing one disease only means living long enough to die of another. This category, usually ignored in theodicy discussion, is significant for our purposes.

---

[11] At least in the United States, "act of God" is a legal term used by insurance companies to describe damage from storm, earthquakes, or other causes that have no apparent human causation. We should not be so quick to make this distinction, however, as human activity may well be causing climatic and other major ecological changes.

[12] Events such the 1883 explosion of Krakatoa are normal geophysical events of incredible energy. The Krakatoa volcanic explosion, occurring in the relatively unpopulated (at the time) Dutch East Indies, blew almost an entire island off the map, killed at least 36,000, and was heard and felt thousands of miles away. It had a force estimated at 13,000 times the nuclear device that destroyed Hiroshima (en.wikipedia.org/wiki/Krakatoa cited: 01/03/2011).

- **Emotional and psychological problems** correlate, but necessarily so, as we will see below, with any of the physical evils in the above categories. We also have the stress of normal life, and mental illnesses unrelated to any external sources.

How can a classification of evil contribute to a belief in God? We can filter out evils of human origin. We do not want to blame God for what people do, neither should we admit as evidence against God an evil of human origin. Some people, however, won't accept this distinction; as cited previously, one writer attempted to hold God responsible for not changing the Nazi leaders' minds. In this worldview, it wouldn't matter if the evil were of human origin. God still had the last word, and could have prevented it. This calls into question the issue of human free choice, and that is our next topic.

Human Free Choice

One solution to the problem of evil would have been for God to create beings incapable of doing evil. Either that, or he might, at every instance, prevent them from doing the evil that they imagine in their hearts. That would also mean such beings would be incapable of doing good, for good and evil cannot exist without the real opportunity to make that choice. The world that would ensue would be free from any morality. Love would go out the window. We would have a peaceable kingdom, inhabited only by animals and automatons.

However, sentient beings with moral capability and the mental faculties sufficient for an awareness of God are a prerequisite for the type of life demanded by the anti-theist sceptic. In other words, for the question of God's existence even to arise, we must have faculties sufficient to conceive of and interact with God. Either we take our world, warts and all, or ask for a world of animal-level mental capability, and for God to programme all of those beings to behave themselves. Ridding the world of moral evil means ridding the world of human free choice. No one would question God's existence, because in an amoral world no being would have the mental equipment to conceive of God. The price we pay for owning the intelligence capable of questioning the existence of God is the possibility of moral evil.

Human Causation

We live a world where people either through intent or accident perpetrate massive harm on themselves and others. United States drivers have for many decades reliably killed 40,000 to 45,000 annually, with noticeable decline only in the past two years. Because these deaths are spread over time in a large country, they lack the emotional impact of an airplane crash. Nonetheless, the toll equates to a medium-sized passenger aircraft going down daily, and that would upset us immensely. Worldwide, the annual death toll due to automobile collisions exceeds one million, and the number of severely injured is many times that. Where are the outcries against God for allowing automobile accidents? Any "argument" based on a great number people dying at once reveals that it is an emotional reaction. Again, singling out some mass-casualty event as the basis for questioning God's existence is a weak argument in the face of comparable evils not as emotionally offensive.

Another datum that unfortunately looks too stable is deaths attributable to cigarette smoking. In the U.S.A., this figure runs about 440,000 annually, more than ten times the number of vehicular accident deaths. These are 100 percent preventable, even though these same people will all die of something. Ought we to blame God for allowing people to smoke? With respect to arguments about theodicy, is there any difference between these deaths and those who die in war or accidents? Whether it's the drunk who kills himself and others in a car wreck, or the victims of their own poor health habits, they're all still dead, and we could say of any of them, "God could have prevented this." If we allow that God will not protect us from ourselves, it's very difficult to establish how God might protect us from others, as degrees of causality and blame make this an impossible criterion to maintain.

On the other side of the ledger, we have no way of knowing how much God does prevent. Perhaps God did not prevent Hitler and the Nazi leaders, but can we assert that God did not prevent them fully realizing their designs? We cannot say that God didn't prevent such and such when the opposite might actually be the case, although to outward appearances and human judgment it might seem that God wasn't involved. Can we expect God to intervene at every entry point of human malice or greed, carelessness or disrespect for others?[13]

---

[13] I have addressed this point in more detail in the articles referenced in footnote 4.

Natural Disasters

There's nothing like a devastating earthquake or other "act of God" to stir up the anti-theist rhetoric. These events seem so utterly preventable (by God), often occur without any warning (earthquakes), cause widespread destruction as well as loss of life, take away the young and old alike, and leave the survivors helpless and terrified. There's no one to blame, so there's no impingement on human free will if God chose to prevent the disaster. A natural disaster that affects a poorer area will do relatively much more damage than the same in a well-constructed area, and this too will all the more arouse our passions— "Could not God have spared these poor people who have already suffered so much?" Finally, natural disasters cause so much damage and take so many lives so quickly that death tolls seem all the more tragic. In just a few seconds of earthquake, tens of thousands of lives can be snuffed out. Except for the Holocaust, natural disasters top the list when it comes to examples thrown into theodicy discussions. And except for the nuclear devastations of Hiroshima and Nagasaki at the close of World War II, no human-engendered evil can take as many lives as quickly as an earthquake or tsunami.

A few days after the 2004 tsunami a clergyman appeared on television to answer the usual question of how could God allow such a thing to happen. He replied tersely, "This was a geological event, not a theological event." The cleric was not being coy. He was making a matter-of-fact statement that I hope realigned people's thinking on the matter. There was nothing about God, existence included, that changed with the tsunami. The same reasoning applies here that I have used above: there is no minimum level of tsunami destruction that would appease an anti-theist. The 2004 event, in our frame of reference, shook us tremendously, but it said nothing that hadn't been said before.

Partly because we feel so vulnerable in the face of natural disasters, and partly because of their sudden destruction, these events raise more doubts about God, even if their toll over the long run is not even what people do to themselves and each other daily. Emotional reactions find their way into what are supposed to be logical arguments about God's existence, and that we must disallow.

Hard But True Arguments

The remainder of this chapter will consider the nature of suffering and evil. Are evil and suffering even well enough defined that they can rightfully take a place in a formal "Problem of Evil" syllogism? Let's start by looking at the fact that human suffering is temporary.

We often say of persons who have just died after a long, painful illness that their suffering is ended and they are at peace. This view of a peaceful state applies regardless of one's beliefs about any form of life after death. Those who assert that the person's soul now inhabits some blissful state should recognize that much misery remains behind in their survivors. God is not glorified, because the earth overall remains a place of much suffering. In the case of those who assert no possibility of life whatsoever after death, then the deceased has gone into oblivion, and suffering remains on the earth. In the case of those who hope for a future resurrection of the deceased and a renewal of the earth, both the individual and collective ills of the earth are remedied. This solution glorifies God and makes sense in many dimensions.

What if the deceased was a scoundrel? Many believe that such a person suffers even worse agonies in hell. The notion of eternal suffering is a mangling of biblical teaching. It requires the mythological concept of an immortal soul, it relies on misunderstandings of terms such as *gehenna*, *sheol*, and *hades*, and it has a just God doling out infinite punishment as the consequence of a finite life of unfaith. The phrase "eternal suffering" is absolutely oxymoronic; only that which is in concert with the character of God can abide forever.

Our point here is that when a person dies, his or her suffering ends. It is gone forever, as if it had never been. This might seem cruel to tell someone who is in great agony, but its veracity remains. A person receiving adequate palliative care can die in peace. A person dying in agony has the same peace upon expiration, and neither has any ability to recall their dying days. At the moment of death, neither peace nor pain abides further.

Let's look at an illustration from real life (or real death, as is the case). A wealthy entrepreneur becomes ill with cancer and dies in great misery. Upon expiring, the pains of his final months vanish, and so do the memories of the pleasures of life he enjoyed. According to his wishes, his body is cremated and the ashes dispersed over a favourite lake. There is nothing left of the person; he is non-existent in all respects, his situation is as it was before he was ever born.

We can't ignore the stark reality of nothingness. We are temporally constrained entities, with a finite life span, no existence prior to our birth and no existence after our death (save for the resurrection of the faithful to eternal life). Death ends all pains and pleasures. It doesn't make any difference at all if a person's life was filled with one or the other, because at the moment of death, it is as if the person never existed. Once life is over, evil and suffering are as non-existent as pleasure and joy.

For the brief time of our vain mortal existence, we seek pleasure and avoid pain. But in the end, it just doesn't make any difference. This is surely the main point of Ecclesiastes, with its proclamation, "Vanity, vanity", calling us to our spiritual senses.[14] Only the development of spiritual character has abiding value, and therefore does make a difference, because it survives death when we reappear in the resurrection.

Part of the reason God allows pain, suffering, and evil is because they are temporary. Temporary means bound by time both at the beginning and the end, and ending the same as it was before it began—non-existent. This is a stiff dose of reality, and of little comfort to those overcome by anguish or pain. It does not mean God condones evil, and it does not mean God lacks compassion or mercy. It does mean that the sufferings inherent to human mortality are limited by that same mortality.

Analyzing Evil Impairs the Argument from Evil

It is unfair to establish a logical argument that purports to disprove the existence of God based on a factor (in this case, evil) that is nebulous and undefined. How can you accuse someone of a crime when you can't even state what the crime is? Evil is easy to assume, but hard to define. The experience of evil is very real, but for purposes of ideological argument, it's hard to characterize. What one person calls treachery, another calls divine duty. What one side calls patriotic acts of heroism, the other side calls infamous deeds of terrorism. Suicide bomber or martyr? One person cries, "injustice"; another responds, "vindication." The same ambiguity applies to suffering. What one person feels as intense pain, another doesn't even notice.

It is impossible to put "evil" into a tidy box. The anti-theist syllogism almost collapses for want of workable definitions of "evil" and "suffering." Evil is not a tangible entity like a termite. Evil is as evasive to

---

[14] The Hebrew word translated "vanity" means "brief, temporary", with the added connotation, "therefore not worth pursuing."

define as beauty: equations and logic are simply misleading. How can the presence of X disprove the presence of Y when X turns out to be a subjective and indefinable entity? Be very careful about using "evil" as a word and as concept.

In an attempt to clarify what evil includes, we will dissect it into three components: moral evil, physical pain, and mental pain. We will look at each of these individually to determine if the presence of any one of them has sufficient reality to merit standing in anti-theist arguments.

Moral Evil

Moral evil implies a moral standard. Most people agree that some kind of moral standard exists in the world, and violations of that standard result in moral evil. Let's illustrate by using a commonly accepted moral tenet: we ought not to harm others. However, people *do* harm each other, so moral evil does exist. I'm only including the actual thought or practice of evil, not its results. If you strike someone, the moral evil is the malicious act against your neighbour. The pain and the psychological trauma suffered by your victim are separate issues discussed below.[15]

If moral evil exists, does that mean God does not exist? Can God make a world in which humans have free will, but never sin?[16] If free will means anything at all, God cannot make a world that guarantees the absence of moral evil. God could have made a world without humans, but humans differ from the animals in that they have the inner and free option to respond to God as creator. If they don't have this, they are not human at all. If anything, moral evil demonstrates the existence of God, for a purely naturalistic world—a world without God—can have no moral system. In a purely naturalistic world, we cannot call the Holocaust an example of evil, because a completely natural world, without God, is amoral. To posit moral evil is to acknowledge a God.

---

[15] In writings on theodicy, "moral evil" usually includes all evils and consequences of human origin, and "natural evil" is used for "acts of God." I am here distinguishing between moral transgression and its effects, and thus using "moral evil" in a restricted sense, approximately equal to "sin."

[16] Moral free will is the human capacity to think and make choices *independent* of external factors or innate drives. Our surroundings and human nature influence us, but we yet are morally responsible in the end. I use the phrase "autonomous moral agents" to describe us. This separates us from other animals, which lack the cognitive governance of a will to override natural impulse and environmental stimuli.

Physical Suffering

This is the category of pure physiological pain. Pain, of course, relates to suffering, which is certainly an aspect of evil, whether it comes from disease, accident, or assault. It is not an evil in that it necessarily arises from malicious intent, but we consider it an evil presence in our life. We think that if we didn't have physical pain, then we would be much happier. However, the story of pain is more complicated than unpleasant neural activity. Pain is far more subjective than it might seem, depending on a number of physical variables, as well as psychological and cultural factors. Does the presence of pain present an argument against the existence of God?

Without pain, we would be in deep trouble, as we would have no way to monitor important interactions with our environment. People who do not sense pain damage themselves severely, not knowing when they have burned themselves, or have appendicitis, or if their shoes are too tight, or if they have broken a bone.[17] People can die from infections and other problems if they lack the warning system of pain.

This response, however, only presses us to ask the next question, "Why did God make us so vulnerable? Why do we need to suffer to stay healthy?" Pain is a warning system because it *is* painful; if pain weren't pain, it wouldn't be doing its job. Pain by definition *must* hurt. It's not a matter of vulnerability; it's a matter of being human. If your fingers didn't hurt when you picked up the hot pot handle, you'd burn your flesh.

We sense pain in our peripheral nervous system, but the brain interprets those sensations in conjunction with other physiological and psychological factors and comes up with the level of pain we actually feel. There is no necessary correlation between physical injury to the nervous system and pain perception. The following examples illustrate the multifactorial nature of pain perception: a person in personal injury litigation with major pain from minor injuries; psychosomatic disorders in which people experience great pain with no physical cause whatsoever; surgery performed without anaesthesia until the mid-nineteenth century; persons in hypnotic states in modern times who undergo major surgery with no anaesthesia; chronic pain patients with social dependency; people

---

[17] Leprosy does not rot off the flesh, but causes loss of sensation from the peripheral nervous system. Hence, injuries and infections go unnoticed and unhealed, resulting in the classic picture of lepers with mere stumps of hands and feet and disfigured faces.

114

with massive injuries from an accident feeling little or no pain until they reach safety; an athlete playing despite injury; a person undergoing acupuncture to relieve pain; the dentist distracting you before an injection; a person reporting significant pain relief after taking a placebo. And what about the "no pain, no gain" crowd, those hard-core endorphin addicts who love pushing their bodies to the point of pain? Does their crusade for discomfort negate the possibility of God?

Even if we need some pain to protect us, couldn't "less pain" still do the job? Wouldn't a loving God subject his creation only to the minimum necessary pain? At this point, the argument parallels the "amount of suffering" discussion we investigated earlier. You can't set a point of acceptable pain reduction, because whatever residual pain humans still experienced would probably register as just as painful as what we have now. Pain is largely subjective, it certainly has some absolute physiological thresholds on both ends, but in practical terms in any conceivable real world, pain, like gas in a closed container, will fill up the space available.

It is unlikely that an adjustment of the nervous system would yield any change in pain experience. As long as we have a nervous system, we will experience the same range of pain, and the question must quickly transfer (again noting the parallel to the "amount of evil" argument) from, "why must pain be so painful", to "why is there *any* pain or discomfort at all?" It's part of our mortal existence. We are back to the question, "Why are we mortal human beings?" That's where the pain question ends, and that's where we shall end this chapter shortly.

Emotional/Psychological Pain

Any physical pain, moral transgression, injustice, or loss of any kind can lead to emotional suffering. We can call it grief, sorrow, stress, anxiety, or whatever; in all cases, what we have is a mental state of great distress, so much so that it too qualifies as suffering, a form of evil, and therefore also enters into the questioning. It is possibly the only form of evil that really counts, for if we suffer great misfortune or pain, but no emotional distress about the matter, is there really any evil? We will approach that idea shortly, but we will first ask the usual question, "Does the presence of mental anguish of any sort present evidence against the existence of an omnipotent, loving God?"

Physical pain is subjective, but mental pain is excessively more so. If someone stabs you in the heart with a knife, it will certainly hurt to some extent, but if someone stabs you in the heart with a cruel remark, or if life stabs you in the heart with a great loss, it will not *necessarily* cause any emotional anguish at all. The emotional anguish response, unlike most physical pain responses, does not ensue automatically. An internal filter, largely of your own making, causes the emotional pain. The fact is this: nothing we encounter in life causes emotional pain except *our own reactions* to the circumstances of life. Scripture teaches this implicitly, for example: "we also rejoice in sufferings" (Rom 5:3); "consider it nothing but joy when you fall into all sorts of trials" (Jas 1:2); and "A cheerful heart brings good healing" (Prov 17:22).

Epictetus and the Stoic philosophers addressed this directly. They taught that we live in a world of unpredictable circumstances, that nature does not always go our way, that life inevitably has its hardships, but nobody and nothing can lay claim on the thinking of our mind. What happens "out there" is neither good nor evil. Peace or suffering result from how we construe these events. Happiness is an internal issue, entirely independent of what happens in life.

> If you are pained by any external thing, it is not this thing that disturbs you, but your own judgment about it. And it is in your power to wipe out that judgment now.[18]
>
> No man can rob us of our free will.[19]
>
> Lameness in an impediment to the leg, but not to the will; say this to yourself with regard to everything that happens.[20]

And Milton wrote in *Paradise Lost,*

> "The mind is its own place, and in it self
> Can make a Heav'n of Hell, a Hell of Heav'n."[21]

If this is a fair parsing of the factors of evil, then the argument from evil is severely diminished. Emotional pain is within our own power to control.

---

[18] Marcus Aurelius, *Meditations* VIII:47. He lived from AD 121-180, becoming emperor in 161.

[19] *Meditations* XI:36.

[20] Epictetus, *Enchiridion* 9. Epictetus (AD 55-135), the most famous of the Stoic philosophers, was born a slave. Lame from birth and poor all of his life, he was exiled when Domitian banned all philosophers from Rome. His writings greatly influenced Marcus Aurelius.

[21] Book 1:254-255.

Moral evil actually argues for the theist position, as it implies a universal moral standard and people being tested thereby. Physical pain is a necessary feature of mortal life. Suffering is mandatory for spiritual development. To rid the world of all these forms of suffering, and still leave a real world with real humans being tested in their humanity, creates an impossible world. Pain, loss, and injustice are inevitable consequences of mortality, but happiness and joy are ours if we want them.

The Real Problem and the Real Answer

As I have repeatedly averred, it is not any amount, distribution, or severity of evil that should be on the table, but the presence of any evil, period. The question then becomes, "Does the presence of mortal humans indicate the non-existence of an omnipotent, loving God?" The real problem is not evil and suffering; it is mortality itself. "Why does God allow mortality?" should be the question on the table.

Mortality is the lynchpin of theodicy. We cannot help being mortal because we are all sinful beings (Rom 5:12). In this condition, evil will of necessity occur, for we will all die of *something*. Unfortunately, when amount becomes the focus, the real evil, mortality *itself*, is ignored. Everyone, regardless of his or her perspective on the Bible, is subject to mortality. We will not all die at the age of 100 with a smile on our face; there can be no conceivable world inhabited by mortals and free of evil and suffering.

The real solution to the problem of evil and suffering must involve a removal of mortality, and that is God's purpose. It is, however, logically and morally necessary to have an antecedent period of mortal existence. Without a period for developing faith, no one could have a place in the divine realm. God can make perfect beings, but he cannot make perfect beings that have free moral choice. God can, however, make a perfect world inhabited by those who *have experienced* mortality and thus prostrate themselves in love and gratitude to their Creator. The theological doctrine of the Kingdom of God on earth is the only possible solution to the present problem of evil and suffering.

A Concluding Thought

The chapter opened with a syllogism that called into question two characteristics of God: omnipotence and omnibenevolence. There's a third "omni" that critics must also account for, omniscience. Regardless of how uncomfortable and miserable our lives may be, and how sorrowful and stricken the earth is in general, we humans ought to recognize the vanity of thinking that we're smarter than God. Calling God into question because we don't like the way things are going trivializes our existence. Better to live a life of faith and accept suffering as part of our mortality and therefore recognize and elevate our humanity, than to degrade it with what are ultimately puerile, emotional, and vain assaults against the one power who can remedy our sad existence. Anti-theist arguments based on the presence of evil only serve to tell us more about the people who propose them than about God.

> He will wipe away every tear from their eyes, and death will not exist any more – or mourning, or crying, or pain, for the former things have ceased to exist (Revelation 21:4)

Now What?

In my psychotherapy practice, clients often ask the "Why?" question; that is, they want to know why something bad happened to them, why they can't be "normal," why they have such stress, and so on. When this happens I redirect them to the "what" question: "what do I do given the situation?" The "why" question is usually unanswerable, and even if answerable, yields no practical guidance. Even when we know exactly, at many levels, the cause of suffering, we still need to deal with it. Knowing "why" doesn't take away the suffering.

I suggest this approach also for the global problem of suffering and evil. At some level, we will never know the "why" of what we perceive as a world so full of suffering and evil. We can answer on a theological level, we can answer on a psychological level, we can answer on a geological level, but we will still have the same pain to deal with.

As Christians, we are content that in the grand plan of the universe ultimately God knows about all the evil there is, and someday God will put it all away. For now, he expects us to exercise our Christian virtue to be clothers of the naked, healers of the sick, feeders of the hungry, consolers of the distraught, comforters of the lonely, and supporters of those in need. Our broken world gives us abundant opportunity for acts of mercy and assistance. It is not enough to have an adequate theodicy that maintains our faith in a world of suffering and evil. If we proclaim that God is present and in ultimate control of the universe, then our next step is to be his presence on earth until that day does come when he wipes away all tears.

Part Two:
Reasons for Believing

Textual Criticism

Jonathan Burke

"Changes in wording and newly discovered sentences and paragraphs will not alter the Ten Commandments or the nature of God or his call to righteous living by faith and obedience" – John R. Kohlenberger III[1]

Two Key Questions

The two questions most commonly asked about the biblical text are 'How accurately has it been passed down to us?' and 'How do we know?' These questions are answered through textual criticism, the scholarly discipline that reconstructs the text from the available evidence. Textual criticism demonstrates that the biblical text we have today is a highly accurate and reliable copy of what the originals would have been.

It is important to consider the reliability of the text. If the text is true to the original, then we have a sound basis for examining its content as a basis for faith.

The Old Testament

Table 1 describes the various textual sources of the Old Testament text we have today.

The Septuagint takes its name from the unsubstantiated legend that seventy scribes in Egypt translated it during the third century BC. Regardless of the details of this legend, it is clear that the original work consisted only of the Pentateuch, and the other Old Testament books were translated into Greek later over some time. Although it is clear that a Greek Old Testament text of some kind existed by the first century AD, and was being used by the Jewish community, later Christians originally used the term 'Septuagint' to refer only to the Greek Pentateuch, and only later to the complete Greek Old Testament editions translated by Aquila

---

[1] J. R. Kohlenberger III, "The Textual Basis of Old Testament Translation", in *The Essential Evangelical Parallel Bible* (Oxford: OUP, 2004), xxxii.

(128 AD), Theodotion (mid-late second century), and Symmachus (late second century).[2]

Table 1: Textual Transmission of the Old Testament		
Text Source	Details	Date
Septuagint (LXX)	A Greek copy of the Old Testament; the history of this text is complex	300–200 BC
Dead Sea Scrolls (DSS)	Hebrew texts of the Old Testament	200 B –50 AD
Samaritan Pentateuch (SP)	A copy of the Old Testament in Samaritan; less valuable than the Dead Sea Scrolls	140 BC–37 BC
Masoretic Text (MT)	A textual tradition of the Old Testament by Jewish scribes	500–1000 AD

The Masoretic Text takes its name from the Masoretes, the Jewish scribes who meticulously copied out the Old Testament text. It is known for the extreme care with which the text was prepared and copied, and the extensive notations indicating vowel points, pronunciation and stress marks, textual variants, and commentary notes.

Prior to the discovery of the Dead Sea Scrolls in Qumran, the Masoretic Text was the oldest Hebrew witness to the text of the Old Testament. The other textual traditions, the Septuagint and the Samaritan Pentateuch, were of limited assistance, as they were translations into either Greek or Samaritan from a Hebrew text. It was difficult for scholars to confirm which textual tradition was closer to the original.

---

[2] "Some scholars use Septuagint (often in quotation marks) to refer only to the Pentateuch, while others intend the term to include the entire collection of Jewish-Greek scriptures ... reserving the rubric Old Greek (OG) for those books which are translations from Hebrew. Others, recognizing that all the extant Greek mss are corrupt and probably only partially representative of what the original translators intended, use the terms 'Ur-Septuagint,' 'Original Septuagint' or 'Proto-Septuagint' to describe the text as it presumably left the translators' hands. Septuagint for some scholars describes a 'critical text,' i.e., one chosen after careful reading and evaluation of all the available witnesses to the book(s) in question, and determined to be the "nearest approach" to the original translation. ... Many other scholars, having subjected the matter to little or no critical scrutiny, use Septuagint to refer to any printed edition so labelled, which may be used to correct/adjust readings in the printed editions of the Hebrew Bible". Freedman, *The Anchor Yale Bible Dictionary* (New York: Doubleday, 1996).

The Dead Sea Scrolls have been the most important Old Testament textual find in the last 100 years, confirming the accuracy of the transmission of the text from its origin to our day:

> (1) The scrolls confirm the reliability of the Masoretic Text, thereby adding almost a thousand years to the antiquity of the Hebrew text. (2) They re-establish the Septuagint as a textual authority. (3) The scrolls are a source of reliable variant readings.[3]

> Again, the Qumran material has diminished the value of the Samaritan Pentateuch as an ancient textual witness, and this on palaeographic grounds. F.M. Cross has shown its text to be a relatively late branch, dating back no further than Hasmonean times.[4]

> The textual evidence of the Dead Sea Scrolls, in fact, confirms the general reliability and stability of the text of the Old Testament as we have it today, while at the same time offers evidence of important early witnesses to textual variants.[5]

With the combined evidence of the Masoretic Text, so carefully copied by generations of scholars, and the Dead Sea Scrolls, scholars are in a much better place to ascertain the reliability of the Old Testament text. Textual scholars have prepared critical editions of the Old Testament text, such as *Biblia Hebraica Stuttgartensia,* which are based upon the Masoretic Text and note possible variants from the other textual witnesses.

Table 2: Textual Transmission of the Old Testament		
Manuscript	**Details**	**Date**
Aleppo Codex	An extremely accurate representation of the Masoretic text; only 294 pages remain intact[6]	10th century AD
Leningrad Codex	An almost intact Masoretic text; corrected with the Aleppo text, and used to reconstruct Aleppo	1008 AD

---

[3] H. P. Scanlin, *The Dead Sea scrolls and modern translations of the Old Testament,* (Wheaton: Tyndale House, 1993), 140, (emphasis added).
[4] S. Jellicoe, *The Septuagint and Modern Study,* (Oxford: Clarendon Press 1993) 244.
[5] Scanlin, *The Dead Sea Scrolls,* 140, (emphasis added).
[6] The location of the 193 leaves that went missing during 1947 is a matter of dispute; it has been claimed that they were burned, but there are no burn marks on the manuscript to indicate this, and two of the leaves were later discovered (in 1982 and 2007).

Table 2 cont.: Textual Transmission of the Old Testament		
Manuscript	Details	Date
Biblia Hebraica[7]	Three editions were printed;[8] footnotes contain alternative readings[9]	1906, 1913, 1937
Biblia Hebraica Stuttgartensia[10]	An edited copy of the Leningrad Codex; footnotes contain alternative readings[11]	1968–1976, 1997
Biblia Hebraica Quinta[12]	A copy of the Leningrad Codex	2004–2010[13]

The New Testament

Greek New Testament texts are identified as belonging to separate 'text types'; groups of texts which emerged in certain geographical locations and which are attested by certain forms of evidence. "Witnesses" are the individual pieces of evidence, whether a manuscript copy (full NT text, single books or small fragments) or quotations from early Christians or early translations in other languages. Scholars group these witnesses into "types", based upon their origins and textual similarities. Table 3 describes the four basic text types and the evidence for each; the dates given are the period when that textual type was in common use.

---

[7] Three editions of this text were issued; the shorthand for Biblia Hebraica is BHK, and edition numbers are indicated with BHK1, BHK2, and BHK3.

[8] First two editions based on the 17th century Mikraot Gedolot, third edition based on the Leningrad Codex.

[9] Suggested corrections in footnotes made on the basis of readings from the Samaritan Pentateuch, LXX, Vulgate, and Peshitta, or 'conjectural emendations' (hypothesized reconstructions of the text on the basis of available evidence).

[10] This is a revision of BHK3.

[11] Suggested corrections in footnotes made on the basis of readings from the Samaritan Pentateuch, Dead Sea Scrolls, LXX, Vulgate, and Peshitta, or 'conjectural emendations'.

[12] This is a revision of the fourth edition of BHS.

[13] The work is still incomplete, and is expected to be finished in 2015.

Witnesses	Alexandrian (2nd-6th C)	Western (2nd-6th C)	Caesarean (3rd-6th C?)	Byzantine (4th-8thC)
Table 3: New Testament Text Types And Witnesses With Dates[14]				
Early papyri[15]	P75, P66, P46, P72	P48, P39, P69	P45	none
Uncials[16]	ℵ01, B 03, C 04, W 032[17]	D 05, W 032[18]	038 W 032[19]	A 02[20] [21]
Patristic citations[22]	Origen (c.185–254), Didymus (c.313–398), Athanasius (296–373)	Irenaeus (c.130–200), Clement (c.96), Tertullian (c.160–225), Cyprian (d.258)	Origen (c.185–254), Eusebius (c.260–340), Cyril of Jerusalem (c.315–386)	Chrysostom (c.347–407), Theodoret (c.393–466)
Early versions[23]	Coptic[24]	Old Latin, Syrs, Syrc, Syrh	Old Armenian, Old Georgian	None

Contrary to popular belief, not all texts of the Alexandrian text type were written in Alexandria in Egypt, and in fact this text type is the earliest, most widespread, and most well attested of all the text types, with the greatest level of agreement with all four text types, since it shares textual

---

[14] Adapted from B. M. Metzger, *A Textual Commentary On the Greek New Testament* (2nd ed.; Deutsche Bibelgesellschaft, 1994).

[15] New Testament texts (complete or fragmentary), dating from the first to the third centuries (papyri after this date are not considered 'early'); they are the earliest textual witnesses to any text type, and the closest texts to the original.

[16] New Testament texts (complete or fragmentary), dating from the third century onwards (typically to the eighth century), written in a majuscule script (all capital letters).

[17] Luke 1:1-8:12, John.

[18] Mark 1:1-5:30.

[19] Mark 5:31-16:20.

[20] Gospels only.

[21] Full NT text only found in eighth century MSS E06 and 045.

[22] New Testament quotations in the writings of early Christians from the first to the sixth centuries; an early text type which was well regarded and widespread will be found commonly quoted in early Christian writings.

[23] Early translations of the New Testament (typically dated from the second to the fourth centuries), into languages other than Greek; most of the versions were translated very early.

[24] Sahidic and Bohairic.

agreement with the Western, Caesarean, and Byzantine types. Textual evidence shows that the Alexandrian text type remained popular until supplanted by the later Byzantine type from the ninth century onwards. Second century papyrus fragments and quotations in Christian writings prove that this type arose in the second century and remained commonly used throughout the next two centuries.

The Western text type contains paraphrases and additions in the gospels and Acts, but is more conservative in the epistles of Paul (in general this text type contains fewer insertions than the Byzantine text type, but more than the Alexandrian). It is represented by some important early witnesses (second century papyrus fragments and quotations in Christian writings prove this type arose in the second century), but is not as well supported as the Alexandrian text.

The Caesarean text type seems to be a combination of the Alexandrian and Western text types, and some scholars have questioned whether or not it should be considered a text type in its own right. Since it is a mixture of two earlier text types (it must have emerged no later than the third century, since it borrows from both the Alexandrian and Western types), it is clearly not the best reflection of the original Greek New Testament (only the gospels have been found in the Caesarean text type), and is not the most reliable witness (it has little early textual support).

The Byzantine is the latest of the text types to have emerged (there are no early papyrus texts of the Byzantine type, and it is not quoted in the early Christian writings until the fourth century). No early translations were made from the Byzantine type, since it did not exist until later, and this text type has the largest number of fraudulent additions and alterations, reflecting later Christian theological inventions.

Contrary to popular belief, the New Testament cannot be reconstructed accurately simply on the basis of quotations from these early Christians:

> The primary authority for a critical textual decision lies with the Greek manuscript tradition, with the versions and Fathers serving no more than a supplementary and corroborative function, particularly in passages where their underlying Greek text cannot be reconstructed with absolute certainty.[25]

---

[25] K. Aland & B. Aland, *The Text Of The New Testament: An Introduction To The Critical Editions And To The Theory And Practice Of Modern Textual Criticism* (trans. E. F. Rhodes; Eerdmans, 1995), 280.

The accuracy with which the text has been preserved (especially in the Alexandrian manuscripts), is well recognized:

> The Alexandrian text is found in manuscripts produced by scribes trained in Alexandrian scribal practices, the best of its kind in Greco-Roman times. <u>Such scribes were schooled in producing well-crafted, accurate copies</u>.[26]

> These manuscripts, produced with acumen, <u>display a standard of excellence</u>.[27]

> In any event, they produced <u>reliable copies that largely preserve the original wording of the New Testament writings</u>. It is to these manuscripts that we look for the preservation of the original wording of the various writings of the New Testament.

The New Testament is not only the most well attested ancient literary work; the earliest copies are closer to their originals than any other ancient work, as Table 4 shows.

Table 4: Proximity of Earliest Copy to Original Text				
Work	Date of original	Earliest copy	Years from original	Copies
New Testament	AD 40-100	AD 125	40-300[28]	24,000
Homer	700 BC	900 AD	1,600	643
Sophocles	496-406 BC	AD 1000	1,400	193
Aristotle	384-322 BC	AD 1100	1,400	49
Caesar	58-50 BC	AD 900	1,000	10

As the atheist Bart Ehrman writes:

> <u>As a result, the New Testament is preserved in far more manuscripts than any other book from antiquity</u>. There are, for example, fewer than 700 copies of Homer's *Iliad*, fewer

---

[26] P. W. Comfort & D. P. Barrett, *The Text of the Earliest New Testament Greek Manuscripts*, (Wheaton: Tyndale House, 2001), 28, (emphasis added).

[27] Comfort & Barrett, *New Testament Greek Manuscripts*, 29 (emphasis added).

[28] Depending on the text; the earliest New Testament text is a fragment of the Gospel of John (the Rylands Fragment), now called 'St John Fragment, Greek Papyrus 457', which is generally dated to around 125 AD, but other books of the New Testament are found only in texts dating to the mid-second or early fourth centuries, though this is still far superior to the record of any other ancient work.

than 350 copies of the plays of Euripides, and only one copy of the first six books of the *Annals* of Tacitus.[29]

Ehrman is more sceptical about the accuracy of the New Testament text than most professional text critics. He rightly argues that the large number of New Testament manuscripts does not prove that the Bible itself is true. He also points out that the reason why the New Testament is attested by so many manuscripts is that Christians were historically more interested in preserving this than any other text. Nevertheless, he still acknowledges the superiority of the preserved witness to the New Testament over any other ancient work.

Furthermore, the agreement between available copies of the New Testament is extremely high; 62.9% of the available texts are free from anything other than insignificant differences between each other, and 85% of the entire text is considered certain.[30]

> Thus in nearly two-thirds of the New Testament text, the seven editions of the Greek New Testament which we have reviewed are in complete accord, with no differences other than in orthographical details (e.g., the spelling of names, etc.). Verses in which any one of the seven editions differs by a single word are not counted. This result is quite amazing, demonstrating a far greater agreement among the Greek texts of the New Testament during the past century than textual scholars would have suspected.[31]

Challenges

Atheists and sceptics typically challenge the accuracy of the scriptural record with claims of textual error. The most prominent recent criticism of this kind was published in 2005 by Bart Ehrman, a professional textual critic and ex-Christian whose work *Misquoting Jesus* has been cited widely as presenting an overwhelming case for the unreliability of the textual transmission of the New Testament.

---

[29] B. D. Ehrman, *The New Testament: a historical introduction to the early Christian writings*, (New York: OUP, 2000), 443, (emphasis added).

[30] Clarke, "Textual Certainty In The United Bible Societies' Greek New Testament", *Novum Testamentum* 44:2 (2002), 116. Clarke's assessment was based on the first three editions of 'Greek New Testament' (the fourth and latest edition provides an even higher assessment of textual accuracy).

[31] Aland & Aland, *The Text Of The New Testament*, 29, (emphasis added).

Despite popular opinion, however, Ehrman's work is neither a breakthrough nor a revelation; anyone even casually familiar with modern textual criticism will be aware of all the issues Ehrman discusses.[32] He raises no new textual difficulties, contributes no new evidence, and in a number of cases his arguments stand well outside the established scholarly consensus.[33] To borrow a phrase, his work is both good and original, but that which is good is not original and that which is original is not good.

It should be remembered that the very identification of error requires first the identification of fact; errors of transmission in the New Testament cannot be established unless we first know what the text said in the first place. For this reason, Ehrman's emphasis on errors is largely misplaced in terms of establishing the reliability of the New Testament text we have today.

Table 5 lists several of Ehrman's more sensational and well-publicized claims, and contrasts them with the views of standard scholarship.

Table 5: Examining Ehrman's Claims	
Ehrman	Response
'We have only error-ridden copies, and the vast majority of these are centuries removed from the originals and different from them, evidently, in thousands of ways.' [34]	'Once it is revealed that the great majority of these variants are inconsequential—involving spelling differences that cannot even be translated, articles with proper nouns, word order changes, and the like—and that only a very small minority of the variants alter the meaning of the text, the whole picture begins to come into focus. Indeed, only about 1% of the textual variants are both meaningful and viable.' [35]

---

[32] "Misquoting Jesus for the most part is simply NT textual criticism 101" (Wallace, "The Gospel According to Bart: A Review Article *Misquoting Jesus* by Bart Ehrman", *Journal of the Evangelical Theological Society* 49:2 (2006): 328).

[33] "Chapter 2 ("The Copyists of the Early Christian Writings") deals with scribal changes to the text, both intentional and unintentional. Here Ehrman mixes standard text-critical information with his own interpretation, an interpretation that is by no means shared by all textual critics, nor even most of them" (Wallace, "Gospel According to Bart", 328; emphasis added).

[34] B. D. Ehrman, *Misquoting Jesus*, (HarperOne, 2005), 7.

[35] Wallace, "Gospel According to Bart", 330, (emphasis added).

Table 5 cont.: Examining Ehrman's Claims	
Ehrman	**Response**
'Mistakes multiply and get repeated; sometimes they get corrected and sometimes they get compounded. And so it goes. For centuries.'[36]	'Yet Ehrman remains well aware that textual critics can, in his words, "reconstruct the oldest form of the words of the New Testament with reasonable (though not 100 percent) accuracy".'[37]
'In almost every instance in which a change of this sort occurs, the text is changed in order to limit the role of women and to minimize their importance to the Christian movement.'[38]	'In a recent contribution to text-critical assessment of Acts, however, <u>Michael Holmes challenges this scholarly conjecture of what he calls an "alleged" antifeminist bias in the Western texts</u>, stating that "the claim, though often repeated, has not, to my knowledge, been examined in a thorough or comprehensive fashion. <u>In his detailed examination he rightly argues</u>, in my view, that many scholars have taken variants or tendencies that appear in Codex Bezae and over-generalized them to describe Western texts as a whole, <u>overlooking that Bezae is only one representative of this text type, and possesses idiosyncrasies of its own</u>.'[39] [40]

---

[36] Ehrman, *Misquoting Jesus*, 57.

[37] Jones, "Misquoting Truth", (2007), 47-48. The quotation from Ehrman is a statement from another work of his, *Lost Christianities: The Battles for Scripture and the Faiths We Never Knew* (New York: OUP, 2003), 221.

[38] Ehrman, *Misquoting Jesus*, 182.

[39] Brock, "Scribal Blunder or Textual Plunder? Codex Bezae, Textual-Rhetorical Analysis, And the Diminished Role of Women", in *Her Master's Tools?: Feminist and Postcolonial Engagements of Historical-Critical Discourse, Global Perspectives on Biblical Scholarship* (eds. C. V. Stichele & T. Penner; SBL, 2005), 257, (emphasis added).

[40] Note that Ehrman, ironically given he is a text critical scholar, does not tell readers that such alterations are so few and far between, so inconsistently found, limited to so few manuscripts, and some of them so much more readily attributable to accidental scribal error or the desire to render the text more grammatically, that they contradict the idea that the New Testament was revised by groups of misogynist scribes; out of the entire New Testament a mere 15 verses are most commonly discussed, and there is no consensus that even all of these are clear indications of deliberate misogynist alterations.

Table 5 cont.: Examining Ehrman's Claims	
Ehrman	**Response**
'The more I studied the manuscript tradition of the New Testament, the more I realized just how radically the text had been altered over the years at the hands of scribes, who were not only conserving scripture but also changing it.' [41]	'Intentional theological changes <u>make up very, very few of the textual variations in the NT</u> and therefore, on a relative scale, <u>have little significance for determining the overall state of the text</u>. The vast majority of scribes, in fact, <u>did not intentionally change the text whenever they felt like it</u>.' [42] 'If, indeed, the number of textual variants is as high as he claims (400,000?), <u>then theologically motivated changes make up such a slight portion of this amount that one wonders why they are being discussed in the first place</u>.' [43]
'Anyone reading a book in antiquity could never be completely sure that he or she was reading what the author had written.' [44] 'We know that this process could be maddeningly slow and inaccurate, that the copies produced this way could end up being quite different from the originals.' [45]	'In order to argue selectively against Christian manuscripts, Ehrman must show that Christian copying was worse than most, which he has tried to do by arguing that Christian scribes were non-professional (even at times illiterate) and therefore prone to mistakes.'[46] 'Even if there were not formal scriptoriums in the second century (and we are not sure), there are substantial indicators that <u>an organized, structured, and reliable process of transmission was in place amongst early Christians</u>.'[47]

It is also worth noting that Ehrman makes a number of acknowledgements of facts that are contrary to the idea that the New

---

[41] Ehrman, *Misquoting Jesus*, 207.

[42] Kruger, "Misquoting Jesus: The Story behind Who Changed the Bible and Why, by Bart D. Ehrman", *Journal of the Evangelical Theological Society* 49:2 (2006): 338 (emphasis added).

[43] Kruger, "Misquoting Jesus", 338. He adds "Not surprisingly, such a discussion of numbers is notably absent from this chapter, because they seem to work against Ehrman's point, rather than for it" (338) (emphasis added).

[44] Ehrman, *Misquoting Jesus*, 46.

[45] Ehrman, *Misquoting Jesus*, 46.

[46] Kruger, "Misquoting Jesus", 338.

[47] Kruger, "Misquoting Jesus", 338, (emphasis added).

Testament text is hopelessly corrupt. These statements are particularly important because they did not receive the same media attention as his more alarmist claims, and are typically overlooked (or deliberately not mentioned), by atheists and sceptics using his work to criticize Christianity.

With regard to textual variants, Ehrman acknowledges that a large number of variants are to be expected in a textual tradition as lengthy and well attested as the New Testament's. He also acknowledges that use of variants 'will show where the first manuscript has preserved an error'.[48] He rightly points out that although the number of variants increases with the number of available manuscripts, it also increases the likelihood of the original text being uncovered.[49]

In fact Ehrman's conclusion regarding the relevance of the large number of variants is that 'they simply provide the data that scholars need to work on to establish the text'; [50] that most are 'completely insignificant, immaterial, of no real importance'.[51]

With regard to the effectiveness of scribes copying the text and the likelihood of them altering it deliberately, Ehrman acknowledges 'the copying of early Christian texts was by and large a "conservative" process', [52] that the scribes' major aim 'was not to modify the tradition,

---

[48] Ehrman, *Misquoting Jesus*, 87.

[49] 'And so it goes—the more manuscripts one discovers, the more the variant readings; but also the more the likelihood that somewhere among those variant readings one will be able to uncover the original text.', Ehrman, *Misquoting Jesus*, 87.

[50] 'Therefore, the thirty thousand variants uncovered by Mill do not detract from the integrity of the New Testament; they simply provide the data that scholars need to work on to establish the text, a text that is more amply documented than any other from the ancient world.' Ehrman, *Misquoting Jesus*, 87.

[51] 'To be sure, of all the hundreds of thousands of textual changes found among our manuscripts, most of them are completely insignificant, immaterial, of no real importance for anything other than showing that scribes could not spell or keep focused any better than the rest of us.' Ehrman, *Misquoting Jesus*, 207.

[52] 'It is probably safe to say that the copying of early Christian texts was by and large a "conservative" process. The scribes—whether nonprofessional scribes in the early centuries or professional scribes of the Middle Ages—were intent on "conserving" the textual tradition they were passing on.' Ehrman, *Misquoting Jesus*, 177.

but to preserve it', [53] that most scribes 'tried to do a faithful job', [54] and that most changes 'have nothing to do with theology or ideology'. [55]

With regard to the aim of textual criticism itself, Ehrman rejects the idea that the recovery of the original text of the New Testament is impossible, 'So at least it is not "non"sense to talk about an original text'. [56] [57] His ultimate decision on this issue is that it is possible to recover 'the oldest and earliest stage of the manuscript tradition for each of the books of the New Testament',[58] and that the oldest form of the text we may find is 'no doubt closely (very closely) related to what the author originally wrote'.[59]

Those of us confronted with criticisms of Scripture based on Ehrman's work should be well aware of the fringe position it occupies in modern scholarship, and of the significant concessions which Ehrman himself makes; the case is far weaker than it appears, and is certainly no real challenge to our trust in Scripture.

---

[53] 'Their ultimate concern was not to modify the tradition, but to preserve it for themselves and for those who would follow them.' Ehrman, *Misquoting Jesus*, 177.
[54] 'Most scribes, no doubt, tried to do a faithful job in making sure that the text they reproduced was the same text they inherited.' Ehrman, *Misquoting Jesus*, 177.
[55] 'It would be a mistake, however, to assume that the only changes being made were by copyists with a personal stake in the wording of the text. In fact, most of the changes found in our early Christian manuscripts have nothing to do with theology or ideology. Far and away the most changes are the result of mistakes, pure and simple—slips of the pen, accidental omissions, inadvertent additions, misspelled words, blunders of one sort or another.' Ehrman, *Misquoting Jesus*, 55.
[56] Ehrman, *Misquoting Jesus*, 210.
[57] 'A number of scholars ... have even given up thinking that it makes sense to talk about the "original" text. I personally think that opinion may be going too far.', Ehrman, *Misquoting Jesus*, 210.
[58] 'For my part, however, I continue to think that even if we cannot be 100 percent certain about what we can attain to, we can at least be certain that all the surviving manuscripts were copied from other manuscripts, which were themselves copied from other manuscripts, and that it is at least possible to get back to the oldest and earliest stage of the manuscript tradition for each of the books of the New Testament.', Ehrman, *Misquoting Jesus*, 62.
[59] 'And so we must rest content knowing that getting back to the earliest attainable version is the best we can do, whether or not we have reached back to the "original" text. This oldest form of the text is no doubt closely (very closely) related to what the author originally wrote, and so it is the basis for our interpretation of his teaching.', Ehrman, *Misquoting Jesus*, 62.

Summary

- The Hebrew text of the Old Testament has been faithfully transmitted by the Jewish scribes – its reliability is confirmed by the Dead Sea Scrolls.
- The Greek text of the New Testament is better attested than any other ancient text, regarding both number and date of manuscripts.
- Recent challenges to the biblical text do not shake the scholarly consensus that the text is reliable and close to the original.

Further Reading

Most modern Bibles note the major textual variants in the margin or footnote so the reader can easily judge for himself or herself the extent to which these variants affect the message.

For more information on the reliability of the Old Testament see Walter Kaiser's *The Old Testament Documents: Are They Reliable?*, and for the New Testament see F. F. Bruce's *The New Testament Documents: Are They Reliable?* Also see *The Books and the Parchments* also by Bruce.

The Old Testament and History

Andrew Perry

"The regularity with which a vocal minority declares the historical worthlessness of the OT has introduced a sense of uneasiness even among those accustomed to regarding the Old Testament differently" – V. Philips Long[1]

Introduction

The subject of the "Old Testament and History" is a large one, and we can only engage here in a summary essay with a discussion of representative examples of the kinds of topic that comprise the area. Our interest in the subject is to outline a reasonable approach to the history in the Old Testament so that it can be read and re-read with a view to adopting and/or building up the faith that is found in the Old Testament.

We use the expression "Old Testament" because it is the Christian faith that we are seeking to foster from these books of the Jewish Scriptures. For Jesus, his disciples and the early church, the "Old Testament" was simply their Scriptures; they did not use the nomenclature of "Old Testament"—this came later as the prophets of the first century church added to these Scriptures new writings that became the "New Testament". The view of Scripture held by Jesus and the first believers was a high one: the Scriptures were given by God, inspired, profitable, and could not be broken (John 10:35; 2 Tim 3:16; 2 Pet 1:21). This is their witness and evaluation, and it is a witness from far nearer the historical times during which the Jewish Scriptures were written than we find ourselves today. This is an important point when we consider modern historical reconstructions that reject the "history" recorded in the Jewish Scriptures. For example, if a historian today regards Moses as a figure of legend because there is no extra-biblical evidence for his existence, such

---

[1] V. Philips Long, *Windows into Old Testament History* (Cambridge: Eerdmans, 2002) 4.

an argument can be countered with the evidential witness of Judaism in the first century, which had no doubt about the existence of Moses.

The evaluation of the Old Testament as history is positive and/or negative according to the scholar that you consult. There are those who offer very negative assessments and those who offer the opposite; no doubt this state of affairs can be explained by pointing to the presuppositions of each kind of person: a critical scholar will have a naturalist standpoint and treat biblical material the same way as other Near Eastern texts, although it may be suspected that there is a bias in favour of non-biblical texts where there is a conflict between the two; in contrast, a conservative scholar will treat the biblical text with an eye on its status as a scriptural text and favour its evidential witness.

The hypothetical and tentative nature of the business of historical reconstruction facilitates the two types of scholarship to the extent that the conservative scholar does not need to appeal to the authority of Scripture (the Old Testament) to settle an issue. Instead, s/he can use the standard methodologies of history but prefer conservative choices in the configuration of the evidence, and so the resulting historical reconstruction will be different. It is because the raw data underdetermines the historical reconstruction that conservative scholars can make conjectures, reject external sources as unreliable, and construe evidence differently from their critical colleagues; the same point applies with regard to critical scholars—they are making choices in their overall interpretation of the data.

Things get left behind, whether it is texts, walls, or pottery, and these things are the stuff of history. The Old Testament refers to many individuals and their lives, but they have left no other traces of their existence. This does not cast doubt on the Old Testament, because the stories in which they occur are not on the scale of the affairs of state. Thus, the stories about Abraham, Isaac and Jacob are family stories; the history of the kings of Israel and Judah, on the other hand, deals with individuals and events on a larger scale. It is not surprising to find corroborative evidence of the history of the kings in the records of other Near Eastern states, but nothing about the Patriarchs. In this latter case, historical corroboration is about the kind of nomadic lifestyle represented—is it true for the times and the place?[2]

---

[2] The historicity of the patriarchal stories is shown in a general way by pointing to correspondences between the stories and other archaeological and textual data from the Early Bronze Age. For a recent discussion, see in D. E. Fleming,

Absence of evidence is not evidence of absence, but it is reasonable to expect extra-biblical evidence, the "larger" the presence of an individual or an event is on the stage of history. Thus, we might reasonably expect "large" individuals and/or events in the Old Testament such as the Exodus, the conquest of the land, or the reigns of David and Solomon to be corroborated; we might not expect smaller individuals and/or events to be confirmed, such as Abraham's visit to Egypt, the existence of Aaron, the women King David married, or the ministry of the prophet Hosea. This is an important point, because it narrows the range of possible conflict that has arisen or might arise about the Old Testament.

A further preliminary point that needs to be made is this: the further back in time we go, the less evidence there is to handle and the more hypothetical is the reconstruction of history. In this regard, we should make a distinction between the "primeval history" of Genesis 1-11 and the history of Israel that begins in Genesis 12 and continues to the end of the Old Testament. Rationalist historians relegate to the status of "myth" and/or "legend" the stories in Genesis 1-11 such as "Adam and Eve", "the Flood" or the "Tower of Babel". Such historians treat the stories about the patriarchs more sympathetically, even if they are regarded as largely "folklore"; yet again, the same historians treat the accounts of the kings more positively. So it is that when investigating the Old Testament and its "history", the further back in time one goes, the more assumptions one finds underlying the scholar's treatment, especially philosophical and theological assumptions.

The Old Testament is a large collection of books and the historical timescale is extensive (1500 years in round numbers if we exclude Genesis 1-11). Accordingly, we have to discuss the topic of "The Old Testament and History" with representative examples. While in scholarship we can find negative appraisals of more or less any aspect of Old Testament history, it is not all of equal value, or a challenge to those who have taken a positive approach. In broad terms, critical scholarship has rejected the accounts of the Exodus, the conquest of the land and the establishment of the monarchy. In addition, little historical value is placed on the so-called "primeval history" of Genesis 1-11. Apart from these "big events", any number of smaller details in the historical record of the Old

"Genesis in History and Tradition: The Syrian background of Israel's Ancestors, Reprise" in *The Future of Biblical Archaeology: Reassessing Methodologies and Assumptions* (eds. J. K. Hoffmeier and A. Millard; Grand Rapids: Eerdmans, 2004), 193-232.

Testament have been questioned and rejected, but it is beyond the scope of our summary essay to make such a list.

A person who comes to the Old Testament, whether s/he is a Christian or somebody seeking faith, should read up on what conservative scholars say about its historical content, as they will provide historical reasons for understanding why Jesus and the early church held a high opinion of the Jewish Scriptures. An even-handed stance would read what both critics and supporters have to say about the Old Testament record. In this essay we will look at the following examples: the primeval history, the conquest, and the kings of Judah. We will finish the essay with a few thoughts about the relationship of faith and history. The Bible has always had its critics, but our thesis is that there is nothing in the world of scholarship that prevents a reader from trusting its history and thereby adopting its faith.

Primeval History

The first chapters of Genesis are widely misunderstood, misrepresented and dismissed as unhistorical; instead, they are valued for their so-called "religious" truth. This observation is about interpretation: if the early chapters of Genesis are not interpreted correctly, any historical judgment is irrelevant. The notion of "history" here is one of the "pre-history" of humankind, the historical "story" that is told about the origin of human civilization on earth in the Near East, and (in Genesis 1) a part of the geological history of the planet. For example,

- If the genealogy of Genesis 5 is counted literally and consecutively, the pre-history is short and recent (including Noah), and this flies in the face of any number of scientific disciplines. If the human ages are notional and the genealogy is non-consecutive, then the length of the pre-history is undetermined.

- If the Flood is global, then the account conflicts with several branches of science. If the Flood is local to the Mesopotamian Basin, then it is to be compared with other traditions about a great flood in the region, and there isn't any necessary conflict with science; the account can be positively appraised as history.

- If the story of the Tower of Babel is about miraculously creating some local languages, then it cannot be verified or falsified by Historical Linguistics—it falls under the radar of that science because it is a localised miraculous intervention.

137

- If special creation is excluded *a priori* from the account of the human species, then there is no prospect that the "Adam and Eve" story could be true. If on the other hand, human ancestry is traceable to a common ancestor pair, then a point in pre-historic time can be identified for Adam and Eve. Furthermore, it is not possible to exclude special creation on a scientific basis because it involves the miraculous and divine agency.

- If the creation week is about the origin of the universe, the observable age of the sun, moon and stars suggests they are in the wrong place on Day 4. However, if the sun, moon and stars, as well as the planet and its water are, instead, presupposed by the account, and the story is about replenishing the earth, then it is not in conflict with current views of the universe or of geological history; the prior existence of the sun, moon and stars is implied by the prior existence of the planet. (This view is known as **Old Earth Creationism**).

- If the creation "week" is a metaphor for the actions of God in relation to the heavens and the earth over time—his work being presented in terms of the "working week" (Exod 20:11), then there is no basis for arguing that the account is in conflict with science; its true value lies in its phenomenological descriptions[3] of the configuration of the land and sea for the placement of human life.

The above brief points are about the interpretation of Genesis 1-11. When someone dismisses this part of the Old Testament, it is often the dismissal of an erroneous interpretation. Any assessment of the historical value of the Old Testament should be focussed on the original intent and meaning of the narrative. What science has done for Biblical Studies is to remove older erroneous interpretations and facilitate a proper appreciation of the text. What science has not done is overturn special creation, divine agency and the miraculous, and our interpretation of Genesis 1-11 should retain these elements, otherwise it will be unfaithful

---

[3] The descriptions of Genesis 1 betray the perspective of subsistence life. For example, humans are given dominion over fish because they catch and eat fish; likewise with fowl and cattle. Or again, the seas are told to "bring forth" the fish abundantly, and the verb reflects what would *appear* to be the case for a fisherman.

to the interpretation of Genesis in the rest of the Bible, for example, with regard to the literal existence of Adam and Eve.[4]

The story narrative that we have in Genesis 1-11 is austere and brief; this is especially so for the creation account of Genesis 1, and it is precisely because that account is a high level description of creation using verbs that would be readily understood to a person working the land, that it is still believed today and valued as a true account of origins. The account lacks any attempt at the "how" of things with which science is concerned, and it is focused on the "that" of things that a person of faith must believe if he is to have an Old Testament faith. It is not like the somewhat fantastic myths of creation native to Mesopotamia.

However, a person coming to these stories today may find some more difficult to accept than others. The element that causes most difficulty for a first-time reader is the genealogies and their numbers. The modern reader initially takes the numbers literally and the generations to be consecutive and without gaps and finds them unbelievable. However, these two assumptions may not be correct for the primeval genealogies. We need to know about the conventions for such genealogies for pre-historic times before we can dismiss them.

Pre-historic Genealogies
The Old Testament scholar, K. A. Kitchen, offers a standard discussion of the genealogy of Genesis 5 in relation to the king lists and reign lengths of Mesopotamian monarchs. In Sumerian and Akkadian king lists, prior to the flood there were eight or ten kings stretching back until kingship was "lowered from the heavens". In the Sumerian King List, for example, the total number of years for the reigns of the eight kings is 241,000 years, whereas the total number of years for the reigns of the kings after the flood is 24,510, and 2310 years for a sequence of 23 and then 12 kings.[5] Whereas the Sumerian King List documents a long pre-history before the Flood in terms of an eight to ten series of kings and their reigns (depending on the tablet), the genealogy of Genesis 5 works with ten generations and fewer years.[6] Both counts break at the Flood; each has

---

[4] While this is a Biblical essay, and not a science paper, it is worth noting that to the extent the sciences do not factor in special creation, divine agency and the miraculous—to that extent they distort the story of our origins.

[5] ANET, 265; K. A. Kitchen, *On the Reliability of the Old Testament* (Grand Rapids: Eerdmans, 2003), 439f.

[6] This comparison is true in a general way if both Genesis and the Sumerian King List are using a decimal system; however, the King List is actually using a

large numbers and the years decline dramatically after the Flood. Their common "8/10" framework[7] allows the suggestion that we have here a **notional use of numbers** to structure an unknown and long period of time.

A second point to make here is that the genealogy in Genesis 5 is not necessarily consecutive—the father-son relationship may in some instances be a grandfather-grandson relationship, or there may be a multiple of intervening generations. The opening entries of the genealogy are,

> And Adam lived an hundred and thirty years, and begat a son in his own likeness, after his image; and called his name Seth: And the days of Adam after he had begotten Seth were eight hundred years: and he begat sons and daughters: And all the days that Adam lived were nine hundred and thirty years: and he died. And Seth lived an hundred and five years, and begat Enosh: And Seth lived after he begat Enosh eight hundred and seven years, and begat sons and daughters. And all the days of Seth were nine hundred and twelve years: and he died. And Enos lived ninety years, and begat Cainan: And Enosh lived after he begat Cainan eight hundred and fifteen years, and begat sons and daughters: And all the days of Enosh were nine hundred and five years: and he died. Gen 5:3-9 (KJV revised)

We would normally read this today as a consecutive sequence without any gaps. However, the early story of Genesis 4 documents the birth of Cain and Abel before Seth. The genealogy of Genesis 5 gives no hint of a Cain or an Abel or any other sons and daughters before Seth, but a reader should take this information and use it to condition his or her understanding of the genealogy of Genesis 5. Seth is a first generation son of Adam (Gen 4:25), and Enosh is likewise a first generation son of Seth

---

modified sexagesimal system. J. H. Walton, *Ancient Israelite Literature in its Cultural Context* (Grand Rapids: Zondervan, 1989), 127-131, shows how the two decimal and sexagesimal systems align very closely in their totals after conversion if the original compiler of the Sumerian King List was using the Genesis 5 genealogy and misunderstood its digits as a modified sexagesimal number. In this way, Walton makes a conclusive case for the Genesis genealogy being the older text.

[7] The use of "ten generations" as a motif to exhaust a period of time is seen in the law, "An Ammonite or Moabite shall not enter into the congregation of the Lord; even to their tenth generation shall they not enter into the congregation of the Lord for ever" (Deut 23:3, KJV).

(Gen 4:26); but Cainan may be a grandson, or a great-grandson, or a more distant "son" of Enosh; the genealogy may therefore have gaps. The birth of Cainan to Enosh may be the birth of a *forbear* of Cainan, the individual in whose line Cainan was born. This possibility is important as it should prevent a reader from treating the genealogy of Genesis 5 as a simple consecutive sequence of father-son relationships—there is a great deal of time after Enos and before Cainan.[8] A further indication that the genealogy of Genesis 5 could be read in a non-consecutive way is the absence of the added information of "calling the name of the son": this detail is recorded for Seth in Gen 5:3, Enos in Gen 4:26, and for Noah in Gen 5:29 but not for the other "sons"; the number of generations in the middle of the genealogy is therefore unknown.

This interpretation makes sense in the light of the nomination of only ten generations; there are ten names that structure the family history of Noah. The colophon in Gen 6:9, "These are the records of the generations of Noah" (NASB), makes the genealogy part of Noah's ancestry.[9] The tenfold stylised arrangement is mirrored in the genealogy of Cain: although it is a 6 generation framework, both end with an individual who has three sons, and both have similarly-named ancestors. Such a selection from history (i.e. the reality of these individuals) supports the interpretation of the ages in the genealogy as notional.

The other difficulty that modern readers have with the genealogy is the longevity of the individuals; the oldest man lived for 969 years and this is dismissed as an unbelievable "fantastic" number. Again, a modern reader is assuming that the ages given are literal, but the modern's case against the ages being real consists simply of the estimates of death given by archaeological anthropologists of the dead that they uncover in any grave sites in the Near East from any point in the past. Furthermore, there is no basis in paleo-biology for supposing that human life spans were much different 10,000 years ago. If we thus assume that men and women lived

---

[8] In addition, we should observe that there were many sons and daughters born to each of the names before the descendent who is named; this is shown by the example of Adam and Eve with Seth and implied by the great age at which the "descendent" (forbear) is born.

[9] That we have a family history in Genesis 5 is indicated by the colophon of Gen 6:9, "These are the records of the generations of Noah" (NASB). On this see, R. K. Harrison, "From Adam to Noah: A Reconsideration of the Antediluvian Patriarchs' Ages" *JETS* 37/2 (1994): 161-168 (162); P. J. Wiseman, *New Discoveries in Babylonia about Genesis* (4th ed.; London: Marshall, Morgan & Scott, 1946), chap. 5.

to what we regard as normal ages (and then some), we should ask: *why* are very long ages given here in Genesis 5 and in the Mesopotamian king lists?

One kind of response would be to reject the ages given as 'real' and regard the numbers as false; we could then reject the historicity of the genealogy as a whole and use this conclusion to cast doubt on the historical value of the primeval history. This kind of reaction would be simplistic, and we should instead ask: if those who composed the genealogy knew very well how long humans typically lived (whatever we say that was; life-spans could have been longer), *why* would they employ very long ages? A preliminary point would be that we are assuming the long ages given were ubiquitous among humans, but the only data we have relates to ten individuals.

Some conservative commentators do see literal ages in the genealogy and they observe that one long age is not associated with a birth or a death, and that is the fact that Enoch "walks" with God for 300 years; this needs further explanation.[10] Moreover, the reduction of human ages after the Flood to between 100-200 years and then to around seventy plus years was gradual over a few generations. Thus, it is suggested that God intervened after the Flood so that human beings had shorter life-spans; the precedent for this is Gen 6:3, "And the LORD said, My spirit shall not always strive with man, for that he also *is* flesh: yet his days shall be an hundred and twenty years" (KJV). These commentators affirm that the speed of ageing was speeded-up.

This approach is problematic for critical scholars of the Bible because it involves the idea of divine intervention. This is a "problem" that occurs in several other places in the Old Testament where the miraculous is recorded or implied. In response, conservative scholars have tried different approaches: for example, it has been said that the Hebrew digits are not decimal (base-10) but base-2 or some other base; or, the numbers are aligned with an old cosmological scheme related to the planets; and, even, the years are not solar years but some other (perhaps lunar) "year". These suggestions, and others, show that scholars do not dismiss the genealogy as poor history; there is a good case[11] to be made for it being older than Mesopotamian king lists in composition. Rather, they seek to explain the *use of large numbers* in the genealogy by scribes perfectly familiar

---

[10] It could be said that God "took" Enoch and it was believed that he then walked with God for 300 years.

[11] Walton, *Ancient Israelite Literature in its Cultural Context*, 127-131.

with the relatively short human life span. Of these approaches, the best harmonizing suggestion is that the numbers are notional[12] and serve the purpose of structuring an unknown long period of time; but that nevertheless the human life span was in fact longer than it is currently. How does this work?

The ages that are given mostly cluster above the 900 mark—just short of a thousand years. Lamech's life is cut short just before the Flood and Enoch is a special case, but otherwise the 900 +/- pattern is carefully chosen, because the choice of a "thousand years" as a limiting period isn't arbitrary. In the "Prayer of Moses", it is said that, "...in your eyes a thousand years are like yesterday that quickly passes, or like one of the divisions of the night time" (Ps 90:4). The comment is, no doubt, a metaphor for the passage of time and how God marks the ages. The New Testament writer Peter makes a comment on this verse when he says, "Now, dear friends, do not let this one thing escape your notice, that a single day is like a thousand years with the Lord and a thousand years are like a single day." (2 Pet 3:8).

This language is relevant to Genesis 5 because in Genesis 2 God had declared that were Adam to sin, he would die in the day that he sinned (Gen 2:17). If the poetic understanding of time expressed in the Prayer of Moses is at work in Genesis 5, the limitation of the antediluvian ages to just under a thousand years is one way in which the compiler of these traditions (traditionally Moses[13]) shows the fulfilment of God's edict of death: the refrain of the genealogy is "and he died" (8x). If a thousand years are as a day in God's eyes, all these men did die in the kind of "day" that God had decreed for Adam's dying.

The understanding implicit in the Prayer of Moses is relevant to our reading of Genesis 5. The prayer starts off (vv. 1-5) as a meditation on the early chapters of Genesis with its references to "all generations", "giving birth to the earth", "children of Adam", "destruction" and a "flood". If a

---

[12] The genealogy uses two verbs: the days 'were' so many years and an individual 'lived' for so many years. This choice means that the names are not the names of ages, such as the 'Adamic Age' or the 'Age of Lamech', following the convention of monarchies (e.g. Tudor, Hanover or Windsor). A lived long age is the meaning and therefore it is the genealogy as a whole that would be notional not the individual ages.

[13] W. C. Kaiser, *The Old Testament Documents: Are they Reliable and Relevant?* (Downers Grove: InterVarsity Press, 2001), 57-58; Wiseman, *New Discoveries in Babylonia about Genesis*, chap. 8.

long and unknown period of time was going to be structured with ten generations, ages just under a thousand years would be chosen to conform to God's attitude to the passage of time and the edict that Adam was to die in the "day" that he sinned. The opening verses of Moses' prayer reconcile the apparent contradiction between Genesis 2 and 5 in its meditation.

The Old Testament account of creation is often ridiculed because the genealogy of Genesis 5 is conventionally totalled up to give an age for the earth of around 6000 years. The historical reliability of the whole of the Old Testament is then thrown into doubt. This is a poor stance to adopt. The genealogy is "of its times" in using large numbers; if we reject the literality of the numbers, this does not mean the individuals are not historical individuals. However, once we observe that there is no name-calling from Cainan onwards until Noah, we have a basis for treating the genealogy as having substantial gaps and the pre-history of Genesis becomes an indeterminate period.[14] The genealogy itself does not engage in totalling up. Whether we treat the genealogy mentioned in a literal way or a notional way can remain an open question.

Exodus and Conquest

Did the exodus happen? Were the Israelites in bondage in Egypt? As a preliminary point, we might say that the exodus is integral to the witness of the rest of the Old Testament—the religion and theology of the Israelites revolves around the exodus. The exodus is also referred to many times in the New Testament. This is powerful evidence for the Exodus having happened; it is not an incidental story in the Old Testament that can be dismissed. Nevertheless, critical scholars have dismissed the account as legendary, while conservative scholars have regarded the story as faithful to its historical setting and the most likely explanation of Israel's origins as a nation. The most recent full-length defence of the historicity of the Exodus is that of J. K. Hoffmeier;[15] here we will consider the Old Testament account of the "conquest".

---

[14] The start of the age of civilization is usually dated to about 10,000 BCE, which is one way to estimate the time period of the genealogy.
[15] J. K. Hoffmeier, *Israel in Egypt: The Evidence for the Authenticity of the Exodus Tradition* (Oxford: Oxford University Press, 1997).

The historicity of the account of Joshua's conquest of the land has been questioned from an archaeological point of view. However, critical[16] and conservative[17] scholars have given different evaluations of the evidence. This divergence of opinion is the result of the "silence" of the archaeological data—it has to be interpreted in a context. Conquest leaves behind evidence of destruction, but it is difficult to be certain of any alignment of archaeological data to a particular conflict; how could an archaeologist positively associate a destruction layer from the thirteenth century BC with the Old Testament record rather than the outcome of a battle between native Canaanite kings? There may be distinctive weapons evidence left behind, or other material remains that identify a particular attacker; a victorious attacker may subsequently occupy the conquered city and leave material remains behind in more recent layers of the site; however, equally, there may be no such remains.

Conservative scholars have generally held that the Exodus is to be dated to the late thirteenth century BC, and they have aligned the conquest with the late thirteenth century or early twelfth century BC destruction layers in Palestinian cities and towns such as Lachish, Ashdod and Hazor, as well as others. P. W. Lapp notes[18] that above the destruction layers of these places, there is evidence of a less advanced culture and of semi-nomadic people. We have archaeological evidence for the presence of Israel as a tribal people[19] in Canaan from the Merneptah Stele in 1209/1208, but no textual reference to their presence before that date. Thus, the historical reconstruction is that the Israelites took over the central highlands of Canaan.

The account in Joshua doesn't detail the destruction of many towns; Jericho, Ai and Hazor are the only ones noted. The various campaigns undertaken by Joshua were from a base at Gilgal. Generally, the army moved on after defeating a town, re-grouping back at Gilgal. After these initial raids, the Israelites moved to occupy the central highlands. The thirteenth century archaeological evidence for the destruction of Hazor

---

[16] M. Weippert, *The Settlement of the Israelite Tribes in Palestine* (London: SCM Press, 1971).

[17] J. Bright, *A History of Israel* (London: SCM Press, 1972); Kitchen, *On the Reliability of the Old Testament*; Hoffmeier, *Israel in Egypt*.

[18] P. W. Lapp "The Conquest of Palestine in the Light of Archaeology" *CThm* 38 (1967): 283-300 (287).

[19] The determinative marker for a "people" rather than a "land" is used in the stela, thereby indicating a tribal association rather than a monarchic land— Hoffmeier, *Israel in Egypt: The Evidence for the Authenticity of the Exodus Tradition*, 30.

has been confirmed, but not for Jericho or Ai. This allows critical scholars to query the conquest account, but some conservative commentators have argued that this shows the archaeological evidence better fits a fifteenth century BC conquest (ca. 1450).

An early date for the conquest would fit Old Testament chronology (1 Kgs 6:1, MT; Jud 11:26). J. J. Bimson has argued[20] the 15c. destruction layers at towns and cities such as Jericho,[21] Bethel, Hazor, Debir, Lachish, Hebron, and Dan are the Israelite "conquest", and it was limited. Settling in the highlands after the military raids and using mostly existing settlements, Israelites would have re-used Canaanite things while adding their own (Josh 24:13), and this accounts for the nature of the material remains of the fifteenth – fourteenth century BC. The countervailing evidence of Ai remains, which most archaeologists affirm was unoccupied both at this time and in the later thirteenth century date, unless the identification of Ai is wrong, which has also been argued.[22] Moreover, the evidence of the Merenptah Stele from 1208/9 presupposes the presence of a tribal people in Canaan, which we may assume requires the Israelites to have "conquered" the land and to have been settled for some time. If we follow the Old Testament chronology and place the conquest at around 1450 BC, most of the archaeological criticism of the account in Joshua becomes irrelevant.[23] J. J. Niehaus and K. L. Younger have shown that the narrative in Joshua is typical of Near Eastern war narratives both of the first and second millennium. Typical of such accounts is hyperbole, war oracles, and divine involvement in warfare. It is this kind of comparative evidence that gives a reader confidence in the historical trustworthiness of the Old Testament account—the account is of its time.[24]

---

[20] J. J. Bimson, *Redating the Exodus and Conquest* (Sheffield: Almond Press, 1981).

[21] The case for a 15c. destruction of Jericho is also argued in B. G. Wood, "Did the Israelites Conquer Jericho: A New Look at the Archaeological Evidence" *Biblical Archaeology Review* 16/2 (1990): 44-59. Wood is cautiously supported by Hoffmeier, *Israel in Egypt: The Evidence for the Authenticity of the Exodus Tradition*, 7.

[22] D. Livingston, "The location of Biblical Bethel and Ai reconsidered" *WTJ* 33, (1970): 20-44; J. M. Grintz, "Ai which is beside Beth-Aven" *Biblica* 42 (1961): 201-216.

[23] Hoffmeier, *Israel in Egypt: The Evidence for the Authenticity of the Exodus Tradition*, 34.

[24] K. L. Younger, Ancient Conquest Accounts: A Study in Ancient Near Eastern and Biblical History Writing (Sheffield: JSOT Press, 1990); J. J. Niehaus, "Joshua and Ancient Near Eastern Warfare" *JETS* 31 (1988): 45-50.

Judges and Kings

Verification or disconfirmation of the Old Testament record becomes a much easier task when the kingdoms of Israel and Judah come to the notice of the Mesopotamian Empires; it is at this time (the 8c.) that the records of those empires can be consulted for any correspondence with Old Testament history. Textual evidence relevant to the Old Testament before this time is rare for several reasons:

- Royal inscriptions on stelae in Jerusalem from the early kings may well have been destroyed, as Jerusalem has been repeatedly destroyed and occupied down the centuries; the same point applies to other cities, towns and villages.[25]

- Royal archives would have been recorded on papyrus, leather, etc. but the climate is not conducive to the survival of such materials.

- The texts that we have are as few as those for neighbouring nations such as the Moabites and Philistines.[26]

Nevertheless, where there has been a mention of the Israelite or Judahite kings on stela, the nomenclature and history has confirmed the Old Testament record. As the field of history is large, we will take a worked example in which there is conflict between critical and conservative historians in order to show how and why the conservative approach is more satisfactory. The example is the Assyrian blockade of Jerusalem from which the Old Testament records a miraculous deliverance—conservative scholars accept this deliverance and critical scholars reject it as legendary.

The Assyrian Blockade of Jerusalem

According to the Assyrian records,[27] the third campaign of their emperor-king, Sennacherib, in 701 was directed generally to the land of Hatti (the

---

[25] The expression 'The House of David' has been found in an inscription from Dan—A. Biran, "An Aramaic Stele Fragment from Tel Dan" *IEJ* 43/2-3 (1993): 1-18.

[26] The Moabite Stone refers to Omri and Ahab, kings of Northern Israel; it may also refer to the "House of David"—see A. Lemaire, " 'House of David' Restored Moabite Inscription" *BAR* 20/3 (1994): 30-37.

[27] For a convenient listing of the sources of the blockade of Jerusalem and the dates of the inscriptions see the table in R. Becking, "Chronology: A Skeleton without Flesh? Sennacherib's Campaign as a Case-Study" in *Like a Bird in a Cage* (ed., L. L. Grabbe; Sheffield: Sheffield Academic Press, 2003), 46-72 (65).

Syro-Judean land-bridge) rather than Judah, which was only a constituent country. The Assyrian records paint a picture of a wholly successful campaign. It involved action against Phoenicia and Philistia as well as Judah; Egypt, who sent an army into the region, was beaten in battle. In relation to Judah, Sennacherib mounted a blockade against Jerusalem, took 46 strong cities, countless villages, forts, a large number of captives (200,150[28]) and domestic animals; he later received a gift from Hezekiah and took his daughters and women from the palace; and he increased Hezekiah's annual tribute (ANET, 287-288).

This summary cannot be reconciled with the biblical account of a miraculous deliverance for Jerusalem, so did this happen?

- 2 Kgs 18:13 has Sennacherib come up against all the fenced cities of Judah and taking them; this agrees with the Assyrian record. 2 Chr 32:1 notes that Sennacherib first *encamped* against the fenced cities, during which time Hezekiah made preparations to strengthen his position in Jerusalem (vv. 2-8).

- 2 Chr 32:10 reports Sennacherib's view of Hezekiah's position: he was under blockade in Jerusalem. This agrees with the Assyrian record that refers to earthworks or forts cast around Jerusalem.

- 2 Kgs 18:14 sees Hezekiah submit to Sennacherib who was at Lachish, and Sennacherib imposes a tribute of 30 talents of gold and 300 talents of silver. The text says that these monies were "appointed" to Hezekiah, and he regards the monies as something "put upon" him; this is the language of annual tribute and this detail agrees with Sennacherib's note of an increased annual tribute.

- Sennacherib's record notes 30 talents of gold and 800 talents of silver that were sent *later* to Nineveh along with valuable commodities,

---

[28] M. De Odorico, The *Use of Numbers and Quantifications in the Assyrian Royal Inscriptions* (SAAS II; The Neo Assyrian Text Corpus Project; Helsinki: Helsinki University Press, 1995), 172., states that the number is an emphasis upon the "very high" (200,000) whilst conveying truthfulness in the exactitude (plus 150). Archaeological calculations place the population of Judah well under 100,000. Y. Shiloh estimates the population of Jerusalem and its outer environs during the eighth century to be between 25,000 and 40,000 inhabitants—"Judah and Jerusalem in the Eighth-Sixth Centuries B.C.E." in *Recent Excavations in Israel: Studies in Iron Age Archaeology* (eds., S. Gitin and W. G. Dever; AASOR 49; Winona Lake: Eisenbrauns, 1989), 97-106 (98).

daughters, concubines and musicians, along with a personal messenger. This would have been construed as a first annual tribute payment, as well as a gift in recognition of subservience. It is the same tribute/gift recorded in Kings, because the Assyrian record (Rassam Cylinder[29]) is dated to 700. It was obviously sent to Nineveh and dispatched before Sennacherib turned the Assyrian army on Jerusalem in an act of treachery (Isa 33:1). We can accept the Assyrian record of the tribute on the grounds that it is detailed, contemporary, and then reiterated in the final edition of Sennacherib's Campaigns in the Taylor Prism; there is no certain conflict with the biblical amounts because the Assyrian basis of calculation may be different or exaggerated.[30]

- The narrative in Kings then goes on to record the sending of (the) Rabshakeh and a large army against Jerusalem from Lachish. Although a new episode account begins in 2 Kgs 18:17, the mention of Lachish ties the narrative to what has been formerly recounted (the sending of an ambassador to Lachish, v. 14). The whole episode is described in great detail and it leads to the deliverance of Jerusalem through the miraculous destruction of the Assyrian army. Obviously, none of this information is in an Assyrian record.

- The Rabshakeh episode climaxes with the promise of deliverance,

  "He will go back the way he came. He will not enter this city,"
  says the LORD (2 Kings 19:33)

  This text picks up on Hezekiah's attempt to get Sennacherib to "return" from him (2 Kgs 18:14) and implicitly criticizes the giving of a gift/tribute to Sennacherib rather than reliance upon Yahweh. While this episode is absent from Assyrian records, we take it as genuine, and see it as in the correct sequence of events.

Scholars will select which elements of the Assyrian and biblical records correspond to the facts.[31] While this is a loaded comment, it is

---

[29] The Rassam Cylinder is the earliest note of the gift/tribute.

[30] The text in Kings has 300 talents but the discrepancy might be due to a number of factors: the Assyrians may have differently calculated the silver and included sundry goods in the tribute/gift. Totals. See Becking, "Chronology: A Skeleton without Flesh? Sennacherib's Campaign as a Case-Study", 67-68.

[31] For a discussion of this issue in relation to 701 see E. Ben Zvi, "Malleability and its Limits: Sennacherib's Campaign against Judah as a Case-Study" in *Like a*

nevertheless expressing the point: that scholars see in historical documents an ideology that expresses the point of view of the author of the document. Certainly, Kings and Chronicles present a different selection of details and emphases on the Assyrian Crisis. The same is true for biblical scholars who will "write up" the history of the campaign rejecting the miraculous account of deliverance: ideology affects the critical scholar as much as the biblical writer—one believes in miracle and divine intervention, the other believes in probability and the human dimension.

The Assyrian records paint a picture of success against all opponents. However, it is unusual that such success did not, on its own terms, mention the capture of Jerusalem. Many other cities are noted as besieged and conquered, so we would have to ask why Jerusalem did not suffer the same fate. Sennacherib defeated the Egyptians at Eltekeh and went on afterwards to besiege and conquer further cities, but the blockade of Jerusalem did not result in it being conquered. It is rather the capture of Lachish that is celebrated in the reliefs in Sennacherib's palace (though not in the *Annals*).[32] Furthermore, E. Ben Zvi notes[33] that the *Annals* give a lot of space to the ordinary tribute gift almost as a way to make up for the lack of any report of Jerusalem's conquest. The conquest of other cities and the submission and/or replacement of their kings are perfunctory notes by comparison. It is puzzling as to why Hezekiah was not removed as a king, given that he was a leader of the rebellion against Assyria. These details support the view that Jerusalem was delivered miraculously, and that this has been omitted for obvious reasons from the Assyrian records.

The nature of the miraculous deliverance is not stated (2 Kgs 19:35; 2 Chr 32:21). The number given for the Assyrians killed is 185,000, which

---

Bird in a Cage (ed., L. L. Grabbe; Sheffield: Sheffield Academic Press, 2003), 73-105.

[32] D. Luckenbill, ed., *The Annals of Sennacherib*, (repr. Wipf & Stock, 2005; Chicago: Chicago University Press, 1924). The reliefs are discussed in C. Uehlinger, "Clio in a World of Pictures—Another Look at the Lachish Reliefs from Sennacherib's Southwest Palace at Nineveh" in *Like a Bird in a Cage* (ed., L. L. Grabbe; Sheffield: Sheffield Academic Press, 2003), 221-305. Uehlinger discusses other reliefs that might picture Jerusalem, but reaches no conclusion, 293-303.

[33] Ben Zvi, "Malleability and its Limits: Sennacherib's Campaign against Judah as a Case-Study", 94.

accords with the canons of the historical reporting of the day;[34] it is an impression of the huge size of the army encamped outside Jerusalem. It is easy enough to hypothesize a natural means for a virulent (water/air borne) virus to sweep through the camp. Such deliverance would not, however, be a defeat from Sennacherib's point of view: there is obviously no acceptance of a miraculous intervention by Yahweh in his records. Interpreted naturally, a water-borne virus, say (or one borne in a new delivery of wine to the camp), having decimated the army, would weaken his military presence in the region and cause him to return to Assyria. His decision not to complete the capture of Jerusalem was a military and logistical decision.

The deliverance by the Angel of the LORD is unusual and is reminiscent of the Exodus from Egypt. It is unusual because Israel and Judah had experienced similar crises and threats in their history, but none of these were resolved through such a dramatic intervention. As R. E. Clements says, "The report that the dire consequences threatened by the confrontation between Sennacherib and Hezekiah were averted by direct divine intervention is highly unusual in Old Testament history-writing";[35] accordingly, some scholars regard the account as legendary.[36] However, the book of Isaiah includes several oracles about the safety of Jerusalem and her deliverance, and this kind of witness indicates that the historical account of 2 Kgs 18:17-19:37 is not a one-off legend. Furthermore, the account coheres with the themes of Samuel and Kings with its interest in the Davidic monarchy, and the choice of Jerusalem as the place where Yahweh would set his Name. We cannot therefore dismiss the account in 2 Kgs 18:17-19:37 without dismissing other aspects of Kings, Chronicles and Isaiah.

Conclusion

By way of conclusion, we will consider the relationship of faith and history. Critical and conservative scholars have argued their cases in monographs and journals. A reader coming to the Old Testament asking the question whether its history can be trusted can infer that its historical record has not been overturned—conservative scholars have provided historical reconstructions of the Near Eastern archaeological and textual

---

[34] Following De Odorico's analysis in *The Use of Numbers and Quantifications in the Assyrian Royal Inscriptions*, 172.

[35] R. E. Clements, *Isaiah and the Deliverance of Jerusalem*, (Sheffield: JSOT Press, 1980), 11.

[36] *Isaiah and the Deliverance of Jerusalem*, 15.

evidence that fits the Old Testament account. These are not partial or *ad hoc*, but are comprehensive, even if there are points of detail where they express uncertainty and a lack of knowledge.

A historian is free to reconstruct the evidence in whatever way s/he chooses; the result is then presented for peer appraisal. There is no burden of proof on a critical or a conservative scholar—the process is a matter of handling some hard data (such as ceramic dates), but there is also a fair amount of subjective interpretation; the critical scholar tends to reject the Old Testament evidence for theological and philosophical reasons—the conservative scholar accepts the Old Testament as evidence and attempts a harmonization of its evidence with the relevant archaeology and any other texts.

In the past, before the rise of Biblical Criticism in the Enlightenment, a Bible commentator might have appealed to theology and/or philosophy to support the Old Testament—he would say that it was divinely inspired and part of the canon of the church. Today, conservative scholars do not *assume* any status for the Old Testament and treat it simply as textual evidence for historical reconstruction. They do not cast it aside for any theological and philosophical reasons, which ironically is the situation with critical scholars. In rejecting any inherent authority for the Old Testament, the Enlightenment replaced such authority with a set of theological and philosophical assumptions that created a sceptical starting point for a scholar working within academia. It was in effect the replacement of one authoritarian structure (church) for another (an academia defined by an Enlightenment philosophy of rationalism, naturalism and scepticism).

For this reason, the better scholarship in Biblical Studies is conservative, and this is because it accepts all the archaeological and textual evidence, making an attempt to reconstruct the history in a maximal way. A reader looking to see if the Old Testament can be trusted should therefore give precedence to the arguments and the reconstruction of conservative scholars. There is an ideological bias in the work of critical scholars which reflects the philosophy of the times; conservative writing is much more self-conscious about the influence of presuppositions on historical research. Conservative scholars value the Old Testament text because it is a substantial witness to the history.

A factor that we have not yet mentioned is the dating of the Old Testament texts. This is a large subject, particularly affected by the shifting sands of hypothesis and theory. Theories of late dates for the texts are likely to be the concomitant luggage of a sceptical view of the Old Testament account of history. The tendency to late-date the Old Testament texts is bound up with source critical theories of composition and theories about the development of religious ideas in Israel and Judah. The point here is that critical scholars then downgrade the evidential witness of books like Joshua or Judges precisely because they regard them as late and etiological[37] in purpose.

Again, the clash between critical and conservative scholars that we have seen in respect of the historical value of the Old Testament is also present in regard to literary theories about the Old Testament. It is beyond the scope of this essay to consider this topic, except to observe that conservative scholars have persuasively argued that the attempt to record and pass on history (orally and then in writing) is early and infused with an integrity that is apparent on the page. Unless there is tangible evidence to the contrary, we should respect this integrity in the text.[38]

What then can we say about faith? The history of the Old Testament cannot be rejected as irrelevant to faith because Christian faith is historical in nature—it is about divine intervention in the affairs of humanity. Moreover, the Old Testament cannot be rejected in favour of the New Testament for the reason that New Testament writers evidently continue the historical story of the Old Testament in the Gospels and Acts. Furthermore, their witness to the Old Testament and their usage of the Old Testament makes it integral to any expression of the Christian faith. While there is a lot of clutter for a reader to work through in the writings of those who have commented on the Old Testament as history, there are reliable guides to the jungle in conservative historians who have refused, for philosophical and theological reasons, to reject the Old Testament as evidence. While they may believe, as a matter of faith, in the authority of the Old Testament as a work of Scripture, they argue for a harmonic approach to biblical and non-biblical evidence, because this makes for the best historical reconstruction.

---

[37] There is a further irony here in that critical scholars will suspect the Old Testament narratives because they are etiological, but accept unquestionably Near Eastern texts even though they may well be etiological.

[38] For example, see W. Hallo, "Biblical History in its Near Eastern Setting: The Contextual Approach" in *Scripture in Context: Essays on the Comparative Method* (ed., C. D. Evans, W. Hallo, and J. B. White; Pittsburgh: Pickwick Press, 1980), 1-26.

Summary

- The way a historian approaches the Old Testament will depend on their presuppositions – many of those who reject the historicity of the Old Testament do so for ideological reasons.
- The early part of Genesis is one of the most disputed texts but also one of the most poorly understood – greater understanding adds to its credibility.
- There are strong reasons for having confidence in the records of the Exodus of the Israelites and their conquest of Canaan, despite current gaps in the available archaeological evidence.
- In later periods, such as that of kingdoms of Israel and Judah, where we have more non-biblical evidence, the Old Testament record is consistent with this evidence.
- Presupposing the harmony between the biblical and non-biblical evidence results in the best historical reconstruction.

Further Reading

For more on the Old Testament as history *On the Reliability of the Old Testament* (K. A. Kitchen) is thorough and readable, if sometimes technical.

Accessible presentations of how archaeology supports the Bible see *Discoveries from Bible Times* (Alan Millard) and *The Archaeology of the Bible* (James K. Hoffmeier).

Bible Prophecy

David Alexander

"The astonishing thing about the Bible is that it has prophesied the most unlikely things" – Alan Hayward[1]

Introduction

In a twenty-seven kilometre tunnel over fifty metres beneath the border of France and Switzerland is a multi-billion euro scientific device known as the Large Hadron Collider. Researchers use it to search for evidence of particles that could help explain our universe – in particular, one important particle theorised by physicists, sometimes grandiosely called in the media the 'God particle'.[2]

The Bible also helps explain our universe – and not just a detail of its working, but its purpose and destiny. Could the same scientific approach applied in the Large Hadron Collider be used to test Scripture? The answer is, emphatically, yes; and Bible prophecy is one of the 'experiments' provided by God to direct our search, not just for a particle popularly named after Him, but for the Creator Himself.

God not only allows His word to be rigorously tested; He encourages it:

> "Test me in this matter," says the LORD (Malachi 3:10)

> Prove all things; hold fast that which is good (1 Thessalonians 5:21 [KJV])

> Faith is the substance of things hoped for, the evidence of things not seen. (Hebrews 11:1 [KJV])

As will be seen, the results of this test are strong witness to the Divine origin of the Bible.

---

[1] A. Hayward, *God's Truth* (London: Marshall, Morgan & Scott, 1973), 7.
[2] Online at: ngm.nationalgeographic.com/2008/03/God-particle/achenbach-text [published March 2008]. The particle is usually called the Higgs boson.

Scientific evidence

The accepted scientific method can be summarised in the following three steps:

1. Articulate a <u>working hypothesis</u> and an <u>alternative hypothesis</u> to be tested.
2. Make <u>observations</u>.
3. <u>If</u> the observations are consistent with the working hypothesis, it is <u>retained</u>; otherwise it is <u>rejected</u> in favour of an alternative hypothesis that better explains the observations.

In the case of the large hadron collider, current physics theory provides the working hypothesis (Step 1) and observations are made using the collider (Step 2). If these observations are inconsistent with current physics theory, but can be explained by the action of new particles, then new theory based on the existence of these particles will be – provisionally – accepted (Step 3). The time and money poured into projects like the Large Hadron Collider demonstrate the importance of obtaining observations in order to prove or disprove a theory. Any theory that is 'scientific' must be able to withstand these types of tests; the more rigorous the testing it withstands, the more confidence is placed in its truth.

This kind of reasoning is common in Scripture. The 'working hypothesis' expected of God's people was a healthy scepticism of the supernatural (Step 1); thus He performed miracles through His prophets (e.g. Exod 4:1-9), providing observations incompatible with this scepticism (Step 2). On this evidence it is rational to accept the alternative hypothesis: that the prophet does indeed carry the power and authority of God (Step 3). Frequent illustrations of this appeal to evidence occur in connection with the Lord Jesus Christ, ' "a man <u>attested</u> to you by God with mighty works and wonders which God did through him" ' (Acts 2:22; cf. John 2:23; 3:2; 5:36; 9:33; 10:25,37-38; 11:45,47-48; 12:10-11; 14:11; 15:24).

But while miracles like this provided compelling evidence to those who saw them, they are difficult to substantiate thousands of years after they occurred. Reasons to believe given in the chapters of this book rely on observations that can be established *today* – evidences provided by God not just for those who saw and heard His prophets speak, but for those also who would read their words centuries later. Chief among these evidences is that of <u>Bible prophecy</u>:

"When the word of the prophet comes to pass, the prophet will be <u>known</u> as one whom the LORD has truly sent." (Jeremiah 28:9 [NKJV])

Fulfilled prophecies are an excellent means of proving the Divine origin of a prophet's words, as they align so well with the steps of the scientific method. The working hypothesis, that the prophet is just an ordinary person with no prior knowledge of the future (Step 1), can, based on the observation of an accurately fulfilled prophecy (Step 2), be rejected in favour of the alternative hypothesis: that the prophet was truly sent from God (Step 3).[3] The very word 'prophet' (the New Testament Greek προφήτης) literally means 'one who foretells the future', since this is such a notable feature of many of God's prophets – though the role is actually more general, that of a spokesperson for God (e.g. Exod 7:1-2). Having proved their authenticity, prophets expected their audience – including modern readers – to pay attention to the rest of the message also.

Importantly, the test of history works unequivocally <u>both ways</u>, confirming true prophets and exposing impostors:

If you say to yourselves, 'How can we tell that a message is <u>not</u> from the LORD?' – whenever a prophet speaks in my name and the prediction is <u>not</u> fulfilled, then I have <u>not</u> spoken it (Deuteronomy 18:21-22)

This point is worth emphasising: Bible prophecy meets the scientific challenge of providing a falsifiable test. The existence of God and inspiration of the Bible *can* be demonstrated by rejecting unlikely alternatives (for example, the origin of life by natural means is impossible; human invention of Scripture is unrealistic; etc) but Bible prophecy goes a step further, presenting bold tests which history could easily have disproved. That history ultimately confirmed, rather than contradicted, these prophecies is powerful positive evidence for their Divine authorship.

Moreover, the test of prophecy still carries its full weight today. The only new condition required by the passage of time is the need for evidence showing the prophecy really was uttered before it was fulfilled (or before

---

[3] Note that replication is unnecessary; the object of study is a *particular* prophesied event, not a general historical theory. Repeated experimentation is required to establish generalisations concerning overall populations, but not for the analysis of individual cases. Scientists routinely provide expert witness in criminal cases without requiring the crime to be replicated!

157

its impending fulfilment became evident). This rules out many short-range prophecies, such as that in Jer 28:16-17 of the death of Hananiah, which was completely fulfilled within months – though this would have been a powerful and dramatic proof to Jeremiah's contemporaries, there is no way to demonstrate today that the prophecy was really given *before* Hananiah's death and not fabricated afterwards. However, many extraordinary examples remain of prophecies fulfilled not just months, or even years, but centuries after they were made. In these cases there is no doubt that the prophecy was made long before its fulfilment; and the accuracy with which history corroborates the details of prophecy admits no other explanation than that its true author is God.

Israel

The most striking example of fulfilled Bible prophecy is that of Israel, treated in detail in the following chapter. In Isaiah God develops this case at length against the false religions of the day, which could offer no proofs in their defence (Isa 41:21-29; 43:9-12; 44:6-8; 45:5-6; 46:9-10).

> "Present your argument," says the LORD. "Produce your evidence," says Jacob's king. "Let them produce evidence! Let them tell us what will happen! Tell us about your earlier predictive oracles, so we may examine them and see how they were fulfilled. Predict how future events will turn out, so we might know you are gods" (Isaiah 41:21-23)

> "Truly I am God, I have no peer; I am God, and there is none like me, who announces the end from the beginning and reveals beforehand what has not yet occurred" (Isaiah 46:9-10)

Israel themselves are the lead witness of God's power to direct history according to His declared purpose (Isa 43:10). The very existence of Israel today in accordance with Scripture – despite their enemies, and the centuries without a land – is dramatic witness of a Divine protector on their side. Psalm 124 makes this point in terms that match exactly the steps of the scientific method:

> "If the LORD had not been on our side, when men attacked us, they would have swallowed us alive" (Psalms 124:2-3)

The hypothesis that Israel is just an ordinary nation (Step 1) is quite incompatible with the observation of their survival through millennia of

158

persistent and extreme opposition (Step 2); thus the alternative hypothesis, that God has protected them, is accepted (Step 3).

The hypothesis of God's existence is proved in this way as conclusively as any (more conclusively than many) of the scientifically established principles that inform modern industry and business. Israel's scattering and re-gathering was foretold centuries before Christ (Deut 28:37, 64-66; Jer 30:10) and fulfilled in the centuries of dispersion following, until the State of Israel was re-established as recently as 1948. That they survived these centuries without a homeland, and were re-gathered exactly in accordance with the prophets' words, is explicable only by the existence and power of Israel's God.

(A numeric discussion of the weight of evidence provided by God in this prophecy and others presented below is given for interested readers in the appendix. But quantifying such evidence is really unnecessary; the facts of history speak eloquently for themselves of the God who revealed them to His prophets centuries before they occurred.)

Contrast with extra-biblical prophecy

The extraordinary accuracy and precision of Bible prophecy is tellingly demonstrated by comparing it with prophecies from other sources.

Recorded predictions of prophets from nations other than Israel are often vague expressions of optimism for worshippers of a particular deity[4] – similar to those of false prophets mentioned in Scripture (e.g. 1 Kgs 22:13; Jer 8:10-11). Prophets from both sides of battles would naturally predict victory for their army; inevitably, one prophet would be proven correct and one false.

The Delphic Oracle was well known for its ambiguous or meaningless prophecies; a famous example is the advice given to Croesus that a mighty empire would be destroyed if he attacked Persia. This 'oracle' could not but be proven true (in the event it was Croesus' empire, not Persia's, that was defeated)!

---

[4] *Prophecy in its Ancient Near Eastern Context: Mesopotamian, Biblical, and Arabian Perspectives* (ed. M. Nissinen; Atlanta: SBL, 2000).

Although the Qur'an is the work of the 'prophet' Muhammad, it contains few explicit predictions of the future.[5] Some of the predictions relate to Muhammad's victories in battle (e.g., Sura 9:14; 48:16, 18-20, 27; 54:45) and are thus no different from the vaguely optimistic predictions made by prophets of many other religions. Other prophecies concern the preservation of the Qur'an itself (e.g. Sura 15:9); given the regard in which Muhammad was held, this prediction required no superhuman foresight. (In any case, this prophecy is incapable of disproof; to discuss it at all presupposes that it *has* been preserved.) The longest prediction into the future of a historical event is in Sura 30:3-4, where Romans are predicted to defeat Persians within nine years. There is of course no way today to verify that this prediction was made before its fulfilment.

A vast chasm separates these limited human forecasts from the inspired precision of Bible prophecy.

Four kingdoms

The Bible prophecies to be considered are miracles on a grand scale; grand enough that secular history can be used to confirm their historical fulfilment. Among the grandest are those in the book of Daniel outlining four stages in the kingdom of man spanning from the prophet's day to the present. The prophecies are symbolic, and not every detail of the interpretation is universally agreed; but even the basic details examined here show a clear framework of history extending millennia beyond the prophet's time – a framework that could not possibly have been predicted so accurately unless God was the true Author.

Nebuchadnezzar, king of Babylon, dreamed of a statue with a golden head, silver chest, bronze middle and iron legs (Dan 2:31-35). A stone struck the statue's feet, where the iron was mixed with clay, breaking them and the whole image in pieces; then the stone grew to a mountain filling the whole earth.

Daniel identified Nebuchadnezzar himself as the golden head, and the three following metals as three future kingdoms (Dan 2:37-43). No other metals are mentioned; the clay represents a dividing of the fourth kingdom, rather than a new empire. 'In the days of those kings' (not 'that kingdom'; the fourth kingdom would be divided among several kings at

---

[5] Online: www.answering-islam.org [cited 27-Apr-10]; cf. J. Thorpe, *The Bible and Islam* (rev. ed.; 2008), 309-316,

160

this point and no fifth kingdom would have risen in their place), God would set up His own kingdom, which would break in pieces all these kingdoms (Dan 2:44). This clearly identifies the action of the stone as the setting up of God's kingdom, much spoken of in the rest of Scripture, which is yet to occur.

Three kingdoms thus remain to be identified: the silver, bronze and iron. As noted, the iron and clay feet do not represent a fifth kingdom (the iron of the feet is not distinguished from the iron of the legs, even when they are not listed consecutively (Dan 2:45)), but a dividing of the fourth. This detail – the number of kingdoms – is the most striking of the prophecy.

The image clearly implies an unbroken sequence in history from head to toe. Dan 2:39 could more literally be translated, "'Another kingdom, inferior to you, shall arise *in your place*'" (that is, directly displacing him and occupying the same territory).[6] The second kingdom replaced Babylon within Daniel's own lifetime (Dan 5:28, 30-31; 6:28): Cyrus the Persian defeated the Medes and then established an empire with major victories over Lydia, Babylon and Egypt. (The Lydian king Croesus defeated by Cyrus was proverbially rich; silver coinage invented in Lydia became the basis of the Persian economy.[7] Perhaps this is one reason why silver was chosen to represent this empire in the dream of the statue.)

A later vision of Daniel identifies the third and fourth kingdoms. Here, a goat identified as Greece defeats a ram identified with Persia (Dan 8:5, 7, 20-21). The movements of the ram west, then north, then south (Dan 8:4) predict the three great conquests of Cyrus mentioned above. The Greek goat flew at this ram, a 'conspicuous horn' representing the first king of the empire (Dan 8:5, 21); the speed of Alexander the Great's conquests 'over all the earth' (Dan 2:39) is famous. Yet 'when he was strong, the great horn was broken' and replaced by four others (Dan 8:8, 22). After Alexander's death at the height of his powers, his empire was split among his generals, four of whom ultimately divided the empire between them. (The Greek empire used not only silver coins but also bronze, and many Greek sculptures in bronze have also been found; this may in part explain why Nebuchadnezzar's dream represented the Greek empire in bronze. Homer famously describes 'brass-coated Greeks' in the *Iliad*, over a century prior even to Daniel.)

---

[6] Dan 7:6-7 uses the same word for the immediate succession of the third and fourth kingdoms also.
[7] Silver remained the standard for monetary systems right through to the British pound sterling, before being replaced by the gold standard.

161

The kingdom that replaced Alexander's empire was <u>Rome</u>, prophesied in Dan 8:9, 11 to grow 'exceedingly great toward the south, toward the east, and toward the glorious land' (a term used of Israel in Ezek 20:6). After the Punic wars with Carthage to their south, Rome moved against Greece to their east and eventually dominated Israel. In AD 70, Rome overthrew the sanctuary in Jerusalem, as predicted in Daniel 8:11 (cf. Matt 24:15).[8] Rome was already identified as the fourth kingdom, replacing Greece, around this time.[9] Daniel describes the fourth kingdom as 'strong as iron' (Dan 2:40-42); the strength of Rome was its army, which adopted iron armour.

All of this was prophesied, decades or centuries in advance, in extraordinary detail – such detail that critics have accused later authors of forging these sections of the book. Other studies refute these accusations[10]. But there is no doubt that the prophecies were written by the time of Christ[11]; and the prophecy continues well past this time, with continued accuracy for which no other explanation but Divine inspiration is possible.

The most significant part of the prophecy for modern readers seeking reasons for belief is the period following the Roman Empire. Unlike all its predecessors, the Roman Empire has not been replaced by another; instead, it was divided (Dan 2:41), first by barbarian tribes, later in the many principalities making up the 'Holy Roman Empire' and its surrounding states, and now in the various nations of Europe, North Africa and the Near East. Many other empires have arisen, but no one from the days of the Mongols or Ottomans through to Napoleon or

---

[8] The Greek Antiochus Epiphanes also defiled the sanctuary, but never destroyed it or grew 'exceedingly great' as described in Daniel 8:9. Israel's attacker is described as a boldfaced king in Daniel 8:23-25, alluding to Deuteronomy 28:48-53, a clear prophecy of the Roman destruction of Jerusalem in AD 70. The last part of the vision is ' "for the time of the end" ' (Daniel 8:17), a time postdating Antiochus (Daniel 11:35) when the iron and clay of the statue (not the Greek bronze) will be struck by the stone and 'broken—but by no human hand' (Daniel 2:34; 8:25).

[9] J. Burke, *A More Sure Word of Prophecy* (Adelaide: CSSS, 2009).

[10] For example, T. E. Gaston, *Historical Issues in the Book of Daniel* (Oxford: Taanathshiloh, 2009), 178.

[11] Copies dating from as early as 125 BC were found in the Dead Sea Scrolls.

162

Hitler has been able to reunite all these territories and establish a kingdom to replace the Roman Empire.[12]

What chance would Daniel have had to predict that *exactly* three kingdoms would succeed Babylon's, with the last to remain divided – as it has now for over 1,500 years? The continuing accuracy of the prophecies rules out the hypothesis that Daniel invented them himself; this observation can only be explained by the alternative hypothesis:

> "There is a God in heaven who reveals mysteries, and he has made known to King Nebuchadnezzar what will happen in the times to come" (Daniel 2:28)

Tyre

The city of Tyre was, from about 1100 BC, the Mediterranean world's leading trading power. Biblical and secular history alike record the maritime expertise of the Phoenicians, who made Tyre the emporium of the world, 'merchant of the peoples' (Ezek 27:3), 'whose traders were the honoured of the earth' (Isa 23:8).

Nebuchadnezzar made a thirteen-year siege of Tyre, ultimately destroying it (as prophesied in Ezek 26:7-11). But the wealth of the city had relocated to an island a kilometre off the coast, beyond his reach. This stronghold seemed impregnable – an island fortress with 45 metre high walls, defended by the greatest naval force in the world.

When Ezekiel prophesied, the siege was already eleven years old. He foretells not only Babylon's impending victory, but also successive <u>waves</u> of attackers:

> This is what the sovereign LORD says: "Look, I am against you, O Tyre! I will bring up <u>many nations</u> against you, as the sea brings up its <u>waves</u>." (Ezekiel 26:3)

The change of pronoun in Ezek 26:12 introduces these later attackers: "'<u>They</u> will plunder your riches'". Ezek 29:18 notes that Nebuchadnezzar in fact gained no spoil from his defeat of the mainland city – this part of the prophecy waited 250 years to be fulfilled in the campaign of Alexander the Great.

---

[12] The Ottomans came nearest to doing so, subsuming almost all the territory of the Eastern Empire, but they made little inroads on the divided territory of the Western Empire (containing Rome itself).

Like Nebuchadnezzar before him, Alexander had no navy by which to reach the island fortress. But, in one of his most famous military exploits, he used the ruins of the mainland city to build a causeway out to the island. When Tyre's ships destroyed the causeway, he scraped every vestige of the mainland city into the sea to rebuild it. Island Tyre eventually fell after a siege of seven months.

Even more remarkable than Alexander's resourcefulness is God's prediction of it centuries before:

> "They will plunder your riches and pillage your merchandise; they will break down your walls and destroy your pleasant houses; they will lay your stones, your timber, and your soil in the midst of the water ... I will make you like the top of a rock" (Ezekiel 26:12, 14 [NKJV])

Even the ruins of the mainland city that withstood Nebuchadnezzar for thirteen years were now totally removed, to the point that modern archaeology cannot determine precisely where the city once stood. (It was probably served by the freshwater spring at Ras al-Ain, five kilometres south of the island; research suggests the city may have sprawled over ten kilometres north and south of the island.) Thus Ezekiel's last prophecy concerning mainland Tyre is fulfilled:

> "I will bring terrors on you, and you will be no more! Though you are sought after, you will never be found again" (Ezekiel 26:21)

The island Tyre (now connected to the mainland – the causeway is still intact) remained inhabited after Alexander's conquest; over the centuries it regained its prominence, until being destroyed again by the Crusaders and Mamluks and finally abandoned. But the mainland Tyre has <u>never</u> been <u>built again</u>, as God decreed:

> "I will make you a bare rock ... <u>You will never be built again</u>" (Ezekiel 26:14)

A new settlement has grown up at Tyre within the last century, now with a population over 100,000. This hardly constitutes a rebuilding of the old power of Tyre, politically or even geographically; the old city extended some kilometres up the coast, while the new city is centred on the old island and encroaches very little on the surrounding land. In fact, the region of the spring was in 1998 established as the Tyre Beach nature reserve, restricting access in order to protect its distinctive wildlife[13] – and ensuring that the mainland city will remain unbuilt.

Ezekiel's prophecy of Alexander is so precise that sceptics have claimed it must not have been written by him, but by an impostor centuries later. This theory ought not to be unquestioningly accepted. There would have been nothing to gain from such an interpolation, since no contemporaries of the impostor would be fooled when the insertion appeared.[14] In any case, the words are ascribed to Ezekiel, so no glory would accrue to his impersonator. If the religious authorities (who maintained the authoritative copies of Scripture) had wanted to boost their hold on the people by augmenting and correcting prophecies in their care, they could hardly have produced such a book as Ezekiel, with its continual strident condemnation of those same authorities (Ezek 5:11; 8:3-18; 9:4,6-7; 11:1-4; 12:9-10; 13:2-23; 14:1-3,9-10; 17:16-20; 20:2-4; 22:6,25-28; 23:38-39; 34:2-10; 43:7-9; 44:7-8,10,12-13; 45:9). Editors 'correcting' Ezekiel would not have left unaltered the prophecies of Tyre's ultimate end (Ezek 27:36), which remained unfulfilled until a millennium after Christ.

Even giving the book the latest possible date, it has still correctly predicted the fate of Tyre for the last two millennia, and it continues to be fulfilled today. The observation of Ezekiel's accuracy is inconsistent with the nature of purely human prognostication; the final destruction of Tyre, great though she was, demonstrates the superior power of the God who had decreed it beforehand.

> "They will destroy the walls of Tyre and break down her towers. I will scrape her soil from her and make her a bare rock ... For I have spoken", declares the sovereign LORD ... "Then they will know that I am the LORD" (Ezekiel 26:4-6)[15]

Other national prophecies

- The kingdom of Edom occupied the arid area south of the Dead Sea, including the mountain fortress Petra carved into the

[13] S. Sheehan & Z. A. Latif, *Lebanon* (Marshall Cavendish, 2007).

[14] Authors of several *apocryphal* books did attribute their writings to long-dead Bible characters, but they are not characterised by extended 'prophecies' of past events as a claim to inspiration; such a ruse could not have succeeded.

[15] For a closer examination of this prophecy see P. Ferguson, "Ezekiel 26:1-14: A proof text for inerrancy or fallibility of the Old Testament?", *Bible and Spade* (2006), available online at www.biblearchaeology.org.

sandstone cliffs. The prophets foretold the destruction and desolation of Edom, including "'you who live in the clefts of the rock, who hold the height of the hill...no man shall dwell there'' (Jer 49:16-18).

The Edomite people eventually disappeared from history by the first century AD, but their cities remained inhabited by the Nabataeans. However, in AD 363, an earthquake wrecked the vital water management systems that made Petra habitable; after another devastating earthquake in AD 551, records of occupation come to an end.

The famous ruins of Petra have remained just that – uninhabited ruins – ever since, just as Jeremiah predicted.

Copies of his prophecy in the Dead Sea scrolls prove it was given at least four centuries before its fulfilment appeared remotely likely; yet the predicted total and continuing abandonment of what was a flourishing city, then and now a wonder of the world, was fulfilled to the letter.

- Babylon, at one time the largest and greatest city on earth, was prophesied to become 'a desert, a land in which no one dwells, and through which no son of man passes' (Jer 51:43). 'It will never be inhabited or lived in for all generations; no Arab will pitch his tent there; no shepherds will make their flocks lie down there' (Isa 13:20).

Babylon remained an important city in the Persian and Greek empires until about 300 BC, when most of its inhabitants were transported to the new city of Seleucia. By about AD 200 Babylon was uninhabited, sinking into almost complete obscurity. While there have been various towns nearby, the ruins of Babylon remain uninhabited – despite the recent unfinished rebuilding efforts of Saddam Hussein.

Although Babylon was built on the Euphrates River, with an extensive canal system, the ruins have for centuries remained devoid of vegetation, and thus of flocks. Various visitors have

166

found Arabs superstitiously unwilling to pitch their tent there[16], again demonstrating the perfect accuracy of Bible prophecy.

- The signs and symbols of Revelation have received an enormous range of interpretations, not all of them accurate. There are, however, striking examples of interpretations that correctly predicted historical events before they occurred.[17] The precise and accurate fulfilment of these predictions provides some validation of those interpretations, and witnesses to the inspiration of the Revelation itself.

  For example, Irenaeus and Hippolytus in the second century correctly foresaw that the Christian church would rise to power in the nations, but that having been corrupted, it would then persecute true believers. This was far from inevitable in their day – the church was then a small, illegal and periodically persecuted minority – but the prediction was eventually fulfilled in the fourth century.

In each case, the question must be asked: how did the prophets know the course of history, centuries in advance? And in each case the answer must be returned: they could not have known if it had not been revealed to them by the God in heaven who knows the end from the beginning.

Jesus Christ

One of the strongest endorsements of Bible prophecy as a reason for belief is its use by Jesus Christ. Even after his own resurrection, he first taught the resurrection not by presenting himself as living proof, but from 'Moses and all the Prophets' (Luke 24:27). When he did show himself to the apostles they still disbelieved, so he 'opened their minds to understand the Scriptures' (Luke 24:43):

> Then he said to them, "These are my words that I spoke to you while I was still with you, that everything written about me in the Law of Moses and the prophets and the psalms must be fulfilled" (Luke 24:44)

Christ thus views prophecy as an even better reason for belief than direct witness of a miracle. Peter describes the evidence of Scripture for Christ's power as even more sure than his own eyewitness and that of the other

---

[16] A. Barnes, *Notes on the Old and New Testaments* (Baker Books, 1983).

[17] J. Burke, *A More Sure Word of Prophecy* (Adelaide: CSSS, 2009).

apostles (2 Pet 1:16, 19). Solid, verifiable historical fact (as, with the benefit of hindsight, his resurrection must be considered; see later chapter), is even more reliable than firsthand evidence of the senses. Indeed, the first three eyewitness reports of Christ's resurrection were all disbelieved (Mark 16:9-13; Luke 24:9-11) — but the 'miraculous' element of prophecy, that the history it described had been written in their Bibles long before its present fulfilment, was clearly indisputable.

The emphasis on prophecy rather than miracle continued in the apostles' preaching of Christ, which never relied solely on eyewitness accounts of his resurrection, but also depended on Bible prophecy (Acts 2:23-36; 3:13-24; 7:2-53; 8:35; 10:38-43; 13:17-41; 17:2-3; 28:23).[18] Prophecy was considered sufficient reason in itself; the many miracles performed by Christ and his apostles go almost without mention.[19]

Old Testament prophecies concerning Christ, including some of those quoted by the apostles in their preaching, are listed in Table 1. The fulfilment of each is demonstrated in the New Testament. Prophecies of which the fulfilment could easily have been contrived, such as Christ's speaking in parables (Ps 78:2; cf. Matt 13:35) are of less value as evidence and thus are not listed.

Old Testament prophecy		New Testament fulfilment
Isa 7:14	Son of virgin	Matt 1:21-25
Isa 11:10	Descendant of Jesse ruling Gentiles	Rom 15:8-12
2 Sam 7:12-13	Descendant of David	Acts 2:29-31; Matt 1:1
Mic 5:2	Born in Bethlehem	Matt 2:1,4-6
Mal 3:1	The way prepared by a messenger	Mark 1:2-4,7
Isa 42:1-3	Not crying aloud in the street; brings justice to Gentiles	Matt 12:15-21

Table 1. Prophecies fulfilled by Jesus Christ.

---

[18] To those unfamiliar with prophecy, Paul reasoned first from creation rather than from modern miracles (Acts 14:11-18; 17:22-31).

[19] In their emphasis on **fulfilled prophecy** the apostles make an interesting contrast with the many Christians whose reasons for faith are (supposed) miracles they have experienced or heard of.

168

Old Testament prophecy		New Testament fulfilment
Isa 53:4	Bore our sicknesses	Matt 8:16-17
Isa 53:9	No sin or deceit	1 Pet 2:21-22
Ps 69:4	Hated by many without cause	John 15:25; Matt 27:18-20,23-24
Ps 41:9; Zech 13:6	Betrayed by a friend	Mark 14:10; John 13:18; 18:35
Zech 11:13	Valued at thirty pieces of silver, which was thrown to the potter in the temple	Matt 26:15; 27:5-10
Ps 2:1-2	Gentiles, Israel, king and ruler plot against Christ	Acts 4:25-27
Isa 53:5-7	Wounded for our healing	1 Pet 2:23-25; John 19:1
Ex 12:46	No bones broken	John 19:33,36
Ps 22:14-17	Crucified, watched by mockers	Luke 23:33-36
Ps 22:18	His clothing divided by lot	John 19:23-24
Zech 12:10	Pierced	John 19:34,37
Isa 53:9	Buried with the rich	Matt 27:57-60
Ps 16:9-11	Raised from the dead	Acts 2:23-33; 13:33-37
Ps 110:1	Ascended to heaven	Acts 2:33-35
Ps 68:18	Received gifts for men	Eph 4:8-11; Acts 2:4,31-33

Table 1 cont. Prophecies fulfilled by Jesus Christ.

The precision of these prophecies is extremely impressive; it would have been utterly convincing to those in whose days they were being fulfilled. Even today, the evidence remains compelling – how could this array of fulfilled prophecy have been fabricated?

Quite obviously, no one except Jesus Christ has fulfilled all these predictions; without Divine foreknowledge, the chances of so accurately foretelling so much of his life would be remote indeed (and Table 1 is far from exhaustive).[20]

---

[20] Over eighty prophecies fulfilled in Jesus Christ are listed in *The Popular Encyclopedia of Bible Prophecy* (eds. T. LaHaye & E. E. Hindson; Harvest House Publishers, 2004).

The theory that anyone could have intentionally gone about fulfilling these prophecies in order to impersonate a Messiah is scarcely credible; such an impostor would gain nothing by so doing but a cruel and early death. In any case, the fulfilment of many of the prophecies could not possibly have been contrived; one cannot plan the location or family of one's own birth; nor one's betrayal, abuse and execution; nor the amount of money paid as bribe and the use of it by the priests; nor the method by which one's executioners divide one's clothing.

The prophecies were certainly not altered after the event; Jews, and solely Jews as opposed to Christians, have preserved the best Old Testament texts. There is no possibility of a Jewish conspiracy to promote Jesus, whom they despised and rejected as a false Messiah. There is no manuscript evidence for such a massive forgery, either in Hebrew or the Septuagint (the Greek translation of Scripture already completed by the time of Christ). Some of the Dead Sea Scrolls, including the complete text of Isaiah containing many of these prophecies, have been dated up to 150 years before Jesus Christ's birth.

The accuracy of prophecies such as that concerning the messenger who prepared Christ's way (fulfilled by John the Baptist) would have been well known at the time, but today can be demonstrated only through the New Testament, not by any independent witness. Histories outside of Scripture, while providing strong historical evidence for Jesus Christ's existence (see later chapter), lack the detail required to confirm most of these prophecies.

Nonetheless, the history of Jewish thought does reveal this: no Jewish writer would have invented a Messiah like Jesus. The Gospels do not present the fulfilment of prophecy expected by Jews – a conquering liberator to restore the rule of Israel and the Law of Moses; instead, there was a humble birth and obscure childhood, preaching to Gentiles, rejection by his own people, betrayal by a friend, death and resurrection. Instead of endorsing the Law of Moses, Jesus fulfilled it and "ended" it (Rom 10:4). None of this was the expectation of the day; yet the four Gospel writers agree on each detail, not because any of it was likely to appeal to their audience, but because it was fact. Scholars confirm the calibre of the Gospels as history[21] – and if their history is fact, then Table 1 demonstrates that it was accurately predicted centuries beforehand.

---

[21] See, C. L. Blomberg, *The Historical Reliability of the Gospels* (Leicester: Inter-Varsity Press, 2008) and F. F. Bruce, *The New Testament Documents: Are They Reliable?* (Eerdmans, 2003).

The climax of all four Gospels is the resurrection of Jesus, an event with such massive implications that it is well verified by history (see later chapter). To the miracle of resurrection may thus be added the miracle of predicting it centuries in advance.

The accuracy of these Old Testament prophecies endorses both the God who authored them and the Son of God whom they foretell. Jesus Christ himself remarked on the evidence of these prophecies to the Jews:

> "You study the scriptures thoroughly because you think in them you possess eternal life, and it is these same scriptures that testify about me" (John 5:39)

Conclusion

This chapter presents some of the evidence of fulfilled prophecy for the inspiration of the Bible, demonstrating accuracy far exceeding that evidenced by prophets of other deities. Any one example would prove the point; science does not demand theories to be proved more than once. The hypothesis that God wrote the Bible does not contradict other scientifically proven results. If an uninspired author could somehow have guessed one of the fulfilled prophecies, the others still provide strong witness; this would be no evidence *against* inspiration, only a weakening of the evidence presented *for* inspiration.

A scientifically valid way to test the hypothesis of Divine authorship is to examine other prophecies to see whether they too have been fulfilled or not. As described above, independent witness of the fulfilment of many prophecies is now lacking, so they provide no objective evidence for or against inspiration. Other prophecies, such as the many foretelling the return of Jesus Christ in power, remain an open question: they have not yet been fulfilled, but there is of course no evidence that they will *never* be fulfilled.[22] For Scripture to offer hope for the future, it must contain some prophecies that have yet to be fulfilled (Heb 11:39-40).

The accuracy of many other prophecies has been doubted. It is perfectly reasonable to seek explanation in these cases, as has been done in a few examples above; however, to explain every prophecy in Scripture is clearly beyond the capacity of this chapter. What has been done, though, is to

---

[22] The obvious objection that Christ died before fulfilling these prophecies is treated in detail in a later chapter, where evidence for his resurrection is discussed.

provide several of the very strongest reasons in Bible prophecy to be confident of the inspiration of the Bible.

At the time of writing, the Large Hadron Collider has not yet uncovered proof of the famous particle it seeks. Perhaps the particle does not exist; or perhaps it does, but the evidence has not yet been found. But ample evidence has been presented that God <u>does</u> exist, satisfying the standard logic of scientific proof. Indeed, the evidence of Bible prophecy is admirably suited to demonstration according to these principles.

The public will immediately accept the findings of the Large Hadron Collider; the integrity of the scientific method is universally approved. This chapter has illustrated how God proves Himself by the same standard, utterly conclusively; it is not for want of evidence that many do not accept His existence. Anyone weighing the witness of Bible prophecy, however, will have absolute confidence in its Divine origin.

> Moreover, we possess the prophetic word as an altogether reliable thing. You do well if you pay attention to this (2 Peter 1:19)

Summary

- The Bible itself asserts that biblical prophecies are given to verify that the Bible is the word of God.
- The Bible contains numerous prophecies that can be demonstrated to have been fulfilled. These include:
    - Prophecies about Israel
    - Daniel's four kingdom vision
    - Ezekiel's prophecy about Tyre
    - Other national prophecies
    - Prophecies about Jesus.
- The testimony of fulfilled prophecy gives us confidence in God's promises for the future.

Further reading

The evidence of Bible prophecy to the divine origin of the Bible is considered in numerous other works. Some recommended titles include *Vox Dei* by Islip Collyer, *Believing the Bible* by A. D. Norris (chapter 7) and *God's Truth* by Alan Hayward (chapters 2-6). Also see *A More Sure Word of Prophecy* by Jonathan Burke.

172

Appendix: Probabilities

It is frequently desirable to quantify how conclusive the results of the scientific method are in a particular situation. Often the observations are not absolutely inconsistent with the working hypothesis, but are so unlikely on that premise that it is more rational to accept an alternative hypothesis that better explains the data. The question then becomes a mathematical one: 'How unlikely is unlikely enough?' This is a matter of judgment, but chances as low as 1 in 20 assuming the working hypothesis is really true are usually considered remote enough to reject it in favour of a more likely alternative. If the chances of the observations occurring under the working hypothesis are as low as 1 in 100, the preference for a suitable alternative hypothesis becomes 'almost certain'. In safety tests, the required mark may be as extreme as 1 in 1,000 or more, to ensure no mistake is made when approving equipment as safe.

While it is impossible to give precise probabilities of the kinds of events Bible prophecy deals with, it should be noted that each of the prophecies considered in this chapter relates to events that are inherently very unlikely to have been guessed. The fates of Israel and Tyre, for example, are without historical parallel.

Stoner[23] gives probabilities for five of the prophecies considered in this chapter (those concerning Israel, Tyre, Edom, Babylon and Jesus Christ), intended to conservatively estimate the chances of such accurate predictions being made under the working hypothesis that the prophet had no prior knowledge of the future. Since the estimates are, of necessity, subjective, no particular confidence can be placed in the exact figures, but in any case each estimated probability is extremely low; on this basis the alternative hypothesis that the prophet did have prior information could be taken as effectively certain. This only formalises what was already abundantly apparent: the prophecies could not possibly have been written so accurately without Divine help.

The evidence of each individual prophecy – already extremely strong – becomes overwhelming when they are taken together. Suppose the fulfilment of each of these five prophecies is independent of the others (which appears reasonable given their separation from each other in space and time); then the probability of all five being fulfilled by chance is the

---

[23] P. W. Stoner & R. C. Newman, *Science Speaks* (Online: www.sciencespeaks.net, 2005). The overall probability of a set of events described in a prophecy is the product of the probabilities of each independent component event.

product of the five individual probabilities. Even taking the probability of chance fulfilment of each prophecy as 1 in 500 only (at least ten times more conservative than each of Stoner's estimates), the probability of observing all five prophecies fulfilled by *chance* would be 1 in 31,250,000,000,000. This is less likely than the same six out of forty numbers winning a lottery on its very first three draws! Such a coincidence is effectively impossible. This illustrates how unlikely it is that these prophecies could have been made without Divine foreknowledge. The analysis may assist to some extent in grasping the degree of certainty with which Bible prophecy proves the existence of the God of the Bible.

Israel: God's Chosen People

Reg Carr

"The very existence of the Jews … together with all that has happened to them in their long turbulent history, is proof that there is a God" – D. W. Torrance[1]

Deeply personal

When Yahweh, the God of Israel, told His people that they were the only people that He had "known" among all the families of the earth (Amos 3:2), He was speaking as a monogamous man might speak to his well-beloved wife, reminding her of his faithfulness as a husband and of the special place that she occupied in his affections.[2]

This special affection of God for Israel is graphically portrayed also by the prophet Ezekiel in a parable about a foundling left to die in the open field, which shows how Israel's God had cared for His people from their birth.

> "I spread My cloak over you and covered your nakedness. I swore a solemn oath to you and entered into a marriage covenant with you", declares the sovereign LORD, "and *you became Mine*" (Ezekiel 16:8)

God's love for Israel is emphasised also in Hosea 11:1, where the metaphor is changed to depict the nation as God's own son. "When Israel was a young man, I loved him like a son, and I summoned my son out of Egypt", says the prophet, in a passage which remarkably prefigures the flight of Joseph and Mary into (and out of) Egypt with the infant Jesus almost eight hundred years later (Matt 2:14, 15). The fact that the nation

---

[1] D. W. Torrance, *The witness of the Jews to God* (Edinburgh: The Handsel Press, 1982) 1.

[2] The Hebrew word **yada**, translated "known" in Amos 3:2, is used throughout the Old Testament to signify acquaintance, or personal knowledge; but it is also used in the more intimate, sexual, sense, as when, for example, "Adam *knew* Eve his wife" (Gen. 4:1).

of Israel could serve in this way as a type of God's own Son shows just how deeply personal God's feelings for Israel really are.

Origins

'Israel' was the new name that an angel of God (Gen 32:28), then God Himself (Gen 35:10), gave to Jacob, the grandson of the patriarch Abraham. The name means 'Prince with God' (Gen 32:28, margin); and it is hard to think of a more highly exalted title for a man and for the nation that took its name from him. And there are no two ways about it: of Isaac's two sons, Esau and Jacob, the younger twin, Jacob, was the one preferred and chosen by divine selection, as God Himself later confirmed:

> "Esau was Jacob's brother," the LORD explains, "yet I chose Jacob" (Malachi 1:2)

Israel, the nation, descended from Jacob, and known initially as "the children of Israel" (Gen. 36:31), is first spoken of as God's people at the time of the Exodus from Egypt. In fact, the very first time that God referred to the children of Israel as "My people" was during His conversation with Moses in Mount Horeb, when Moses was told: "I will send you to Pharaoh to bring my people, the Israelites, out of Egypt" (Exod 3:10). From then on, the nation was able to celebrate its 'adoption' by God – a position that was confirmed immediately after the Exodus by the binding covenant sealed in the Wilderness of Sinai with the solemn words, "We are willing to do and obey all that the LORD [Yahweh] has spoken" (Exod 24:7).

The children of Israel thus became God's people in the most formal sense - a position of privilege in which the nation had every reason to rejoice. And Moses, as he prepared to take his leave of the second generation of Israelites, whom he had led to the edge of the Promised Land, was careful to remind them of their special position:

> When the Most High divided their inheritance to the nations, when He separated the sons of Adam, he set the boundaries of the peoples according to the number of the children of Israel. For the LORD's portion is His people; Jacob is the place of His inheritance. (Deuteronomy 32:8-9)

176

Chosen, elect and precious

It is unfashionable in the modern world to speak of the Jews as 'the chosen race';[3] yet the Bible – both Old and New Testaments – consistently maintains that the Jews are God's people, uniquely chosen and guided by Him from the time of their formation as a nation.[4]

'Chosen' may be a word that smacks of favouritism to the modern mind, but it is nevertheless an important Bible term that underpins the relationship of the God of the Bible with those whom He counts as His. This is emphasised on the first occasion when the word is applied to the children of Israel, embedded as it is deep in the heart of the Deuteronomic code, designed to remind God's people constantly of their privileged position:

> For you are a people holy to the LORD your God. He has chosen you to be his people, prized above all others on the face of the earth (Deuteronomy 7:6)

And yet, as if those words of divine selection to specialness were not enough to underline the point about Israel's unique relationship with God, many more such terms were to be added (and repeated) as the Old Testament unfolded. For the Psalmist, Israel was God's "inheritance" (Ps 78:71); in Isaiah, the nation was called God's "elect" (Isa 45:4; 65:9, 22); and in the same prophecy Israel was described as "precious in [God's] sight" (Isa 43:4). Later on, too, the prophet referred to God as Israel's "husband" and "Redeemer" (Isa 54:5); in Jeremiah, the nation was not only "the LORD's flock" (Jer 13:17), but also God's "firstborn" (Jer 31:9); and finally, God likened Israel to "the apple of His eye" (Zech 2:8). The God of heaven would not use such words lightly.

---

[3] Even the Jews themselves have recognised this: "The idea of chosenness is received negatively nowadays, the political and intellectual climate is against it. The great passion of our time is equality ... Chosenness seems to set one group apart from the rest of mankind as superior" (D. Gottlieb, *The Informed Soul,* (Brooklyn, N.Y.: Mesorah Publications, 1990). Cited 22nd March 2011 from www.heritage.org.il/innernet/archives/chosen.htm.

[4] The term 'Jew' first appears in 2 Kings 16:6, where it is used in the narrow sense of a person belonging to the kingdom of Judah, as distinct from a member of the ten northern tribes of Israel. But the terms 'Jew', 'Jewish' and 'the Jewish people' are used in this chapter in the broader (and later) sense of the *Concise Oxford Dictionary*'s definition of a Jew as "a member of the people whose traditional religion is Judaism and who trace their origins to the ancient people of Israel". This later sense is clearly also the meaning attached to the word 'Jew' in the New Testament (for example, in Matt 27:37, Acts 18:24 and Rom 3:1).

Not cast away

It is important to note that this biblical concept of Israel as God's chosen people does not end with the Old Testament. Instead, the special position of Israel is a persistent theme in the New Testament also; and it is one of the remarkable hallmarks[5] of the divine origin of the Bible that such a key theme runs through both the Hebrew and the Christian parts of a book which, in all its parts, claims to be the revealed Word of God.

When the Christian apostle Paul wrote to the church in Rome, he knew that there were Christians there who wrongly assumed that God's purpose with the Jews had been superseded by His more pressing desire to be a Father to all believers in His Son Jesus Christ. So Paul came quickly to the questions that he knew were greatly exercising his readers: *Had* God really laid aside the centuries-old privileges of the Jew? Was the 'special relationship' now forever at an end? These were the issues that Paul addressed in his letter to those who thought that the Jews were no longer 'special' to God in the new Christian dispensation and that they had been permanently set aside in favour of the Christian church.[6]

"So I ask", Paul writes, "God has not rejected his people, *has he?*" (Rom 11:1). And Paul's categorical answer was a resounding "Absolutely not!" (v. 1). "God has not rejected his people", said Paul (v. 2). And why not? Because He "foreknew" them (v. 2) – that is to say, because God, in His knowledge of the future, knew very well that the Jews would turn away from worshipping Him, that they would reject His Son when He sent him, but that ultimately they would turn again to serve Him. God knew all of this, and His ultimate purpose in saving Israel from permanent destruction would not be frustrated by their waywardness. And so the

---

[5] A 'hallmark' is defined by the *Concise Oxford Dictionary* as "a mark stamped on articles of gold, silver or platinum ... certifying purity". In the same way, the unifying themes of the Bible (of which God's special relationship with the Jews is simply one among very many) 'mark' it out as a genuinely superhuman work.

[6] Although some in Corinth appear to have made this false assumption, the doctrine (later known as Supersessionism) was not properly developed until the second and third centuries AD, by 'Church fathers' like Justin Martyr, Tertullian, Hippolytus of Rome and Augustine of Hippo. Still later theologians, both Catholic and Protestant (including Martin Luther) also believed that the Jews had been replaced in God's affections as a punishment for bringing about the crucifixion of Jesus. The early Christian apostle Paul, however, was very clear in teaching that the Jews' fall from grace was only temporary: "... if their fall is riches for the world, and their failure riches for the Gentiles, how much more their fulness!" (Rom 11:12).

apostle asked again about his own people, the Jews, who, in their first-century subjection to a Roman yoke, might well have been thought to have been abandoned by their God: "I ask then, they did not stumble into an irrevocable fall, did they?" (v. 11). And back came Paul's answer again, just as categorically: "Absolutely not!" (v. 11).

Throughout Romans 11 Paul was at pains to explain that it is through Jesus Christ – himself a Jew – that "all Israel will be saved" (v. 26).[7] There is simply no getting away from it: the Jews still continue to be right at the heart of the unchanging purpose of God with the earth. For, as Paul concluded: "The gifts and calling of God are irrevocable" (v. 29).[8]

The long-term purpose of God

It is another key theme of the whole Bible that God's ultimate purpose is to fill the earth with His glory (Num 14:21; Isa 11:9; Hab 2:14). He will achieve this through the work of His Son Jesus Christ, whom He has promised to send back to the earth to set up an everlasting kingdom of peace and righteousness (Ps 2 and 72; Acts 1:9-11).

This long-term purpose of God with the earth is explicitly declared on many pages of the Old Testament. The prophet Malachi, for example, complained about Israel's unfaithfulness to the marriage covenant with God, and reminded them that, from Creation onwards, it had always been God's intention for married partners to remain "one" and not to practise adultery (Mal 2:11-16). And why did God want this? Malachi explains: the purpose of monogamous marriage was because "He (God) seeks godly offspring" (Mal 2:15). In other words, it was always God's purpose to fill the earth with people who, from their own free will, would choose to remain faithful to their Creator in love and obedience. Mankind were designed to be "godly"; and yet the freely-made choice of Adam and Eve to disobey, and to break that 'oneness' with God, brought about a state of

---

[7] The expression "all Israel" includes not only those Jews who turn again in faith to God (Rom 11:23), but also those faithful non-Jews ("Gentiles") who, by baptism into Jesus Christ, are entitled to share in the blessings promised to Abraham and his seed (Gal 3:26-29).

[8] The unalterable permanence of God's special relationship with Israel is heavily underlined by *The Message*'s translation of Romans 11:29: "God's gifts and God's call are under full warranty – never cancelled, never rescinded".

alienation between themselves and their Creator, which God in His goodness has been working ever since to repair.[9]

And that process of reparation, which began in Eden with God's provision of animal skins to cover our first parents' nakedness (Gen 3:21), is what the Bible's gospel of human salvation from sin and death is all about. As the triumph of God's Son Jesus Christ over sin and death on the cross so beautifully illustrates, the goodness and love of God will ultimately triumph over the sinfulness of man, the breach between man and God will be permanently repaired, and the earth will at last be "filled with the knowledge of the glory of the LORD" (Hab 2:14).

From the 'sons of God' to Abraham

God's long-term purpose, however, requires time to be worked out in human history. And, in order to bring His purpose forward, from Eden onwards God has been seeking that "godly offspring" to whom He might reveal His will. The child of Adam and Eve who chose to worship God acceptably was Abel, described by the Jesus as "righteous Abel" (Matt 23:35) because he obeyed God and offered the prescribed sacrifices (Gen 4:2-4). Not many recorded generations after Abel, however, "the sons of God" – those to whom God was looking for faithful service – were deviating from God's way and mingling with those who defied God, as Cain had done (Gen 4:5-15; 6:1-6).

It was in this increasingly ungodly context that one man stood out: Noah. He alone was behaving like the "godly offspring" that God was seeking; and so Noah is described as "a just man, perfect in his generations" and as one whom, like Enoch before him (Gen 5:24), "walked with God" (Gen 6:8, 9).[10] Hebrews 11:7 highlights Noah's confidence in God's warning that the world was going to be flooded as a judgement on its wickedness.

---

[9] 'Repairing the breach' that exists between man and God as a result of Adam's disobedience is precisely what lies behind the word 'religion': "As a word, it is derived from the Latin *religio*, from *religare*, which signifies, *to bind again*: hence, *religion* is the *act of binding again*, or, that which *heals a breach* previously existing between two parties" (J. Thomas, *Elpis Israel: being an exposition of the Kingdom of God, with reference to the Time of the End, and the age to come* (5th rev. ed.; Birmingham: Robert Roberts, 1884) 139).

[10] In describing Enoch and Noah as men who "walked" with God, there is an echo of the experience of Adam and Eve in the Garden of Eden, where the LORD God Himself "walked" in their presence (Gen. 3:8, where the same Hebrew word – *halak* – is used).

180

It is clear from the Genesis record that, once the waters of the Flood had abated, the Creator was in effect making a new beginning with this faithful man, who had shown himself to be the kind of godly seed that God was looking for: "… be fruitful and multiply", said God to Noah and his sons, "increase abundantly on the earth and multiply on it" (Gen 9:7).[11] And that new beginning, designed once again to fill the earth with children with whom God Himself could be pleased, was accompanied by a binding promise from the Creator: "Look! I now confirm my covenant with you and your descendants after you… never again will a flood destroy the earth" (Gen 9:9,11).

Eleven generations on, however, and the earth was filled with wickedness again – witness the infamous depravity of Sodom and Gomorrah (Gen 19); and God was still looking for some sign that mankind would choose to exhibit those godlike qualities of righteousness and faithfulness to which he had been calling each generation since Creation. And then He found Abram, a man with the same qualities as Noah, and who responded to God with a faith that became archetypal in its own right.[12]

God appeared to Abram at least seven times, renaming him 'Abraham' in the process (Gen 17:5); and, having found in him the kind of faith that made God willing and able to treat him as if he were wholly sinless, God focussed His long-term purpose on Abraham, with promises about the land of Canaan, about eternal life, about the nations that would descend from him, and about a seed (descendant) who would bring divine blessings to all nations (Gen 12:1-3,7; 13:14-17; 15:18-21; 17:3-8,19; 22:15-18). And so it came about that God's way of saving mankind from sin and death became centred in this faithful man and in his descendants through his son Isaac, the child of promise (Gen 17:19), and through Isaac's son Jacob (Gen 28:1-5, 13-15).[13]

---

[11] These are more or less the same words that God spoke to Adam and Eve before the Fall (Gen. 1:28).

[12] Even two thousand years later the Christian apostle Paul could still write about Abraham as "the father of all those who believe" (Rom. 4:11).

[13] Through his other sons Ishmael and Esau, of course, Abraham became, quite literally "the father of many nations", with various Arab peoples tracing their lineage back to Abraham through them; but, as Jesus Christ himself made clear, "salvation is of the Jews" (John 4:22).

So why *did* God choose Israel?

From all this it is abundantly clear that, in choosing to favour the offspring of Abraham through Isaac and Jacob, God was not so much *excluding* other peoples as selecting the children of Israel for a heavy dual responsibility, both as the custodians of the knowledge of God's continuing purpose and as an example of godliness in practice, at individual and national level. Just as Abraham had remained faithful to God, so the nation that came from him was intended to be "a people holy to the LORD" (Deut 7:6), in order to show the world what God's purpose was all about.

And God Himself explained to the children of Israel, in case they might have ideas above their station, that "it is not because [they] were more numerous than all the other peoples that the LORD favored and chose [them]. Rather it is because of... his faithfulness to the promise he solemnly vowed to [their] ancestors" (Deut 7:7, 8). The Apostle Paul confirms this in saying that the Jews are "dearly loved for the sake of the fathers" (Rom 11:28); and the fact that the Jews are still 'God's chosen people', almost four thousand years after Abraham's time, proves that, in spite of the many reasons God may have had not to keep Israel as His people, He *always* remains faithful to His promises. As one writer puts it: "... all that has happened to Israel, her preservation through appalling suffering, exceeding the suffering of any other nation in history, her preservation through the horrors of the Holocaust of Nazi-dominated Europe, and the restoration of a remnant to the Promised Land, testifies to God's faithfulness".[14]

The Jews: a living witness

It is also the case that, having established His permanent promise of favour with the descendants of Abraham through Jacob, God is able to point to the continued existence of the Jews as evidence of His own existence. This point is made graphically in Isaiah 43, where the nations of the earth are challenged to prove their gods really exist (v. 9). Then, when they are unable to do this, the God of Israel is able to say to His own people: "You are my witnesses ... and my servant, whom I have chosen ... you are my witnesses ... that I am God" (vv. 10-12). The nation of Israel itself, therefore, is a living witness to the existence of the God Who first chose them so long ago.

---

[14] Torrance, *Witness of the Jews*, 7.

It can be said with complete confidence that if there ever came a time when the Jews no longer existed, then that would be the day when atheism and agnosticism would find their complete justification. As it is, however, a careful reading of the Bible leads the open-minded reader to the conclusion that such a day will **never** dawn; for God Himself declares that He will "not make a complete end" of the Jews (Jer 30:11). This is a bold claim indeed, but it is one that we can monitor quite easily for ourselves.

Against all the odds, and unlike so many of the nations, large and small, that once populated the ancient Near East, Israel still exists as an identifiable nation; and every time we see, or read of, a Jew in our modern world, we are in effect being given a pointed reminder of the existence of God and the truth of His Word.

The witness of Israel to the existence of the God of the Bible is therefore much more than merely historical: it is evidence that relies not simply on the records of history to support it. It also receives strong corroboration from the evidence of our own twenty-first-century eyes and ears. *The presence of the nation of Israel in the land of Palestine is, in itself, a living witness that challenges us to believe what the Bible says about God and His long-term purpose with the Jews and with the world.*

"Not altogether unpunished"

It is also remarkable that the Old Testament – the Jews' own Scriptures – actually records the nation's failure to keep God's laws. At the time of Samuel, the children of Israel added to their sins by rejecting God as their king while asking for a mere man to rule over them (1 Sam 8:6,7). The succession of kings who followed – some faithful, but others not – led the people into many errors, with God sending a succession of prophets to encourage them to stay faithful to Him, as well as many foreign armies to bring them to their senses (2 Chr 36:15-17; Ezek 21:25-27; Dan 11).

Jeremiah was sent by God to foretell the nation's captivity because the people were not keeping God's ways. The prophet's task was to pronounce God's coming judgements: "I will turn my beloved people over to the power of their enemies" (Jer 12:7). It was Jeremiah's unpleasant duty to say, on behalf of God: "I will do to this temple

[Solomon's Temple] what I did to Shiloh,[15] and I will make this city [Jerusalem] an example to be used in curses" (Jer 26:6).

Yet Jeremiah never foretold the nation's complete destruction. He spoke often about a long captivity to come; but he also promised that the scattered nation would be re-gathered:

> Hear what the LORD has to say, O nations. Proclaim it in the faraway lands along the sea. Say, "The one who scattered Israel will regather them. He will watch over his people like a shepherd watches over his flock." (Jeremiah 31:10).

The nation's punishments, though severe, would never be allowed to extinguish their existence:

> I will completely destroy all the nations where I scattered you. But I will not completely destroy you. But ... I will not allow you to go entirely unpunished (Jeremiah 30:11)

Such passages of prophecy (and there are many more) about the long-term survival of Israel are evidence in themselves that the prophet was inspired to make such unerringly accurate predictions. So much so, in fact, that they have prompted another writer to conclude: "What prophet, be he Jeremiah or any other, would dare to foretell his nation's downfall, to be followed not by her extermination, but ultimately by her triumph, unless he were moved by God, and knew himself to be so moved?"[16]

"Your house is left to you desolate"

During the period when the Romans were the dominant power in Palestine, Jesus Christ was born a Jew. In spite of the fact that the common people heard Jesus gladly (Mark 12:37), the Jewish rulers did not, and they persuaded the Roman governor to crucify him. One of the many reasons why the Jewish rulers hated Jesus so much was that he foretold the destruction of the great Temple of which they were so proud. Not one stone of that marvellous building would be left standing on top of another, Jesus had said (Luke 21:6); their "house" would be "left ... desolate" (Matt 23:38); and Jerusalem itself would be "trampled by the Gentiles" (Luke 21:24). These prophetic words came dramatically true

---

[15] That is, an abandoned ruin (see Jer. 7:12-14).
[16] C. Cooper, *Modern Israel*, (Birmingham: The Christadelphian, 1973) 127.

within decades of the ascension of Jesus to heaven: in 70 AD the Romans besieged Jerusalem, and Israel's existence as a sovereign nation came to an end.

Yet throughout the centuries since then, the purpose of God through His people and through His Son has still remained unchanged. Jesus, descended from Abraham and David the king of Israel, is the seed promised by God to both of these faithful men. He will sit on David's throne in Jerusalem and reign over the Kingdom of God - Israel restored and enlarged – bringing about the widespread blessings promised to Abraham. That will be the time, envisaged by Zechariah, when "ten people from all languages and nations will grasp hold of – indeed, grab – the robe of one Jew and say, 'Let us go with you, for we have heard that God is with you.'" (Zech. 8:23). In those days, there will be no doubt as to who God's chosen people really are.

The witness of prophecy fulfilled

In the meantime, the return of so many Jews to their former homeland after the horrors of World War II, their establishment as a nation-state in 1948, and their survival against all the odds for more than sixty years, are in themselves a powerful witness to the truth of the Bible's prophetic promises about their ongoing centrality in the purpose of God. From Bible passages that we can read and check for ourselves emerges the clear promise of their restoration as a nation prior to the return of Jesus Christ from heaven and their ultimate recognition of him (see, for example, Deut 28:15-68, Isa 11:1,10-16, Jer 30-31 and Ezek 37:21-28).

So clear, in fact, is the biblical promise of Israel's long-term restoration to their ancient land that it ought to come as no surprise to learn that generations of Bible students looked for its fulfilment long before it actually happened around the middle of the twentieth century; that fact in itself argues strongly for faith to be put in the prophetic word of God. From Thomas Brightman's *Shall they return to Jerusalem again?* (1615), through Joseph Eyre's *Observations upon the prophecies relating to the restoration of the Jews* (1771), and on to John Thomas's *Elpis Israel: an exposition of the Kingdom of God* (1850), there was a long line of Christian writers predicting the Jews' return to Palestine;[17] this is evidence for the reliability of the Old Testament prophets that cannot be lightly dismissed.

---

[17] These remarkably prescient words, for example, were written almost exactly a century before the establishment of the state of Israel: "The pre-adventual

185

"The hope of Israel": the true Christian gospel

There is, however, still one element missing from the chosen people of God: their present religion, Judaism, based more on the traditions of men than on the commandments of God (Matt 15:9), continues to reject Jesus Christ as the nation's Saviour from sin.

Nevertheless, Israel's own prophets make it clear that the nation will yet have a change of heart (Ezek 36:24-26). They will eventually come to acknowledge Jesus as their king, and they will turn back to the God of their forefathers and become God's true children. A great invasion of Israel from the north will temporarily overwhelm the nation, but Jesus Christ will be revealed to them as their Messiah, and a remnant will welcome him. All this is clear from such passages as Ps 118:22-26, Isa 59:19-21, Ezek 37-39, Joel 3, Mic 5:4,5, Zech 12-14, Mt 19:27,28, 23:37-39, Rom 11:25-29, Rev 1:7 and 16:15-18. And this promise of good things still to come for the children of Abraham is what the Apostle Paul himself looked forward to, calling it "the hope of Israel", and being prepared for the sake of it to be held in chains in a Roman prison (Acts 28:20).

The gospel message of Jesus and his early disciples is firmly based on the promises given earlier in the Hebrew Scriptures. As one writer puts it: "Christianity has an identity of hope and purpose with that of the Old Testament".[18] The Apostle Paul even tells us that the Christian gospel he preached was also "preached ... beforehand" to Abraham (Gal 3:8). A true Christian will therefore appreciate the Israelitish nature of the hope of a future life beyond the grave (Dan 12:1-3). The partial return of the Jews to Israel, which began in the mid-twentieth century, is a God-given sign that the return of Jesus from heaven, the resurrection of the dead, the judgement of all those responsible to God, and the setting up of God's everlasting Kingdom on earth, will all shortly follow, according to God's own timetable (Luke 21:24-33; Acts 17:30,31). Those who have been baptised into the saving name of Jesus Christ are to think of themselves not only as followers of Jesus, but also as "Abraham's descendents, and heirs according to the promise" (Gal 3:29). In God's great mercy they will

---

colonization of Palestine will be on purely political principles; and the Jewish colonists will return in unbelief of the Messiahship of Jesus, and of the truth as it is in him. They will emigrate thither as agriculturists and traders, in the hope of ultimately establishing their commonwealth" (Thomas, *Elpis Israel*, 395-6).

[18] H. Tennant, *What the Bible teaches*, (Birmingham: The Christadelphian, 2004) 250.

186

live to see the glorious things that are yet to be fulfilled in Israel, the land promised to God's chosen people forever (Gen 13:14-18).

> The restoration of a remnant to the Promised Land, in itself the fulfilment of prophecy, points forward to the fulfilment of those greater prophecies concerning the new creation, to the renewal and perfection of all God's people living on an earth renewed and made perfect[19]

Summary

- The Bible (both Old and New Testaments) makes many references to God's special affection for the Jews, the children of Israel.
- Israel, the name given by God to Jacob, the father of the twelve tribes, is an exalted title meaning 'Prince with God'.
- Israel became God's people in a formal sense at the time of the Exodus.
- The special position of Israel is a 'hallmark' theme of the whole Bible and an integral part of the Christian gospel: God has not 'cast away' His people.
- God's kingdom on earth will be the kingdom of Israel restored, with God's Son Jesus Christ as king.
- It has always been God's purpose to call people to eternal life through their faith and willing obedience as 'godly offspring': Abel, Noah and Abraham are key examples of this continuing call.
- God's promises to Abraham saw God's plan of salvation become focussed on this one man and his descendants through Isaac and Jacob.
- God chose Israel:
    1. Because of His regard for the 'fathers' of the nation (Abraham, Isaac and Jacob);
    2. So that Israel might serve as the custodians of God's Truth and be an example to the world of how a godly nation should live;
    3. To show that God keeps His promises;
    4. So that Israel might be witnesses (evidence) to others of God's own existence and faithfulness.

---

[19] Torrance, *Witness of the Jews*, 11.

- The Old Testament prophets predicted that Israel would be scattered and subsequently re-gathered.
- Jesus predicted the destruction of Jerusalem and its restoration prior to his Second Coming.
- The 'hope of Israel' (the restoration and immortalisation of "all Israel" at the coming of Messiah) is a central feature of the true Christian gospel.

Further reading

For further exposition of the witness of Israel as God's people see particularly John Carter's *God's Way* (chapter 5 "The Nation of God") and Harry Tennant's *What the Bible Teaches* (chapters 5, "God's Covenant with Abraham" and 25, "The Enigma of Israel").

You may also like to consult *Israel – Land and People of Destiny*, by J. V. Collyer, and *Modern Israel*, by C. Cooper.

The Historical Jesus

Andrew Perry

"I don't know of any historians today, who doubt the existence of Jesus" – N. T. Wright[1]

Introduction

In this summary essay we will briefly review what scholars have said about the possibility of describing the historical Jesus. After this, we will consider how we can evaluate the earliest written records about Jesus for historical reliability. Finally, we will discuss how and why history is important for the Christian faith. Our argument is that there are good reasons to trust the canonical gospels for historical information about Jesus, even if we come to the gospels with reservations about the extraordinary details such as the virgin birth, the miracles and the resurrection. In trusting the gospels regarding the ordinary things about Jesus, we take the first step towards belief in the extraordinary claims about Jesus made in the gospels. The full grounds for belief in the extraordinary are broader than that with which historical arguments can furnish a reader. The role of this essay in *Reasons* is one of encouraging a reader to get to know about Jesus in the gospels and to not let any initial doubts about the extraordinary to get in the way.

Scholarship

Scholars have been self-consciously aware of the business of researching and writing about the historical Jesus since the Enlightenment. Since that time, scholarly debate in the area has waxed and waned and many accounts of the life of Jesus have been produced. Those who write histories of Bible interpretation typically record three periods, or "quests", for the historical Jesus during the last two hundred years or so; periods interspersed with "quieter" times when scholars were not so occupied

---

[1] N. T. Wright, "The Self-Revelation of God in Human History", in *There is a God*, 188.

189

with deciding what can be known about Jesus.[2] During this time, conservative scholars were positive in their appraisal of the gospels as historical records and critical scholars were more negative.

The catalyst for inquiry into the historical Jesus is <u>doubt</u>: can the gospels be trusted as historical accounts? The basic methodological presupposition that defines the modern era of Gospel Criticism is that the gospels are to be treated like any other historical record. The doubt arises from the distinction between the Jesus of History and the Christ of Faith: it is asked to what extent the gospels are coloured by a later story-telling fabricated by believers, and to what extent they record an accurate portrayal of Jesus of Nazareth. German critical scholars in the nineteenth century concluded that the gospels contained many legendary stories and that they also give expression to common myths of the day. They also took the view that many stories were fabricated by the early church and then included in the gospels. As a result the critical "Lives of Jesus" that were written tended to reflect just the liberal moral values of the German Enlightenment.

The German scholar Albert Schweitzer is credited with bringing to a close this first "quest" for the historical Jesus with the publication of his book, *The Quest of the Historical Jesus* (1906).[3] In reviewing the work of German scholars of the nineteenth century, he observed that they had created a Jesus in their own image, which was Jesus as a liberal moral teacher stripped of the supernatural. After Schweitzer, critical scholars focused on the analysis of the individual units of narrative and sayings in the gospels, and they sought to explain their origins and their placement in the gospels as a result of the needs of the early church. This approach, known as "the form critical study of the gospels", went hand in hand with less interest in producing a "Life of Jesus". Of course, "Lives of Jesus" were produced during this time, and from conservative and critical scholars, but as a trend, German critical scholarship moved into other areas of research.

The reason why critical scholars have been sceptical of recovering the Jesus of History has been their predilection to see the <u>agenda of the early church</u> in the gospels. Conservative scholars have been more ready to see

---

[2] Two accessible recent reviews of the field are, D. B. Gowler, *The Historical Jesus?* (New York: Paulist Press, 2007). See also P. R. Eddy and J. K. Beilby, "The Quest for the Historical Jesus" in *The Historical Jesus: Five Views* (eds. P. R. Eddy and J. K. Beilby; London: SPCK, 2010), 9-54.

[3] A. Schweitzer, *The Quest of the Historical Jesus* (ed. J. Bowden; London: SCM Press 2000).

in the gospels an attempt to record an accurate history of Jesus, something similar to a biography. While critical scholarship has waxed and waned in its interest in the Jesus of History, conservative scholars have been more consistent in defending the historicity of the gospels. Subsequently, it was not until the 1950s that critical scholars once again focussed their attention upon determining what can be known about Jesus from the gospels. Thus, the German scholar Ernst Käsemann in his essay, *The Problem of the Historical Jesus* (1953),[4] argued that scholars were duty bound to find the continuity between the Jesus of History and the Christ of Faith, and that therefore they must determine what can be known about Jesus in order to preserve the doctrine of his humanity. Accordingly, such scholars renewed their efforts to find the historical Jesus in what has come to be known as a "second quest". In addition to analysing the individual stories and sayings of gospels, they did so with a renewed sensitivity to the role of the author in bringing the individual units together in a gospel, a method of analysis that was dubbed "redaction criticism".

German critical scholars once again drove this second quest, but as a scholarly fraternity it gradually lost its significance in the 1970s as American critical scholarship gained greater prominence. As a result, in 1982, the scholar N. T. Wright coined the phrase, "third quest", to refer to the work that mostly American scholars were doing in recovering the Jesus of History from the available records.[5] This trend is still ongoing today and it is characterized by the use of new methodologies involving the archaeology, sociology and cultural anthropology of Jesus' times.[6] There is among these scholars less emphasis on the analysis of the canonical gospels and more an emphasis on situating their record within a plausible context. This latest quest has been inter-disciplinary and overtly conscious of the role of method in reaching historical conclusions. To some extent, during this period, there has been a coming together of critical and conservative scholars in a more positive appraisal of what can be known about the Jesus of History.[7]

---

[4] E. Käsemann, *Essays on New Testament Themes* (London: SCM Press, 1964), 14-47.

[5] N. T. Wright, "Towards a Third 'Quest'? Jesus Then and Now" *ARC* (Montreal, McGill In-house Journal) 10 (1982): 20-27.

[6] G. Theissen and A. Merz, *The Historical Jesus: A Comprehensive Guide* (London: SCM Press, 1998), 1-15.

[7] For an overview of recent research into the historical Jesus, and a review of key scholars identified with the so-called 'third quest', see D. S. Du Toit, "Redefining Jesus: Current Trends in Jesus Research", in *Jesus, Mark and Q: The Teaching of Jesus*

In the history of scholarship there have been both conservatives and liberals. A layman coming to the question of what can be known about Jesus is faced with a wide choice of opinion. The movements in the discipline have been dominated by critical scholars; these have formed fraternities in which a common goal has been sought, and historians have identified such fraternities as "a liberal quest", "a second quest" or "a third quest" for the historical Jesus. Conservative scholars have only really been part of the last fraternity and have positively assessed what can be known about the Jesus of History from the *realia* of history. Their writings have offered plenty of reasons for trusting the canonical gospel records.

Historical Analysis

Although it may seem an odd thing to affirm, the consensus is that Jesus did exist; we have several notices of his existence in contemporary histories of the times. The contemporary Jewish historian, Josephus, mentions Jesus when describing Pilate's governorship of the region. He was a "doer of wonderful works",[8] opposed by the Jewish leaders and crucified (*Ant.* 18.63-64). The Roman historians Tacitus and Suetonius also mention Jesus as 'Christ' (*Annals* 15, 44; *Life of Claudius*, 25, 4).

Luke refers to the existence of various written accounts[9] about Jesus in his day:

> Now many have undertaken to compile an account of the things that have been fulfilled among us, like the accounts passed on to us by those who were eyewitnesses and servants of the word from the beginning. So it seemed good to me as well, because I have followed all things carefully from the beginning, to write an orderly account for you, most excellent Theophilus, so that you may know for certain the things you were taught (Luke 1:1-4)

---

and its Earliest Records (eds., M. Labahn and A. Schmidt; Sheffield, Sheffield Academic Press, 2001), 82-124.

[8] The consensus of scholars is that this particular expression is original to Josephus and that in this respect his text has not been altered by later Christian copyists—see G. Vermes, "The Jesus Notice of Josephus Re-examined" *JJS* 38/1 (1987): 1-10

[9] Luke's prologue has an emphasis on written accounts although, no doubt, there was oral tradition that he took on board.

We have four canonical gospels, but other gospels of later dates are known.[10] Scholars have long observed literary relationships between the first three gospels, and the most common view is that Mark was used as a source for both Matthew and Luke. Consequently, scholars approach the gospels with a view to establishing their sources. Luke's comment about his own gospel is a statement of an historical method, an attempt to set things in order using eyewitness testimony. He states,

- Tradition was preserved and delivered by eyewitnesses and "ministers of the word" to second-generation believers.

- There were other written records, from which it was possible to gain an accurate understanding of Jesus' life.

- New converts were instructed in the things of Jesus' life, and this was supported by written accounts, of which Luke's gospel was to be a 'perfect understanding'.

The scholar H. J. Cadbury asserted that,

> ...it is the bare fact of his [Luke] using a preface rather than in its details that Luke's relation to literature is apparent.[11]

Cadbury also argued that Luke's "prefaces and dedications at once suggest classification with the contemporary Hellenistic historians".[12] The use of prefaces was common in the Hellenistic era (but not earlier), for example, *Dionysius: Roman Antiquities*,[13] and *Polybius: Histories*.[14] Thus the presence of

---

[10] Scholars have tended to date the canonical Gospels after AD70, except perhaps Mark which is often dated to the mid-60s AD; for a critical review see J. A. T. Robinson, *Redating the New Testament* (London: SCM Press, 1976), who dates all the NT writings to before AD70. The most recent scholarship argues a date for Mark just twenty years or more after the death of Jesus— J. G. Crossley, *The Date of Mark's Gospel* (London: T & T Clark, 2004). For an introduction to the non-canonical Gospels see H. Klauck, *Apocryphal Gospels* (London: T & T Clark, 2003).

[11] H. J. Cadbury, *The Making of Luke-Acts* (London: SPCK, 1968), 196, 344.

[12] H. J. Cadbury, "The Greek and Jewish Traditions of Writing History" in *The Beginnings of Christianity: Part 1: The Acts of the Apostles: Vol. II: Prolegomena II: Criticism*, (eds., F. J. Foakes-Jackson & K. Lake; London: Macmillan, 1922), 15.

[13] Dionysius: *Roman Antiquities* (trans. E. Cary; Loeb Classical Library; Cambridge: Harvard Univ. Press, 1937), Bk I.1-8. All citations are from this edition.

[14] Polybius: *The Histories* (trans. W. R. Paton; Loeb Classical Library; London: Heinemann, 1925), Bk I.1-5.

a preface in Luke and a brief recapitulation[15] in Acts is taken to be evidence that Luke-Acts was meant as a species of a single genre — Hellenistic history writing. Classic and Hellenistic historians such as Herodotus, Thucydides and Polybius advocated an objective historiography, which is reflected in Luke.

This is important information for someone investigating the gospels for reliable historical information about Jesus; it is significant because one of the gospel writers has stated that an historical record was his intention, and that other historical accounts existed (which he may have used). Matthew and Mark are sufficiently like Luke to be placed within the same genre – something resembling a "biography"[16] of Jesus.

The priority of Mark gives it precedence in evaluating the gospels as historical accounts of Jesus' words and deeds; further, early church tradition records that it was written under the direction of Peter, an eyewitness and close disciple of Jesus.[17] Luke was a companion of Paul the apostle, while Matthew and John are held by early church tradition to be of the original disciples and therefore eyewitnesses.[18] Since Luke refers to many prior accounts about Jesus, we can surmise that Matthew and Mark were also aware of a variety of sources—other eyewitnesses, oral traditions,[19] as well as written accounts—all close in time to their subject

---

[15] The preface to Acts is not sharply delimited and a matter of scholarly dispute; we will take vv. 1-3 as the preface, with v. 4 beginning a new scene; vv.1-3 have a summarizing quality indicated by the time period of forty days.

[16] Scholars debate whether the Gospels are formally to be classified as "biographies"; see D. E. Aune, *The New Testament in its Literary Environment* (Philadelphia: The Westminster Press, 1987).

[17] The fourth century church historian, Eusebius, cites the testimony of Papias, an apostolic father (c. 115 AD) on the relationship of Mark and Peter in his *History of the Church*, 3.39.14-16 (ed. A. Louth; trans. G. A. Williamson; rev. ed.; London: Penguin Books, 1989).

[18] See D. Guthrie, *New Testament Introduction* (Leicester: Apollos, 1990), 43-53; 113-125; 269-275, who discusses Papias' mention of Matthew (*History of the Church*, 3.39) and another early church father, Irenaeus (c. 120-200 AD), who mentions the common view that John the disciple was the author of the Fourth Gospel.(*Adv. Haer.* Iii. 1).

[19] The transmission of oral traditions is indicated in Luke's prologue, incidental comments by Paul—1 Cor 15:1-3; 2 Thess 2:15, as well as the character of the first three Gospels themselves, which at times have a certain oral quality. For further reading see J. D. G. Dunn, *A New Perspective on Jesus* (London: SPCK, 2005), ch. 2.

matter, Jesus. This gives a reader confidence in the historical veracity of what s/he is reading in the first three gospels.

Criteria of Authenticity

It might be thought that Jesus' ordinary words and deeds cannot be proved to be authentic or inauthentic. How could anyone prove or disprove whether Jesus visited Bethany or caused a commotion in the temple? It is claimed that the ordinary everyday happenings in Jesus' life and the words that he spoke cannot be historically verified by any independent measure. This is trivially true, but irrelevant to the business of historical reconstruction. There are several criteria that can be used to authenticate the records:

1) First, we might ask whether the ordinary things that happened in Jesus' life were common for an itinerant preacher. Are his attributed words of their times? These two questions articulate criteria of assessment[20] for the authenticity of Jesus' ordinary words and deeds and they need to pass muster if we are to accept the gospel records as historically accurate. Thus, scholars assess whether Jesus' message is consistent with the Judaisms of his day. Generally speaking, even critical scholars judge that Jesus' words are of their times as a prophet who preached a message about the last days of the Jewish state and the need to repent and turn to God. Jesus' thought only makes sense within Judaism before AD 70; early church writers have not made changes to reflect their needs after the destruction of the Temple and the Jewish state.

2) In the same way, if Jesus' message is to be judged authentic, it needs to be consistent with early Christian writings – if Christian teaching in the letters, Acts or in Revelation was different from that of Jesus, we would have reason to question either the Christian teaching or the record of the words of Jesus. This issue is really about the degree of any difference and whether we can see a trajectory from Jesus' words and deeds to the preaching and teaching of the early church. Again, even critical scholars do not see anything that decisively casts doubt on Jesus' words and deeds when we apply this criterion.

These two criteria, (1)-(2), are about whether we can exclude any of Jesus' preaching as inauthentic, but they are not absolute rules. Jesus should be

---

[20] For a recent study of such criteria see S. E. Porter, *The Criteria for Authenticity in Historical-Jesus Research* (JSNTS 191; London: T & T Clark, 2000), 63-102.

of his times, but this does not mean that he cannot be original. The early followers of Jesus should be faithful to his message, but they themselves may have written about different things. The criteria are useful as ways to counter the critical rejection of Jesus' words as recorded in the gospels, but they do not license the inclusion of such words in a canon of authentic words.

It would be somewhat sceptical to hold the opposite point of view—to say that we can only accept as authentic those sayings that cannot be attributed to the gospel writers (the early church) or to the general cultural environment of the day. This would be to focus on the original to the detriment of what would be familiar to Jesus' contemporaries. Identifying the <u>dissimilar</u> may give us greater confidence that this is what Jesus said, but identifying what is <u>similar</u> should not suffer as a result.

We have four canonical gospels and three give <u>multiple attestations</u> to the same words and deeds of Jesus. This is important as corroborating evidence for the authenticity of the records when it is clear that the gospels are independent of each of other in their record of a particular episode. However, from another point of view, a literary relationship among the first three gospels is a validation by the writers of the material they are using; moreover, these writers are close in time to their subject matter. So, with Luke's and Matthew's use of Mark, we have a confirming use of Mark as a reliable early source for Jesus' words and deeds. The same point applies if we consider Matthew or Luke to have used each other's gospel or any other sources.[21] Furthermore, if we consider not just written sources but the forms in which traditions were passed on orally, we find that they are mutually supportive.

The choice of the four canonical gospels by the church of the second century would also be confirming evidence of their value as historical records provided we could show that the church used the gospels as an historical record about Jesus rather than as just the story of Jesus; the church could have chosen other gospels or more gospels. As such, <u>their canonical choice is a witness to the quality of the records</u> in terms of their teaching.[22]

---

[21] There is a large body of scholarship on the sources of the Gospels. When considering the historical veracity of the Gospels, the use of disparate early sources adds to their credibility; see Guthrie, *New Testament Introduction*, ch. 5.

[22] For an introduction to the formation of the canon, see A. G. Patzia, *The Making of the New Testament* (Downers Grove: InterVarsity Press, 1994).

One way that you can build up your picture of Jesus from the gospels is through acceptance of the basic facts about his words and deeds, followed by acceptance of what <u>coheres</u> with this basic story. Critical scholars accept that Jesus was crucified, but having accepted this, they are required to consider the causes that led to his execution. This throws up the question as to whether Jesus' conflict with the Jews and the authorities is coherent and plausible in the light of their lobbying for his death. The answer is that it is a coherent and likely cause of his crucifixion, and in this way, a historian would ascribe greater credence to the gospel accounts in this regard; another test of coherence would be to ask whether the story reflects the Palestinian environment or the legal framework in Jerusalem at the time—again, the gospel accounts pass this test.

Another criterion that can be used to validate some stories in the gospels stipulates that <u>unfavourable material will likely be genuine</u>—material that casts Jesus in an unfavourable light. This kind of material creates a tension with material that presents Jesus favourably. The inclusion of both kinds of material in the gospels is best accounted for if we infer that the intention of the gospel writers was objective and historical. For example, in the story of the healing of Jairus' daughter, the synagogue leader is portrayed in a favourable light, yet other stories place Jewish leaders in opposition to Jesus, and the Jewish authorities persecuted the early church. These considerations speak to the authenticity of the story of the healing of Jairus' daughter.

Another example of the inclusion of unfavourable material is the Beelzebub Controversy. The gospels record in different places the accusation that Jesus was able to perform miracles because he wielded the power of the devil; in addition, the story also recounts how his friends thought that Jesus was mad (Matt 12:24; Mark 3:21-30; Luke 11:15). It is significant that Jesus' opponents did not deny the miracles, but attributed them to the devil or, in the second century, to magic (Irenaeus, *Adv. Haer.* Ii.32.3-5). There is also recorded Jesus' failure to perform miracles albeit because of a lack of faith in his home village (Matt 13:58).

It is not possible here to consider each of the stories in the gospels and argue for their authenticity using criteria of assessment; some combination of criteria will be used in each case and conservative and critical scholars will offer different assessments that reflect their differing presuppositions. What is noteworthy in the debate is not that there are those who reject and those who accept the gospel records, but that there are so many different lines of argument to support a positive evaluation of the gospels.

Historical Difficulties

The difficulties that are had with the gospels' portrait of Jesus lie in the areas of putative factual inaccuracies; inconsistencies within and between the gospels; Jesus' nature miracles; his healings, and his resurrection. Otherwise, there are no decisive historical objections to the "ordinary" in the gospel accounts. Those who investigate the life of Jesus are more likely to disbelieve the "extra-ordinary" than the "ordinary", and therefore those happenings require separate comment.

Factual Inaccuracies
There are many characteristics of the gospels that indicate their accuracy; additionally, there are a small number of well-known so-called inaccuracies. Conservative scholars have written positive assessments of the nuts and bolts of the gospel records. Since the gospels are a social history of a charismatic teacher and his followers, any inaccuracies would be limited to the "public" side of Jesus' ministry—names, dates, places and the cultural environment. Thus, for example, we are able to verify Luke's political facts—the emperor Augustus, Herod the Great, Quirinius and Pilate, or Annas, Caiaphas and Ananias. Furthermore, we are able to verify Luke's reliability as a historian by examining his follow-up book, Acts.

Inaccuracies in historical texts are expected by the historico-critical method; there is no presumption that the gospel texts are divinely inspired in such a method and so historians will point out errors where there is other evidence that points to different facts of the matter. For example, the reference to a tax census of Quirinius when Jesus was born (commonly dated to sometime in 6-4 BC) has been dubbed an error because he is known to have become the legate of Syria in 6 AD and initiated a census in that year (Josephus, *Ant.* 18.1.1; cf. Tacitus, *Annals* 3.48).[23]

There are two preliminary points to make about this "error": first, it is representative of the type of error that could be identified in the gospel records, i.e. errors to do with the more public facts of names, dates and places—the possible errors in this regard are very few indeed; secondly, where there is a conflict between two different sources (Josephus and Luke), critical scholars will favour the non-biblical evidence and conservative scholars will favour the biblical evidence.

---

[23] This view is defended in the standard academic bible dictionary—D. S. Potter, "Quirinius" *ABD*, 5:588-589.

It is accepted by conservative scholars[24] that Quirinius was a legate of Syria in 6-7 AD and that there was a census then which caused unrest in Judea (a province of Syria), and which is referred to by Luke in Acts 5:37: "After him Judas the Galilean arose in the days of the census, and incited people to follow him in revolt. He too was killed, and all who followed him were scattered". Luke's use of the expression "the census" and his reference to Judas the Galilean establishes that he is referring to the census of 6-7 AD, against which Judas led a rebellion.

The census at the time of Jesus' birth is mentioned in this way:

> Now in those days a decree went out from Caesar Augustus to register all the empire for taxes. This was the first registration, taken when Quirinius was governor of Syria. Everyone went to his own town to be registered. (Luke 2:1-3;1 emphasis added)

In this narrative aside[25] Luke refers to a first census, or a former or earlier census than the one made in 6-7 AD. This is an important qualification as it coheres with Acts 5:37 which refers to the later and more famous census. Since there is no record of any more census enrolments happening after 6-7 AD in relation to Quirinius, we can deduce that the census of Luke 2:2 is not that of 6-7 AD but an earlier one. Because Josephus does not record two such census enrolments, critical scholars work with just one and infer that Luke makes a mistake with his placement of a first census at the end of the reign of Herod the Great.

However, an incidental detail of Luke's account makes it unlikely that he is making a simple mistake (after all, his chronology in Luke 3:1 is flawless). Mary and Joseph travel to Bethlehem of Judea to enrol for tax purposes. Just before the birth of Jesus, Herod was ruler of Judea and Galilee and a census initiated in his region could have been one that required travel to Judea for those born in the south. After Herod's death, the kingdom of Judea was divided and Galilee came under the jurisdiction of Antipas. In the census of 6-7 AD there is no particular reason why those residents in the north would have been required to travel south for enrolment. This makes the census of Luke 2:2 more likely to have been a different and earlier one than that of 6-7 AD.

---

[24] A representative treatment is that of W. Brindle, "The Census and Quirinius: Luke 2:2" *JETS* 27/1 (1984): 43-52.
[25] For a discussion of this narrative aside see S. M. Sheeley, *Narrative Asides in Luke-Acts* (JSNTSup 72; Sheffield: JSOT Press, 1992), 102-103.

Although no extant record other than Luke's requires the suggestion, some scholars have therefore proposed that Quirinius could have been a special military legate anytime between 6-4 BC in addition to the domestic governor of Syria at the time (who was Sentius Saturninius until 6 BC and thereafter Quintilius Varus between 6-4 BC[26]). It is known that Quirinius was conducting a long campaign from the north of Syria (and maybe Galatia) against the Homonadensus at this time and had been since about 10 BC. He could have assumed a temporary legateship in Syria during any interim period between the two documented governors.

Upon hearing of Jesus from the Wise Men, Herod sought to kill the children in Bethlehem up to two years of age, but Mary and Joseph had been warned to flee this danger. They fled to Egypt and only returned when Herod had died, which is dated to 4 BC. The inference therefore is that Jesus was born most likely in the years 6-5 BC, and that the census Luke mentions took place in one of these years.[27] A temporary military governorship on the part of Quirinius is not implausible. Herod's relationship with Augustus had broken down by the end of his reign and a direction from the military legate of Syria to conduct a census would have been heeded.

Our discussion of Luke's chronology is an example of the kind of discussion that conservative and critical scholars have about the reliability of the gospel records. It is a choice to allow Luke's evidence to stand in a reconstruction of Roman History, but it is because Luke shows himself to be reliable on other names and dates that it is best to do so in this case and conjecture a second interim legateship on the part of Quirinius. In the relatively few cases where the historical veracity of the gospels can be challenged with apparently contrary external evidence,[28] conservative scholarship has provided plausible harmonisations of the data.

---

[26] It is known from Josephus (*Ant.* 10, 9-10) that Quintilius Varus was legate until at least 4 BC and the death of Herod but not thereafter—when it is next known that Gaius Julius Caesar was the governor in 1 AD.

[27] Tertullian, *Adv. Marc.* 4.19, dates the census to the governorship of Sentius Saturninius.

[28] A. N. Sherwin-White, *Roman Law and Roman Society in the New Testament* (Oxford: Oxford University Press, 1963), 162-171 (162) observes that the presence of Quirinius' name has caused the most controversy in Luke's Roman History.

Inconsistencies

We have four canonical gospels and several non-canonical ones. As a matter of historical method, the main reason for preferring the canonical gospels lies in the second-century witness to their authorship among the apostles or their disciples—the dispute over which gospels were accurate and reliable took place in the church towards the close of the second century and the canon is their settlement of the question. The non-canonical gospels proliferated during the second century but were rejected as authoritative by the church.

Critical scholars point to inconsistencies between the gospel records and thereby cast doubt on the picture of Jesus in a given gospel. Historians are used to handling discrepancies between different accounts of the same person and his/her life. The problem raised by such putative inconsistencies was known as early as the second century and at the time, "harmonies" of the canonical gospels addressing the problem were produced.[29]

It is beyond the scope of a summary essay to discuss this area in detail. We will take two examples of "inconsistencies" in order to illustrate how conservative scholars support the historical veracity of the gospels.

1) The wording above the cross is given as, variously, "THIS IS JESUS THE KING OF THE JEWS" (Matt 27:37), "THE KING OF THE JEWS" (Mark 15:26), "THIS IS THE KING OF THE JEWS" (Luke 23:38), and "JESUS OF NAZARETH THE KING OF THE JEWS" (John 19:19). This different testimony could be described as an inconsistency between the records; on the other hand, the gospel writers could be selecting their words from "THIS IS JESUS OF NAZARETH THE KING OF THE JEWS" in order to convey the accusation. Whether we see an inconsistency is a matter of our attitude to the evidence. This example is typical insofar as a reader will find differences in the wording of what Jesus says in several places. Such differences are due to Jesus having spoken the same things on different occasions and/or the gospel writers recording *what* Jesus said rather than the actual words of Jesus.

2) A second example concerns sequencing events in Jesus' life. Luke opens his gospel narrative with Jesus' confrontation in Nazareth (Luke 4:16-30). This episode is placed in a different place in Matthew and Mark (Matt 13:53-58; Mark 6:1-6). Did the confrontation occur at the beginning

---

[29] See Tatian, *Diatessaron* (ed., S. Hemphill; London: Hodder & Stoughton, 1888).

201

of Jesus' ministry as in Luke, or later as in Matthew or Mark? We could see this as an inconsistency between the gospel records in terms of the sequence of events in Jesus' life, although the three witnesses testify to the historicity of the actual episode. However, equally, it is possible that Luke has moved the episode to the beginning of his gospel narrative to form a prologue of two episodes in Jesus' life: the temptation in the wilderness and the rejection of Jesus at Nazareth. The point of such a prologue would be to introduce the character of Jesus' ministry as Luke will go on to narrate. Alternatively, it could be that there are different episodes of conflict being recorded: Luke records a rejection at Nazareth while Matthew and Mark record a conflict "in his own country" (Matt 13:54; Mark 6:1). The conflict is similar because the same sort of questions and objections to Jesus will have occurred throughout the villages of Galilee.

These two examples, (1) and (2), illustrate the kind of discussion that critical and conservative scholars have about the consistency of the gospel records. Conservative scholars have produced harmonies of the gospels that show how they are consistent.

Legend and Myth
It is argued by rationalist historians that some stories in the gospels are legendary and overlaid with contemporary mythology. Of itself, this does not detract from the historicity of the gospels because the mythology is "of the times". Thus, some historians further embed the gospels in their first century milieu with this kind of argument. This is an important point of evaluation for the historicity of the gospels. The claim that a given story is legendary is a claim about historicity—the story is not a true account—and it is a claim about currency—the story is being told to enhance the reputation of the hero. Given the brief time that has elapsed between Jesus and the writing of the gospels, it is not certain that any stories can be properly regarded as "legend" on any cultural anthropological measure. The claim that stories reference mythological beings such as Satan or Beelzebub, however, is credible and it enhances the historicity of the accounts.

Miracles
One area where historians reject the gospel accounts as factual is that of the miracles.[30] In terms of historical plausibility, there are differences to note in the evaluation of miracles. Jesus' exorcisms and healing miracles are deemed more likely than the nature miracles, because Jesus'

---

[30] The classic expression of this view is that of D. Hume—see "On Miracles" in *Hume on Religion* (ed. R. Wollheim; London: Fontana, 1963), 205-229.

contemporaries viewed him as an exorcist and healer. Some scholars will offer rationalist explanations of the nature miracles, for example, it might be said that the account of Jesus walking on water has its basis in an optical illusion: Jesus was walking in shallow water and appeared to be walking on water and a historian might say that the story was embellished in its telling.

Rationalist explanations can be offered for each of the nature miracles in the gospels, but to do so is a philosophical choice; it reflects a philosophy of history in which such miracles are ruled out *a priori*. This is a form of naturalism that assumes natural law cannot be contravened, but such an assumption begs the question as to whether the God of Jesus exists and intervenes in the world. The Gospel writers would certainly have had such a view and therefore do not misrepresent their thought world with the accounts of Jesus' nature miracles. If you do not subscribe to the naturalist assumption, then you must remain open to the possibility that Jesus performed nature miracles.

Jesus' miracles are attributed to his possession of the Spirit of God (Matt 12:28; Luke 4:14) and they are therefore presented as acts of God through Jesus; they represent divine intervention in the natural order. As such, the gospel writers do not present miracles as happenings that contravene laws of nature; nor are they presented as inexplicable according to contemporary standards of knowledge; they are simply presented as the outcome of Jesus' actions. Depending on how you make the count, there are about thirty-forty miracles in the gospels, with the vast majority occurring in Mark, who is then used by Matthew and Luke. This is historically significant as Mark is the earliest gospel and his re-use by Matthew and Luke is a confirmation of his account by contemporaries.

It is a modern point of view to take the presence of miracle in an historical narrative to be something that detracts from the evidential value of that narrative for constructing a portrait of Jesus. The gospels would have had a more favourable reaction in their own day on this score; we know this because miracles appear in histories around at the time. For example, the classical historian, Herodotus (fifth century BC), accepted a role for the gods in human affairs as unseen forces in some events, and attributed natural events to the actions of the gods. For example, victory at sea with the enemy ships destroyed by a wind from Poseidon (*The Histories*, VII. 189-192); or again, victory over an enemy through a thunderstorm and a fall of rocks from Parnassus (History, IX. 64) - in both cases oracles predicted the victory.[31] Plutarch (50-120 AD) is another historian and man of letters who believed in the intervening activity of the gods in the affairs of men. With the examples of Herodotus and Plutarch in mind, we can see that first-century readers of the gospels would not have had the same difficulty in believing Jesus performed miracles as a modern person; we have already noted above that Josephus records that Jesus was a wonder-worker. In assessing the historicity of the account of a miracle, certain points support a positive appraisal of the evidence:

- Miracles are attested in different and early sources (Mark, John); the earliest source (Mark) is re-used by other gospels (Matthew, Luke).

- Within the gospels, miracles are described and referenced in sayings, parables and controversial stories, as well as straightforward narrative accounts. The variety of material shows that the gospel writers are incorporating the oral traditions of the first generation of Christians; two of the miracle stories contain obvious Aramaisms[32] that show the use of the original and early oral tradition (Mark 5:41; 7:34).

- Various characters in the gospels, sympathetic and hostile, acknowledge Jesus' miracles (Mark 6:2, 14; John 3:2).

- The accounts are not included for entertainment as in a novel;[33] the gospels have a serious purpose—a miracle is not incidental or *ad hoc* to the narrative. Luke's prologue states that he was careful to record Jesus' words and deeds.

- Miracle accounts have a teaching purpose; they are signs for those that can see their significance (Luke 11:29; John 20:30); they demonstrate the power of God associated with the coming kingdom (Luke 11:20).

---

[31] A. H. Macdonald, "Herodotus on the Miraculous" in *Miracles* (ed. C. F. D. Moule; London: Mowbray, 1965), 83-91; see Herodotus, *The Histories* (ed. A. R. Burn; trans. A. De Sélincourt; London: Penguin Classics, 1972).

[32] While the Gospels are in Greek, scholars have noticed evidence of the use of Aramaic—see M. Black, *An Aramaic Approach to the Gospels and Acts* (3rd. ed.; Oxford: Oxford University Press, 1967).

[33] This has been defended by R. I. Pervo, "The Ancient Novel becomes Christian" in *The Novel in the Ancient World* (ed., G. Schmeling; Leiden: E. J. Brill, 1996), 685-711.

- Miracles continued with the disciples and the early believers (Mark 16:17; Acts 2:43; 2 Cor 12:12).

- There are later "third-party" witnesses to Jesus' miracle-working, including, as we have noted above, Josephus, but also the Babylonian Talmud (*Sanh.* 43a)

These considerations encourage a reader to accept the accounts of miracles, but in the first instance a reader will consider whether the ordinary facts of Jesus' life as presented in the gospels are reliable.

Healing, Exorcism and Cosmic Mythology

Historians observe that Jesus' exorcisms are detailed using a contemporary mythology, viz., one that involves Satan and his demons. There are some distinctions to be observed with this proposal: Jesus mentions Satan and his demons in dialogue with others; he doesn't engage in any teaching on the subject; further, his remarks are very brief. We do not have sufficient basis for asserting that Jesus believed in demons. The case for such a belief is more likely for the disciples and the Galilean populace, and this reflects the history of the times. Whether the gospel writers believed in demons at the time of writing their accounts is not known.

The narrative accounts reflect the language of the day and are consistent with Jewish rather than Hellenistic thinking. The dimension that Jewish literature adds to Hellenistic ideas about demons is the nomination of a leading demon: the Devil and Satan. In Greek religion, demons might be the intermediaries of the gods, but no one particular "god" is signalled out as a leader of demons.[34] So, for example, in the Jewish work *Jubilees* (c. 161-149 BC), Mastema or Satan is given a recurring adversarial role in Israelite history.[35] [36] This is confirmatory evidence for the accuracy of the gospels account of Jesus' exorcisms.

There are other aspects of Jesus' exorcisms that cohere with his times. In *Ant.* 8.46-48, Josephus describes an exorcism that bears comparison with Jesus' practice. In Josephus' example, Solomon's name is invoked and a ring with a root attached is placed into the nostrils of the demoniac. The

---

[34] W. Burkert, *Greek Religion* (Oxford: Basil Blackwell, 1985), 179-181, 329-332.

[35] See *Jubilees* 11:15, 17:15-18:13, 23:29, 46:1-2, 48:2, 12, and 50:5.

[36] See further A. Perry, *Demons and Politics* (2nd ed.; Sunderland: Willow Publications, 2010).

demon is adjured to depart, and the exorcism is then demonstrated by the disturbing of a basin of water. Jesus' exorcisms likewise involved adjuring demons, and in the case of the Gaderene demoniac, the exorcism was demonstrated by an external sign—pigs went down a hill (Mark 5:13); Josephus' exorcist commands the demon to enter no more into its victim, and this is what Jesus does with an epileptic boy (Mark 9:14).

Another example that bears comparison with Jesus' exorcisms is in the fragment 4Q560 from the Dead Sea Scrolls, which contains a Jewish incantation against various demons associated with various ailments. The text mentions a fever-demon and this can be compared with Jesus' healing of Peter's mother-in-law, as Jesus likewise adjured and rebuked this fever (Mark 1:30: cf. Luke 4:39). Other examples of similarity could be given, but these are enough to illustrate that the gospel records are "of their times" in their account of Jesus' exorcisms. There are therefore no grounds for doubting their historicity on the basis of their use of a cosmic mythology.

J. Robinson comments on Mark that, "the exorcisms, rather than being the nearest point of approach to history in a myth, are the points in a historical narrative where the transcendent meaning of that history is most clearly evident".[37] Robinson is referring to the cosmic aspect of the exorcisms in which Jesus is portrayed as in conflict with Satan or the demons under his command. This aspect is transcendent in the sense that Jesus is not just healing a possessed man, but the possession is symptomatic of a struggle between God and Satan over Israel, and Jesus, as representative of God, is confronting the enemy. The Beelzebub controversy interprets the exorcisms in this light. Robinson's argument is that apart from the interpretative context of the Beelzebub Controversy, the exorcisms would resemble other exorcism stories from the Ancient World, but "in the Markan presentation they depict a cosmic struggle in history to inaugurate the eschatological reign of God".[38]

Resurrection
The next chapter will consider the resurrection in detail; here it is only necessary to make three brief remarks. The resurrection is an act of God in history; it is something that was done for Jesus—it is not part of his

---

[37] J. Robinson, *The Problem of History in Mark* (London: SCM Press, 1957), 33. This cosmic conflict is also seen by some scholars in Pauline Christianity, e.g. in Eph 6:12, Col 1:16, 2:16.
[38] Robinson, *Problem of History*, 38.

life. The issue for a questioning reader is whether the God of the Jews exists and acts in history, and the only way to answer this question in respect of the resurrection is to look at the <u>after-effects of Jesus' death</u> to determine how they are best explained.

1) The main after-effect is the existence of the Christian church; we could account for this phenomenon in terms of ordinary factors such as the ethical and social teaching of the first Christian preachers and leaders, or we might explain it in terms of their message of religious hope. So, for example, the early Christians gave greater freedoms to women in the church than other Jewish sects, and this would explain the attraction of the church to women; or again, Christians promoted a view of the church as the focus of worship in contradistinction to the temple in Jerusalem—there was then a ready understanding that could handle the dissolution of the Jewish state. However, such explanations of the growth of the church do not necessarily explain the <u>conviction</u> of the early believers, a conviction that would lead many through persecution. The point here is that the witness of the church to the resurrection was not relinquished in the face of persecution.

2) The resurrection of Jesus is not the most obvious teaching for a Jewish sect to promote. The doctrine of the general resurrection of the dead was common enough in Judaism, but the gospel accounts do not end with the vindication of Jesus in terms of his participation in that resurrection. He is not presented as a prophet who will be raised from the dead in "the last days". This would have been a natural end to the gospels, one that would have fitted the Jewish world-view, but instead the gospels end with an individual resurrection. This is an uncommon choice but would be explained if it was in fact what actually happened.[39]

3) The gospel stories do not make the strongest case for the resurrection in terms of the witnesses. Women had no legal status as witnesses, yet they are the ones who first see Jesus raised from the dead. Further, the response of the disciples is one of doubt in respect of the testimony of the women. If the stories in the gospels are a true reflection of events, these details are explained on that basis, but if the stories were self-serving in any way, then one would have expected them to be more robust.

---

[39] In fact, the resurrection might have been problematic to Jesus' followers as it interrupted what they had anticipated as the coming Kingdom of God.

These points, (1)-(3), are about the best historical explanation for the church and its story: is it true, or is the resurrection something that is capable of being explained away?

The Jesus of History and the Christ of Faith

This essay is not concerned with describing the Jesus of history; there have been many portraits. The task is valuable and necessary and, of course, it would take a book to do the subject matter any justice. We will conclude our remarks with a consideration of the relationship between faith and history.

It might be supposed that the job of the historian is to uncover the facts and strip away any faith-tradition or later interpretation of the facts. It might be said that the Gospel writers have included their faith in the narrative and that it is the job of the historian to strip out this layer of faith. This is a common view and scholars routinely separate that layer in the text that they attribute to the author or an editor and which reflects a later point of view; the method of analysis they employ is known as Redaction Criticism. However, the existence in the gospels of the author's point of view is not inimical to the portrayal of the Jesus of History; rather, it is part of the history of the times that such points of view are included in a contemporary history. It is a cliché to observe that history writing involves perspective and interpretation; Jesus comes to the modern reader in a package. We may doubt the package, but it is substantially of its day.

We might ask: to what extent does historical investigation have a role to play in engendering Christian faith in a believer today? The question concerns the relationship between history and faith. Some would argue that history has no relevance and argue that faith consists of a belief in a **story** regardless of any historical veracity. Many have rejected this view on the grounds that the Christian faith has at its centre the belief that God has intervened in history in the person of Jesus of Nazareth. If he has so intervened, Christianity cannot disassociate itself from historical commitments and it is therefore vulnerable to any doubts put forward by historians. We cannot avoid engaging with such doubts and presenting the positive historical case for belief in Jesus. History has value for Christianity. It offers a basis for preaching the faith—a preacher can lay claim to facts; such facts also form a basis for doctrine—they prevent doctrine from distorting the faith. This is our position but there is an important qualification. The apostle Paul declared that "So faith *comes*

208

from hearing, and hearing by the word of Christ" (Rom 10:17, NASB). We can equally say that faith comes by reading the Word. An historical inquiry, of itself, cannot engender faith; only reading and/or hearing the Word will engender a Christian faith.

Older (mainly German) critical scholarship on the question of the historical Jesus has largely been fruitless because it was founded on faulty Enlightenment philosophical assumptions. It presumed that the task of scholarship was to extract the Jesus of History from the Christ of Faith—that the early church had infused traditions about Jesus with their faith perspective. The dichotomy is false; it presumes that traditions were not preserved with regard to their historical veracity. Instead, Luke's method makes it plain that such veracity was fundamental to the existence of the written gospel(s). Furthermore, in the description and recording of Jesus' words and deeds, the perspective of faith is itself part of accurate historical writing and not a dispensable overlay. Faith is an understanding of the words and deeds and a way of seeing what actually happened. If we exclude a faith perspective we do not thereby gain a neutral description of what was said and done, we obtain another competing way of understanding. However, that faith is the *correct perspective* with which to describe Jesus' words and deeds is shown by the fact that they were directed to engendering faith.[40] If you try and represent a Jesus without the apparatus of faith in a modern "Life of Jesus", you falsify the intention of his words and deeds.

The faith with which the gospel writers record Jesus' words and deeds is however not the same as that which the Christian church developed in subsequent centuries. The average person starting out on a consideration of Jesus and the Christian faith might assume that the Christian churches today preach the faith of the first-century church. In many aspects this is demonstrably false, and it was an advance of older critical scholarship to strip away the anachronistic superimposition of the later Christian faith upon the gospels. In rendering this service, they went too far, because they also took away the notion that the faith of the gospel writers was a valid historical perspective with which to present the words and deeds of Jesus.

A reader coming to the gospels for the first time will want to know if they are historically reliable. Our answer is that they are and that in order to establish this you should read conservative scholarship, preferring the reasoning therein over and above that of critical scholars. While scholars

---

[40] Dunn, *A New Perspective on Jesus*, ch. 1.

of all persuasions have insights to offer, the historiographical approach of conservative scholarship is sounder and should be preferred where you come across scholarly conflict.

Summary

- Previous "quests" by critical scholars to discover the historical Jesus have recently given way to a more positive analysis of the gospel records.
- There is broad consensus on the existence of Jesus and the core of the gospel records.
- The gospels can be shown to be early and based on eye-witness testimony.
- Alleged inaccuracies and inconsistencies can be explained and should be balanced against the general reliability exhibited by the gospels.
- Having established the reliability of the "ordinary" elements of the gospel records, we can test the "extraordinary" elements in a balanced way.

Further Reading

For more on the historical reliability of the gospels see *Jesus and the Eyewitnesses: The Gospels as Eyewitness Testimony* by Richard Bauckham.

The Resurrection of Jesus

Simon Dean

"Jewish revolutionaries whose leader had been executed ... had two options: give up the revolution, or find another leader. Claiming that the original leader was alive again was simply not an option. Unless, of course, he was." – N. T. Wright[1]

The Importance of the Resurrection

The resurrection of the Lord Jesus Christ from the dead lies at the heart of God's dealings with this world and transformed the course of history. It changed men of fear into men of faith; it changes everything for believers today. The apostle Paul tells the young church in Corinth that the Gospel, the good news for the world, is that Jesus died, was buried, and rose again - and that death is defeated by the resurrection. The curious Athenians are confronted by the apostle's challenge that there is only one true God and that the resurrection was God's stamp of approval on the life of His Son Jesus who will judge the world. In his first letter, Peter announces that the resurrection makes possible renewed life for the believer now: "[God] gave us new birth into a living hope through the resurrection of Jesus Christ from the dead" (1 Pet 1:3). The link between Christ's resurrection, our belief and our salvation could not be set out more clearly by the apostle Paul – a man most dramatically affected by his encounter with the risen Jesus on the road to Damascus: "if you confess with your mouth that Jesus is Lord and believe in your heart that God raised him from the dead, you will be saved" (Rom 10:9). The hope of the resurrection, mentioned over one hundred times in the New Testament, "has been the comfort of the children of God since the earliest days. It is the hope. It is the only hope."[2]

---

[1] N. T. Wright, *Who Was Jesus?* (Eerdmans, 1993), 63.
[2] H. Tennant, *The Christadelphians: What They Believe and Preach* (Birmingham: CMPA, 1986).

If believing the resurrection is the basis of our salvation, we want to be convinced that its historical foundations are sure and that there are sound reasons for believing that it actually took place. Without the resurrection there is no Gospel, no good news for a world in despair. Paul said, "if Christ has not been raised, your faith is useless; you are still in your sins" (1 Cor 15:17).

First we need to clear the ground and set out what we should understand by the resurrection. The eyewitness disciples were adamant that the resurrection of Christ was an event that actually happened and was not just in their minds. Their testimony was that they saw the risen Jesus, spoke with him and touched him. Indeed, Jesus appealed to his followers to handle his body, calling attention to his wounds and scars so that they would know for sure that it was real and not a disembodied spirit (Luke 24:39). His encounter with the disciples by the Sea of Tiberias is not suggestive of a visionary experience but has all the physical ordinariness of a real event. There are fishermen's nets, a charcoal fire, Peter standing sodden after his strenuous night's work - and Jesus offering bread and fish for breakfast (John 21:1-14). Luke concludes that Jesus' appearances gave his disciples demonstrable "proofs" (Acts 1:3); inescapable empirical evidences that he had been raised from the dead. But it was more than just a resuscitated Jesus. Lazarus experienced a temporary renewal of life and yet it was not permanent. The New Testament writers explain that a transformation had taken place in Jesus' nature following his resurrection. He was the same person in his risen state as he was before he died - yet totally different. The apostle Paul tells us that the raised Jesus had a "spiritual body" that was imperishable and supernatural. He was no longer subject to natural laws; he could appear and disappear at will. He was never going to die again as "death no longer has mastery over him" (Rom 6:9). He has become the prototype for all who share in the hope of rising to eternal life at the last day.

Assessing the Evidence

In this chapter we will look at the formidable range of evidence that shows that the best explanation for what took place on resurrection morning nearly 2,000 years ago was that Jesus was raised by 'the glory of the Father' to eternal life. How should we go about assessing that evidence? We cannot categorically prove the resurrection took place – there are no photographs or other contemporary recordings available for us to study. But this should not overly concern us – it is common not to be able to prove a lot of things one hundred percent. What we do all the time is review the facts available and then decide which scenario best fits the data. Some kinds of evidence will prove more persuasive than others and we need to ensure we give priority to that which should carry more weight. Here are some principles to assist in appraising the evidence.

Principle 1:   The existence of a number of independent sources for an event provides stronger evidence than a single witness.

Principle 2:   The shorter the time between the event and the testimony, the more reliable the witness, as there is less time for exaggeration or legendary additions.

Principle 3:   Eyewitness testimony should be allowed more weight than second or third hand accounts.

Principle 4:   The confirmation of facts by a source that is neutral or unsympathetic, who will not profit from the account, serves as a mark of authenticity; a friendly witness is more likely to be biased.

Principle 5:   If a witness reports an event that causes him embarrassment or weakens his position when arguing with opponents, the event is more likely to be true.[3]

Those defending a belief in the literal resurrection use these principles, but they are "borrowed from the approach to ancient texts regularly employed by secular historians" and we will refer to them when evaluating the data.[4]

The Gospels: Early Testimony from Eyewitnesses

The Gospels are unanimous in claiming that the followers of Jesus began proclaiming right away that he had been raised from the dead. The four different accounts of Jesus' life and ministry are generally agreed to have been written in the first century by eyewitnesses or those who knew them. There is debate about precisely when they were first composed, but there is good reason to date Luke to about A.D. 61-62 and, assuming Mark was the first Gospel, this would date his Gospel to the late 50s. Historians estimate that it takes at least two generations for false legends to develop, as it takes that long for those witnesses who might contradict the story to

---

[3] G. R. Habermas & M. R. Licona, *The Case for the Resurrection* (Kregel, 2004), 36-40.

[4] See *Recent Perspectives on the Reliability of the Gospels* (Online at: www.garyhabermas.com [cited May 2011]).

die.[5] In the case of the resurrection accounts, there is just too short a timeframe for a legend to develop before the Gospels are composed [Principle 2]. In addition, not only were the Gospels early, but also they are based on eyewitness testimony. In Luke 1:2-3, the Gospel writer tells us that he has information handed down from reliable eyewitnesses and that he has carefully investigated the information from these eyewitness accounts so that he is in a position, as an inspired narrator, to write an orderly account [Principle 3].

The resurrection narratives in the Gospels have notable features that point to them being authentic and early. Firstly there is the surprising lack of references to the Old Testament. If the Gospel accounts had been fabricated much later by writers who wanted to invent eyewitness resurrection narratives from scratch, it is most likely that they would have woven in quotations of fulfilled OT prophecies - proof texts to help them make their case. In the ministry and crucifixion sections of the Gospels, the writers reference the Hebrew Scriptures to show how Jesus' life is fulfilling God's plan, but these 'so-it-was-fulfilled' statements largely disappear when we get to the resurrection narratives. A reasonable explanation for this absence of quotation is that, under inspiration, the Gospel writers have incorporated very early, raw first-hand accounts of those who were not expecting Jesus to be raised and, like the disciples on the road to Emmaus, were "slow of heart to believe" both Jesus' predictions and OT pointers to his resurrection. This remarkable silence is in stark contrast to the situation a short time later when Peter who, having had the benefit of Jesus' teaching after the resurrection and the insight gained from the Holy Spirit, declares at Pentecost that David "foreseeing this spoke about the resurrection of the Christ" (Acts 2:31). Additionally, the resurrection narratives never mention the hope of a future resurrection for the believer, whereas the rest of the N T repeatedly sets out the link between Jesus' resurrection and the expectation that his followers will one day be raised (see e.g.1 Cor 15:20). If the resurrection narratives were put together much later, we would undoubtedly have seen this note of a future hope written into the narrative. In summary, the resurrection narratives neither explicitly look back to the OT nor forward to the resurrection at Jesus' return, which suggests that they have precisely the simple, matter of fact qualities we would expect of eyewitness material of the kind Luke refers to at the beginning of his Gospel.[6]

---

[5] A. N. Sherwin-White, *Roman Society and Roman Law in the New Testament* (1963), 189-190.

[6] For further details see N. T. Wright, *The Resurrection of the Son of God* (SPCK, 2003), 599-604.

The resurrection accounts are also free from sensational elements. They describe a series of extraordinary events in an ordinary, blunt style with no overwrought emotionalism or unnecessary colour. We can contrast these plain retellings of the story with the apocryphal resurrection account of the so-called Gospel of Peter, written in the second century. In this faked Gospel, a voice rings out from heaven during the night, the heads of the angels stretch beyond the clouds and Jesus' cross emerges from the tomb speaking.

A News Flash from the Resurrection: 1 Corinthians 15

Some of the letters of Paul are believed to predate the Gospels. Furthermore, it has been argued that his letters contain oral traditions (in the form of early statements of belief, songs, or sayings) that are older than the letter in which they are recorded. Paul makes it clear that his Gospel is not constructed from man's words but is from God (see Gal 1:12). But we know that Paul, in his first letter to Timothy, includes and therefore approves "faithful sayings" then in circulation.[7] Similarly it has been argued that the apostle's important testimony about the appearances of Jesus in 1 Cor 15:3-5 incorporates a statement of belief of the early church which is likewise fully compatible with the Gospel revealed to Paul from heaven and receives the endorsement of inspiration.

> For I passed on to you as of first importance what I also received:
>
> > that Christ died for our sins according to the scriptures,
> > and that he was buried,
> > and that he was raised on the third day according to the scriptures,
> > and that he appeared to Cephas, then to the twelve

The evidence is technical and fascinating - the broad outlines are as follows. Paul uses the language the rabbis used when formally passing on a body of accepted teaching in oral form: "received" and "delivered". Verses 3-5 have a repeating four-line rather stylized formula – "and that" is repeated. Peter is referred to by his Hebrew/Aramaic name *Cephas* – suggestive of an early Judean origin. This has convinced virtually all scholars that Paul is quoting what is already in use in the early ecclesia,

---

[7] See A. H. Nicholls, *Letters to Timothy and Titus* (Birmingham; CMPA, 1991), 49.

and may go back to Paul's fact-finding[8] visit to Jerusalem. This was around AD 36, when he spent two weeks with Cephas and James (Gal 1:18), who are interestingly both separately mentioned in the list of appearances (1 Cor 15:4, 7). Why is this piece of analysis so important? It shows that between three and five years following Jesus' death there was a fixed way of talking about the Gospel amongst believers and at the heart of it is the fact of Jesus' resurrection. Based on this one text alone few today would dare suggest that the idea of the resurrection grew up slowly over time [Principle 2]. Even sceptical scholars cannot deny that what Paul refers to is extremely early. The atheist scholar Gerd Ludemann writes: "the elements in the tradition are to be dated to the first two years after the crucifixion . . . no later than three years after the death of Jesus."[9] This section of Paul's writing has been described as a "news flash" from the resurrection, the "kind of evidence a historian drools over", and demonstrates powerfully that the belief in the resurrection did not emerge over time but was at the centre of the Gospel from the outset.

What lay behind these early and widespread claims? The actual resurrection of Jesus, in the sense of his exit from the tomb, is not narrated in the NT. The teaching that he did rise from the dead was a conclusion drawn from two simple facts: (i) the tomb was empty and (ii) Jesus appeared in a transformed body to numerous individuals and groups.

Empty Tomb

The founding of the church in Jerusalem, the same city where Jesus was publicly killed and buried requires as a minimum an empty tomb. If the tomb still contained the body, no one would have believed the disciples' story of the resurrection. When Peter claimed that Jesus had risen, the authorities could have produced the body and stopped the new movement in its tracks. The Jewish religious leaders did in fact agree the tomb was empty, claiming that the disciples stole the body (Matt 28:13). As the Jewish leaders are an unsupportive and unsympathetic source, they provide high quality evidence that there was no body to be produced and the tomb was empty [Principle 4].

---

[8] Paul's describes his visit with Peter and James by the participle ιστορησαι (Gal 1:18-19), which literally means "to visit and get information".
[9] G. Ludemann, *Resurrection of Jesus: History, Experience, Theology* (Fortress Press, 1995), 38.

The fact that women, and not the male disciples, are listed as the first witnesses of the empty tomb lends powerful credibility to the accounts. Women were of such low status in first-century Jewish society that their testimony in court was considered worthless. The contemporary historian Josephus, expressing a view widely held, wrote: "But let not the testimony of women be admitted, on account of the levity and boldness of their sex."[10] Given this low view of women, it seems improbable that the Gospel authors would invent testimonies, place them in the mouths of those who would not be believed by many, and then make them the first witnesses to the empty tomb. If the Gospel writers had invented the story about the empty tomb, they would most likely have depicted men making the discovery – Joseph of Arimathea, Nicodemus or even the disciples. But the male disciples, future leaders of the young church, are hiding and afraid. The Gospel writers faithfully recorded what happened, even though it was embarrassing to their cause and potentially weakened their case [Principle 5]. Michael Grant concludes, "The historian cannot justifiably deny the empty tomb... if we apply the same sort of criteria that we would apply to any other ancient sources, then the evidence is firm and plausible enough to necessitate the conclusion that the tomb was indeed found empty."[11]

The Appearances

The empty tomb alone did not produce a belief in the resurrected Jesus.[12] For most it was Jesus physically appearing to them that led them to conclude that Jesus had been raised. Even though there is seeming interdependence between many of the pre-resurrection Gospel narratives, the post-resurrection appearance accounts are independent of one another [Principle 1]. This independence gives rise to the problem of surface contradictions that we will address later. The evidence from five independent historical sources (Gospels and Paul's letters) indicates that on more than ten separate occasions, various individuals and groups in differing locations and circumstances saw Jesus alive after his death. The four Gospels tell us about appearances to:

1. Mary Magdalene (John 20:11-17)
2. The women returning from the tomb (Matt 28:9-10)
3. The two disciples on the road to Emmaus (Luke 24:13-35)

---

[10] Josephus, *Antiquities* 4.8.15.
[11] M. Grant, *Jesus: An Historian's Review of the Gospels* (Collier, 1992), 176.
[12] With the exception perhaps of John (John 20:8).

4. Peter (Luke 24:34; cf. 1 Cor 15:5)
5. The disciples with Thomas absent (Luke 24:33, 36-43; John 20:19-23; cf. 1 Cor 15:5)
6. The disciples with Thomas present a week later (John 20:26-29)
7. The seven disciples at the Lake of Tiberius in Galilee (John 21:1-22)
8. The eleven disciples and others on a mountain in Galilee (Matt 28:16-20)
9. The disciples at the ascension (Luke 24:50-52; Acts 1:3-11; cf. 1 Cor 15:7)

Paul, besides repeating the appearances to Peter, the twelve and to all the apostles (probably the larger group of followers on the mountain in Galilee), also mentions appearances to James, himself, and to over 500 people at one time (1 Cor 15:5-8). This is an impressive list of witnesses. Jesus was seen not once, but many times; not by one person, but by several; not only by individuals, but also by groups; not at one location, but at many; not by believers only, but by sceptics and unbelievers as well. Paul's reference to the 500 is especially powerful. He was not naïve and knew that the resurrection would be doubted and challenged. He would have been very wary of making a claim that there were still three or four hundred people alive who claimed to have seen Jesus if he was not sure of his facts. His meaning is clear: "If you don't believe me, there are plenty of people who can confirm this statement. Go and ask them."[13]

Transformation

Following his arrest, Jesus' followers denied him and took flight. His crucifixion left them stunned, leaderless and in despair. The account of Peter's denial is particularly embarrassing for him (although paradoxically has the ring of truth as no one would write such an unflattering story about the future leader of a movement if it were not true [Principle 5]). But after the resurrection, Peter and the other disciples were utterly changed. Peter risks his life at Pentecost by boldly telling those in Jerusalem that he had seen Jesus alive from the dead. Men who had been afraid to identify with Jesus are changed into bold proclaimers of his death and resurrection. The NT is explicit about the fact that it was Jesus' resurrection appearances that were the catalyst that changed them. They claimed that "God has raised this Jesus to life and we are all witnesses of

---

[13] N. Anderson, *The Fact of Christ* (InterVarsity Press, 1979), 5.

218

the fact" (Acts 2:32). The disciples willingly faced persecution precisely because they were absolutely convinced that they had seen the risen Jesus. Paul summarises the new position in which they now found themselves: they had seen Jesus (1 Cor 15:1-11), and this is what confirmed their eternal life, for if Jesus was raised, so they would be raised (vv 17-20) - death had no more sting for them (vv 53-55). Peter similarly declared that because Jesus' resurrection secured a "living hope", the serious struggles of life could be faced with rejoicing (1 Pet 1:3-7). The disciples had an experience based on evidence that no one else ever has, before or since. Something tremendous must have happened to change these men's lives. Without the resurrection, we have no other reasonable explanation for this change. Pinchas Lapide, an orthodox Jew and not a Christian, summarises the power of this testimony: "When this frightened band of apostles suddenly could be changed overnight into a confident mission society... Then no vision or hallucination is sufficient to explain such a revolutionary transformation." Although Lapide remained an Orthodox Jewish rabbi, he conceded that the evidence showed that Jesus must have risen from the dead.[14]

The Testimony of Opponents - James and Paul

And it was not just followers, but sceptics and enemies who were transformed by seeing the risen Christ. Saul of Tarsus hated the Christian "heresy" even to the point of killing in order to stop it. But his encounter with the risen Jesus changed Saul, the number one persecutor, into Paul, the number one proponent of Christianity. His conversion was no half-hearted affair. He gave up the prestige and comforts of being a respected rabbi and took on the life of a travelling missionary who experienced terrible suffering.[15] Something incredible, something as momentous as the appearance of the living Jesus must have happened to change him.

James, and Jesus' other brothers, did not believe in Jesus during his lifetime. But later James not only believed but became the leader of the Jerusalem Christian movement and may have died a martyr's death. The strong unbelief of James prior to the crucifixion (Mark 3:20-21; John 7:5) would have been an embarrassment for a leader in the early church. "Not even his own brother believed him", the critics would have taunted [Principle 5]. These are strong indications that the accounts of James' opposition and then sudden transformation are authentic, and it is surely

---

[14] P. Lapide, *The Resurrection of Jesus: A Jewish Perspective* (Fortress Press, 1988), 125.
[15] See e.g. 2 Cor 11:23-33.

219

the appearance of the risen Lord to James (1 Cor 15:7) that accounts for this remarkable change.

This absolute conviction that Jesus was alive began the chain reaction of Gospel proclamation that transformed the Roman Empire. If the resurrection were not true, the early preaching would have lost its early momentum. But despite great persecution, the church increased. So great was the drive and power of this new movement that in a few years after the resurrection, its opponents were claiming that the preaching of the risen Jesus was turning the world upside down (see Acts 17:6). The existence of Christianity from such unpromising beginnings requires the miracle of the resurrection.

Naturalistic Explanations

Excellent evidence exists to demonstrate that Jesus was miraculously raised from the dead, and this explanation fits all the historical facts without distorting them. However, from the very beginning, natural explanations have been put forward to counter the claim of a supernatural resurrection. We will see that these theories do not provide a satisfactory explanation for all the facts; they only attempt to explain one small portion and require other speculations to account for the rest.

Legend theory. This states that as the teaching of Jesus spread, the accounts of his life and death changed – miraculous stories were added and then the miracle of his resurrection was developed before they were written in the letters and the Gospels. The problem with this theory is that the resurrection account can be traced back to the experiences of the early disciples and the separate and independent experiences of Paul and James.

Stolen body theory. It is argued that the body was stolen from the tomb by the disciples or removed by others such as the Jewish authorities. This theory can withstand little scrutiny. To steal the body, the disciples would have had to overcome the Roman guard and then defend what they knew to be a lie in the face of persecution and the threat of death. This would make them frauds and deceivers, quite inconsistent with the ethics of the teachings of Jesus and their own writings. The Jewish religious leaders had little motive to remove the body. Even had they done so, they would have been able to produce it and confound the disciples' claims of resurrection. In addition, this theory does not address the fact that the disciples, Paul and James, believed that they had seen the risen Lord.

Swoon (or Apparent Death) theory. Although largely discredited today, this theory was once popular amongst sceptics. It proposes that Jesus only came close to death and revived in the coolness of the tomb. He somehow managed to exit the tomb, in spite of the large stone, and convince his disciples of a falsehood – that he had risen from the dead. We know much more about the nature of scourging and crucifixion than those who first proposed this idea. Scourging often killed the victim before crucifixion could take place. The piercing of the nails and a spear in the side would undoubtedly have proved fatal. A study published in the Journal of the American Medical Association concluded that Jesus' death resulted "primarily from hypovolemic shock and exhaustion asphyxia", and that "modern medical interpretation of the historical evidence indicates that Jesus was dead when taken down from the cross."[16]

Psychological theories. These theories suggest that the disciples experienced hallucinations or delusions, or that their resurrection experiences were the result of wish fulfilment. Hallucinations are private experiences, whereas the evidence in the NT is that groups of people claimed to have seen Jesus. Furthermore, the disciples' despair indicates that they were not in the proper frame of mind to see hallucinations, and they certainly did not expect Jesus to rise from the dead (John 20:9). Indeed the reverse is the case; the resurrection caught the disciples by surprise, and each appearance is unexpected and leaves them incredulous. The facts show that it was not the disciples who convinced themselves that Jesus was alive - Jesus had to convince them. Perhaps the most serious problem is that there were far too many different times, places and personalities involved in the appearances for a separate hallucination on each occasion. As with other theories, for this view to be correct, Jesus' body should still have been located in the tomb. Finally, there remain the two significant problems of the conversions of both Paul and James, neither of whom had a desire to see Jesus.

Other theories have come and gone – one claims that Jesus faked his death and that the resurrection was a hoax. There is even a twin brother theory! Some were once popular; now they are widely dismissed as fanciful. Although many books have been written to promote them, they have failed to convince, largely because they lack explanatory scope and power – they do not adequately account for all the data, or they force data to fit their hypothesis. Each one fails at key points: the stolen body theory fails to account for the fact that very early after the resurrection

---

[16] W. D. Edwards, W. J. Gabel & F. E. Hosmer, "On the Physical Death of Jesus Christ", *Journal of the American Medical Association* 255 (1986): 1455-1463.

individuals and groups claimed they'd had experiences of the risen Lord; the apparent death theory flies in the face of the evidence, attested to by dispassionate medical analysis, that Jesus clearly died from torture, crucifixion and the spear thrust; and all the psychological theories (e.g. mass hallucination) fail because the body would have been produced to disprove the claims. When we consider carefully what we do know historically about Jesus' resurrection, there are simply no opposing theories that can account for the facts. Faced with the impossible challenge of producing a viable alternative account to the resurrection, some sceptics find it easier to shift the argument and claim that Jesus never existed - but such a move avoids the issue, and only a minority of non-believing scholars hold this extreme position.

Contradictions

Some claim that there are discrepancies or contradictions in the resurrection narratives that call into question whether the accounts are factual at all.[17] However, the reality is that there is a consistent core account which is the same in all the Gospels: Jesus' body is placed in the tomb by Joseph of Arimathea; a small group of women disciples visit the tomb early Sunday morning and they discover that the tomb is empty. They encounter angels, who tell them that Jesus is alive. The apparent discrepancies are minor in the secondary detail and can be reconciled.[18] For example, the Gospels mention one (John 20:1), two (Matt 28:1) and three (Mark16:1) women visiting the tomb. But just as the Gospels do not set out to provide exhaustive accounts of Jesus' life, it is clear that the accounts do not pretend to give a complete list of the women. They all include Mary Magdalene and other women, so it would appear there was a group of disciples including those named, as well as others. Furthermore, the lists cannot be described as contradictory: no one list excludes any other, and none of the accounts speak of these being the only women to travel to the tomb. Quite why the lists differ we cannot be sure. It may be that the readers of Mark in some way know Salome, only mentioned in the second Gospel, whereas Matthew's readers had no knowledge of her. What time did the women visit the tomb? The times are variously described by the Gospel writers: "as it began to dawn," "very early in the

---

[17] Dan Barker's Easter Challenge (Online: http://bit.ly/h6sQYx [cited: May 2011]) provides a representative example and a sample of his objections are addressed in this paragraph.

[18] See for example J. Wenham, *Easter Enigma: Are the Resurrection Accounts in Conflict?* (Zondervan, 1984) and A. D. Norris, *The Gospel of Mark* (Birmingham: CMPA, 1977), 164-5.

morning," (twice), and "when it was yet dark." All of these are observations that are all fully capable of describing the point where the night transforms into pre-dawn twilight, just before the sun fully emerges over the horizon. It could have been undeniably dark when the women first set out and then become light as they arrived at the tomb. In an era when all but the very rich lacked the means to precisely mark the time, these observations are hardly contradictory. Who was at the tomb when they arrived: one angel (Matt 28:2-7); one young man (Mark 16:5); two men (Luke 24:4) or two angels (John 20:12)? The mention by one Gospel of two angels and by another of one is in no way a contradiction. If there were two, there was one. In the case, as we have here, where one person is the chief speaker, it would often be perfectly natural not to make reference to the chief individual's companion. Luke and Mark both do not use the term 'angel' in their accounts, but rather "men" or "young man." This does not contradict Matthew, who is clear to use the term "angel." Angels are normally depicted in Scripture in the form of men. In Mark, the awe and fear that seizes the women, as well as the man's white robe, make it clear that he was a supernatural young man, and therefore an angel. Also, the description in Luke 24:4 of the men's "dazzling apparel" implies that these are supernatural beings. This is confirmed later in the same chapter - the women's encounter at the tomb is described as a "vision of angels" (Luke 24:23). The Gospel records are different because they record additional, but not contradictory, information, and none claims to be exhaustive.[19] Word for word agreement might suggest one writer had copied from another, whereas the differing accounts provide the stronger historical evidence of separate and independent eyewitness accounts [Principle 1].

Finally, critics claim that miracles simply do not happen. However, we must be clear that the resurrection cannot be ruled out because of a pre-existing assumption that miracles are impossible. When a sceptic proposes that the resurrection accounts are legendary because they describe something miraculous, the presupposition (that miracles are impossible) has become a part of the argument for the hypothesis, and the argument is circular. As long as it is possible that God exists, miracles, like the resurrection, are possible.

When faced with the compelling evidence of the appearances, those who reject the miraculous fall back to the position that the historical facts cannot be recovered with any certainty. This standpoint is well summed up by the historian Paula Fredriksen: "I know in their own terms what

---

[19] See John 20:30; 21:25.

they [the disciples] saw was the raised Jesus. That's what they say and then all the historic evidence we have afterwards attest to their conviction that that's what they saw. I'm not saying that they really did see the raised Jesus. I wasn't there. I don't know what they saw. But I do know that as a historian that they must have seen something."[20] The view of many, like Dr Fredriksen, is that the door must be left ajar to allow for the possibility of a risen Jesus. However, a pre-disposed unwillingness to accept a miraculous explanation prevents them from believing the simplest explanation – that Jesus was alive.

The Son Rises

So what can we conclude? Days after seeing Jesus put on a cross to die by Roman soldiers, the followers of Jesus stated that they had seen him alive. It was their firm belief, declared to all, that he had appeared to individuals and groups, that they had touched his living body, and that they broken bread with him. They were unshakeably sure in this belief. The tomb was empty. Even the adversaries of Jesus had to agree. And there is just no credible alternative theory to account for the missing body.

The apostle Paul, perhaps the greatest sceptic of the new religion, turned his life around completely when faced with the risen Jesus. This powerful man, a scholar of huge intellect and full of authority was absolutely convinced of the reality of the resurrection and became Christianity's greatest advocate.

The appearance of Jesus alive after being seen categorically dead by both friends and enemies had the effect of galvanising the despondent followers and energising them with a force that changed the world for all time. For the sake of Jesus, the believers cheerfully "risked their lives" (Acts 15:26). They had seen evidence that Jesus, having been dead was alive, and that he promised them the same if they believed. This conviction changed everything for the early followers, compelling them to go out and preach the message to the ends of the earth. They affirmed that God's promises had come rushing together in a wondrous climax, triggering the beginning of God's new creation: "in Christ all will be made alive. But each in his own order: Christ, the firstfruits; then when Christ comes, those who belong to him" (1 Cor 15:22-23). This is their message, which it is our privilege to have received and to believe. Jesus rose from

---

[20] Dr. Paula Fredriksen, Boston University cited in Habermas and Licona, *Case for the Resurrection,* 60.

the dead. Death is not the end; it has been reversed, cancelled and destroyed. There is hope.

Summary

- The testimony to the resurrection of Jesus, both in the gospels and in other Christian writings, is early and based on the accounts of eyewitnesses.
- All ancient sources claim that the tomb of Jesus was empty – a claim that could have been easily contradicted by the Jewish authorities, but never was.
- Numerous appearances of the risen Jesus to both individuals and groups are recorded.
- These appearances convinced the early Christians, transformed the disheartened disciples into powerful evangelists and even converted enemies like James and Paul.
- Attempts to explain away this evidence lack plausibility.
- The historical reality of the resurrection of Jesus gives us confidence in the Bible's promise of life after death.

Further Reading

One of the most important scholarly works on the resurrection is N. T. Wright's seminal work, *The Resurrection of the Son of God.*

Accessible treatments of this subject including Frank Morrison's *Who Moved the Stone* and Habermas & Licona's *The Case for the Resurrection of Jesus.* Older works of interest include *The Trial: Did Christ Rise?* by C. C. Walker.

Several shorter works on the resurrection can be found online, such as "The Resurrection of Jesus" by W. L. Craig and "The Resurrection of Jesus Christ" by A. D. Norris.

For wider treatment of the Gospel records consider commentaries, such as A. D. Norris' *The Gospel of Mark* and H. A. Whittaker's *Studies in the Gospels.*

Epilogue
Alan Eyre

"Seek and you will find"

All the authors of this volume are convinced that there are good, sound reasons for believing that "there is one God and one intermediary between God and humanity, Christ Jesus, himself human, who gave himself as a ransom for all" (1 Tim 2:5-6). They are urging you to consider seriously the appeal of the apostle Paul to seek God "and perhaps grope around for him and find him, though he is not far from each one of us. For in him we live and move about and exist" (Acts 17:27-28). They have argued, as persuasively as they know how, that godless unbelief and agnosticism are quite literally a dead end. They are beseeching you, for reason's sake, to live a life of "faith, hope and love" (1 Cor 13:13). The Lord Jesus himself expressed this in his inimitable fashion:

> I tell you: Ask and it will be given to you; seek and you will find; knock and the door will be opened for you. For everyone who asks receives, and the one who seeks finds, and to the one who knocks, the door will be opened (Luke 11: 9-10)

Solomon, or whoever wrote the early chapters of the book of the Proverbs, expressed the same idea in a poetically colourful way:

> If you call out for discernment – raise your voice for understanding – if you seek it like silver and search for it like hidden treasure, then you will understand how to fear the LORD, and you will discover knowledge about God. (Proverbs 2:3-5)

Watch your children's excitement with a treasure hunt at a Christmas party. Read Stevenson's *Treasure Island*, or read about the almost incredible determination of the thousands of 'forty-niners' during the California gold rush. We are being told that that is the way in which to 'seek'; like our very life depends on it, as indeed it does! All the authors of this book are convinced of this. In some cases it has been true in their own experience.

Three Seekers for the Extra-Special Pearl

The Lord Jesus told two little parables or stories about how people find and come to appreciate the value of Jesus' teaching. Here is one of them:

> Again, the kingdom of heaven is like a merchant searching for fine pearls. When he found a pearl of great value, he went out and sold everything he had and bought it. (Matt 13:45)

I have chosen the experiences of three men to illustrate this short but profound parable. The first two are recounted in the Acts of the Apostles.

The first example was an African, a very senior civil servant. We do not know his name, but we do know the name of his employer. He was "an important official in charge of all the treasury of Candace, queen of the Ethiopians" (Acts 8: 27). He was seeking a faith to live by that would be more credible, satisfying and fulfilling than the pagan cults of his homeland. He made a special pilgrimage to the temple of Yahweh in Jerusalem, by-passing on the way many other famous temples such as those in Egypt. By chariot and horses, the journey must have taken him at least three months. But he was seeking the one true and living God, and he was seeking diligently and in the right place. He believed that the Bible (our Old Testament) held the key to his quest. Acts 8: 26-40 tells us the sequel.

> [He] was returning home sitting in his chariot, reading the prophet Isaiah. Then the Spirit said to Philip, "Go over and join this chariot." (Acts 8:28-29)

The evangelist Philip explained that the passage the Ethiopian was reading was a prophecy of the saving work of Jesus Christ.

> So Philip started speaking, and beginning with this scripture proclaimed the good news about Jesus to him. (Acts 8:35)

Even though the road was through desert, very conveniently they came upon a pool or cistern with water, and this devout African was baptized. A sincere seeker became a joyful finder.

The second man was an officer in the Roman army. His name was Cornelius, "a centurion of what was known as the Italian Cohort. He was a devout, God-fearing man, as were all his household; he did many acts of charity for the people and prayed to God regularly" (Acts 10:1-2). That is just the kind of seeking soul that God is constantly looking out for. The

Holy Spirit directed Peter, the leader of the Christian church at that time, to bring the search for truth by this pious Italian to a happy conclusion. He was baptized, with all his extended family, and they became pillars of a church in the city of Caesarea that was famed as a beacon light of Christianity for centuries thereafter.[1]

The third seeker was arguably the greatest figure in the history of science. Three hundred and fifty years ago, in 1661, in the great university of Cambridge in England, Isaac Newton plunged into an emotionally driven search for 'ultimate truth'.

> [He] sought knowledge in everything he came across, a man who was driven to investigate all facets of life he encountered, everything that puzzled him...but the work that emerged from these explorations changed the world[2]

And he came to this conclusion:

> He must be blind who from the most wise and excellent contrivances of things cannot see the infinite wisdom and goodness of the Almighty Creator, and he must be mad and senseless who refuses to acknowledge them[3]

However, Sir Isaac went further, much further.

> In millions of words, mostly unpublished to this day, Sir Isaac systematically taught the unity of God, the divine Sonship and sinlessness of Jesus Christ, the nature and mortality of man, the Abrahamic and Davidic covenants of promise, salvation by grace, faith and believers' baptism, the atonement, the second coming of Christ, resurrection, the day of judgment, the hope of Israel, the return of the Jews to their ancient Land, the biblical devil, the Kingdom of God on earth, the Millennium with immortal rulers and mortal subjects, and many other Scriptural doctrines which we as Christadelphians espouse and proclaim.[4]

---

[1] A. Eyre & G. Gordon, *Cornelia's Story* (Hawthornedene: Christadelphian Scripture Study Service, 2010).
[2] M. White, *Isaac Newton, the last sorcerer* (London: Fourth Estate, 1998) 4.
[3] I. Newton, *The Mathematical Principles of Natural Philosophy by Sir Isaac Newton: Translated into English by Andrew Motte, 1729* (repr. with intro. by I. Bernard Cohen, 2 vols.; London: Dawsons, 1968) 1:xxv.
[4] A. Eyre, "Sir Isaac Newton: Our Brother in Christ?", *The Caribbean Pioneer* (2003) 169.

It should be stated here that these significant conclusions of Newton's are shared today by all the authors of this volume, arrived at by the same process - an ever-deepening conviction that the words of Jesus Christ will continue to stand the harsh test of time and are an enduring standard for our lives: "heaven and earth will pass away, but my words will never pass away" (Mark 13: 31).

Newton's friend Roger Cotes stated in his preface to the second edition of the masterwork *Principia mathematica,* "Newton's distinguished work will be the safest protection against the attacks of atheists, and nowhere more surely than from this quiver can one draw forth missiles against a band of godless men".[5]

The African finance minister, Cornelius, and Isaac Newton were all like the man in Jesus' little story of the pearl merchant, searching for truth, serious seekers over many years. Like many others of the same mind, they came to be totally committed Christians, convinced in their minds and hearts that Jesus is "the way, the truth and the life" (John 14:6), and that "there is salvation in no one else, for there is no other name under heaven given among people by which we must be saved" (Acts 4:12). They were the same kind of people who might find encouragement and faith from reading and pondering the evidence in this book. At least, that is our hope and our prayer.

Finding Hidden Treasure

This is the second little story about the kingdom of heaven that Jesus told:

> The kingdom of heaven is like a treasure hidden in a field,
> that a person found and hid. Then because of joy he went and
> sold all that he had and bought that field. (Matt 13:44)

In this parable, Jesus is reminding us that God's word and work are far more powerful than any of our feeble human efforts. By His providence He works miracles. "For God all things are possible" (Matt 19:26). By the most seemingly trivial incidents, God guides those whom He wishes to save. Often, there is no long search, just a sudden, perhaps dramatic, find.

Andrew, a fisherman from Bethsaida in Galilee, met Jesus and spent most of one day with him (John 1: 39). Before the end of that day, he told his

---

[5] *Sir Isaac Newton's Mathematical Principles of Natural Philosophy* (trans. A. Motte and F. Cajori, 2 vols; Berkeley: Univ. of California Press, 1934; 1962) 1:xxxiii.

brother Simon, "We have found the Messiah, that is, the Christ" (v41). A hasty, credulous, superficial and emotional conversion? Hardly. On the strength of that one day, Andrew the fisherman was a changed man. He became a lifelong "fisher of men", and, according to tradition, forty or fifty years later, he was converting many to Christ in the land we know today as the Ukraine.

Andrew, though long dead, was still in a sense 'preaching' in the Ukraine nineteen centuries later. The second of our finders is Natasha, a terribly disfigured victim of the Chernobyl nuclear disaster in 1986. She learned from a booklet in the Ukrainian language given to her by a Jamaican scientist, researching the effects of the catastrophe, that the good news that Andrew had proclaimed in the first century AD was being proclaimed and taught in 1993. She jumped for joy and was baptized in Christ.

Finally, amongst the sudden, unexpected finders, we can read about the unnamed Roman jailer at Philippi (Acts 16:16-36). Within the brief compass of one exciting night, he met a couple of Christians for the first time, heard them sing hymns in his prison, and was so impressed that he asked to be taught the basic elements of God's way of salvation, and was baptized in the name of Jesus Christ.

Beyond Argument

I will conclude this Epilogue by presenting a glimpse into the life (yes, life not lives) of Enos and Estrina Campbell of Argyle Mountain, Jamaica, a Christadelphian brother and sister in the Lord, mighty in the Scriptures, in words and in deeds. More than any other man or woman I have ever known, they exemplified and embodied faith, hope and love; and they were, and after they fell asleep in the Lord, they remain, an overwhelming 'proof' that "Jesus is the Christ, the Son of God, and that by believing you may have life in his name" (John 20: 31).

Enos and Estrina were poor farmers and lived in a rural community of poor farmers. There was no school, no regular water supply, no electricity or any other public services. As the area has a rainforest climate, there are lots of tall trees, and so the tiny houses were made of either wood or 'spanish walling' consisting of a mixture of laths and clay.

Just over sixty years ago, Estrina found a small Christadelphian booklet called *Preaching the Truth* by William Brown. It had no cover, so there was no contact address, and they were unable to get in touch with the author or publishers.

Enos and Estrina studied their Bibles with the help of the little book, and they both came to a deep and spiritual understanding of "the faith that was once for all entrusted to the saints" (Jude 3). They baptized each other, and then decided to preach their newly found faith. With their own hands and simple tools they built a Christadelphian meeting hall holding about sixty people, made out of hardwoods cut from the forest. It was hard going building up a congregation, because many people in the district were illiterate, ignorant and superstitious. Because Enos and Estrina did not know of any other Christadelphians, for nearly thirty years, the Campbells and their little 'ecclesia in the bush' were known all around as "the people who can't find their church".

There were other reasons for slow growth and a limited harvest. Besides poverty and illiteracy, corrupt and venal political 'enforcers' controlled the whole area. Illegal drugs were grown and traded. Young men and women were trafficked too; some were even sold into slavery in other countries. Family life was often chaotic, with many abused and neglected children. Enos and Estrina decided to concentrate on uplifting the young people of the area. They saved several youngsters from abuse and ill treatment and arranged for some in a serious condition to be adopted. They quietly demonstrated all the Christian virtues without a thought for their own convenience. No one – good, wicked or in between – was beyond their incredibly selfless generosity, their love, and the message of the Gospel. Many lives were totally transformed. Enos became an informal, unpaid 'schoolmaster' for the area. The young people loved him, and some were brave enough to spurn the drug gangs and crime and support the lonely church.

Like finding hidden treasure in a field, in 1985 they saw a newly built Christadelphian meeting hall in a city twenty miles from their home in the mountains, and their joy knew no bounds. My first visits to them were thrilling, and glorious evidence of the veracity of the apostle Peter's words: "I now truly understand that God does not show favouritism in dealing with people, but in every nation the person who fears him and does what is right is welcomed before him" (Acts 10:34-35). There was a 'youth circle' of more than fifty, and some of those young people in later years became ambassadors for Christ and for Jamaica in Canada, England, the USA, and the Cayman Islands. My wife and I opened our home to several of them, and what joy it was!

Three years later, in 1988, hurricane 'Gilbert' destroyed the village. The meeting hall collapsed into a shattered pile of broken lumber. Within a few days, although their own home was wrecked, the Campbells had erected a temporary shelter from debris, which leaned alarmingly. Triumphantly, they invited me to the fellowship of the Lord's Table. My own home, two hundred miles away, had also been totally destroyed. Nevertheless, I could not refuse that invitation. Sharing the bread and wine, lovingly displayed on a rickety table in a tumbledown shed, on an immaculate white tablecloth, was a privileged moment of my life for which I ever thank the Lord.

Today, except for those made rich by the 'drugs for guns' trade, many of the people in the area are poorer than ever before, and more ignorant. Enos and Estrina fell asleep in the Lord nearly twenty years ago, but the lighthouse of hope they founded in Argyle Mountain is still flourishing, surrounded by modern day barbarism.

I can never forget the day I said goodbye to Enos. He was in hospital, behind the usual screen to hide the dying. As I looked at this saint, propped on his pillow, his eyes were shining with faith, hope and love. His countenance was joyfully serene. As he saw me, he smiled. I asked Enos if he would like a prayer. "Of course, my brother", came the response in a clear voice, "and who would you like me to pray for?"

When scoffers mock my faith (and there are plenty of them in this day and age) I do not try to think up a convincing and rational argument. Instead, I think of the wonderful face and faith of a dying man, and his fervent prayer – for me and for others, not for himself. The face of a true saint is beyond argument as evidence for a God of love, indeed, who *is* love (1 John 4:8).

Whenever I recall the life and love of Enos and Estrina Campbell, I find it utterly incredible that they, and we all, could possibly be merely a valueless product of the mindless and random shuffling of microscopic blobs of matter on twisted strands of nucleic acid – and nothing more. It makes me long with all my heart for that Age which is surely coming, when, the final chapters of the Bible promise:

232

The residence of God is among human beings. He will live among them, and they will be his people, and God himself will be with them. He will wipe away every tear from their eyes, and death will not exist any more – or mourning, or crying, or pain, for the former things have ceased to exist (Revelation 21:3-4)

Let the one who is thirsty come; let the one who wants it take the water of life free of charge. (Revelation 22:17)

Amen. Come, Lord Jesus (Revelation 22:20)